Deer Hunting
with
DALRYMPLE

Deer Hunting
with
DALRYMPLE

Byron W. Dalrymple

ARCO PUBLISHING, INC.
NEW YORK

The author and publisher express gratitude to the following publications for permission to reprint from the indicated articles by Byron W. Dalrymple:

SPORTS AFIELD: "An Advanced Course in Deer Hunting," November 1959, © 1959. "Guarantee Your Whitetail," October 1960, © 1960. "What's Wrong With Being a Meat Hunter?" March 1961, © 1961. "Timing Your Deer Hunt," October 1961, © 1961. "What Every Deer Hunter Should Know," October 1968, © 1968. "Challenge of the Desert Mule Deer," August 1970, © 1970. "Sure Way to Take Your Mulie on Opening Day," August 1972, © 1972. "Warm-Weather Whitetails," October 1972, © 1972. The Hearst Corporation. All rights reserved.

SPORTS AFIELD HUNTING ANNUAL: "Surefire Deer," 1966 Edition, © 1965. "How to Rattle Up a Buck," 1967 Edition, © 1966. "Hunting Western Whitetails," 1976 Edition, © 1975. The Hearst Corporation. All rights reserved.

OUTDOOR LIFE: "The Art of Mule-Deer Hunting," November 1962, © 1962 Popular Science Publishing Company. "How My Sons Improve My Deer Hunting," August 1974, © 1974 Times Mirror Magazines, Inc.

FIELD & STREAM: "Boat Float Bucks," July 1964, © 1964.

THE AMERICAN HUNTER: "Hunting Desert Whitetail and Mule Deer," © 1975. Reprinted by permission from the AMERICAN HUNTER magazine, August 1975, a publication of the National Rifle Association.

FAWCETT'S HUNTING JOURNAL No. 2: "Zeroing in on Spooked Deer," © Fawcett Publications, Inc.

DEER SPORTSMAN: "How to Hunt Different Kinds of Cover," July-August 1976, © 1976.

First Arco Edition, First Printing, 1983

Published by Arco Publishing, Inc.
215 Park Avenue South, New York, N.Y. 10003

Library of Congress Cataloging in Publication Data

Dalrymple, Byron W., 1914–
   Deer hunting with Dalrymple.

   Includes index.
   1. Deer hunting.   I. Title.
SK301.D35   1983   799.2'77357   83-3891
ISBN 0-668-05868-4 (Cloth Edition)
ISBN 0-668-05870-6 (Paper Edition)

Printed in the United States of America

For my two favorite deer-hunting compadres of the past 15 seasons, Mike and Terry.

CONTENTS

VIEW FROM A HIGH PLACE

There's a common joke passed around among hunters in Texas that whitetail bucks in that state aren't very surefooted. They stumble over downed logs, trip on low vines, bump their shins on rocks, and upend themselves from bumbling into varmint burrows. The reason for such missteps is that the bucks go around all during deer season trying to look up. I'm not at all certain that sitting in a tree or in a high-stilt blind to hunt deer originated in Texas, but a lot of Texans claim it did.

Regardless, a tremendous number of Texas deer hunters do look down on their quarry, and in the past few years the practice has spread from wherever it started to all over the country, except for the few states where it has been made illegal. You'll hear endless pro and con arguments about the high-stand technique. One substantial disadvantage, of course, is that sitting up in a tree or a commercially built high seat forces you to stay put, to choose the nonmobile-nonprowling-stand technique, unless you decide to change trees or move to a high seat that is portable.

The advantages, on the other hand, if you accept the basic stand-hunting premise (that sitting still in a likely spot is virtually certain in due time to bring a deer to you), are multiple and provocative.

● In some situations you can see down into cover that your vision couldn't penetrate usefully at ground level.

● You can shoot down into openings that wouldn't be apparent from ground level.

● You get your scent above the level that the deer is on.

Deer don't expect danger from above, and they're physically built so that looking up is not easy anyway.

When I first came to live in Texas, where we've been settled in now for some 20 years, I had hunted deer from New England to the Great Lakes region to the Western mountains to the Deep South. But in all that time, I had never had the experience of climbing a tree to hunt a buck. In northern Michigan, a couple of us had even discussed that idea years before. Maybe it would be a crafty approach. But at that time it was not legal in Michigan to hunt that way. There were even tales (it always had happened to a hunter who was known by a friend who had an uncle who heard . . .) about the gent wearing the black cowhide coat, hair on, who climbed a tree and was shot out of it by a hunter who thought he was a bear.

At any rate, we arrived in Texas late in summer, and a rancher invited me to come out and look around his place. You don't go gallivanting around private land in Texas without being invited. You might not get mistakenly shot for a bear. You'd more likely get shot because the owner realized you were a man who didn't belong there. This gentleman took me bass fishing at a pond on his place.

We did some walking here and there, and I kept seeing big live-oak trees with several two-foot lengths of two-by-four nailed in ladder fashion horizontally to the trunk. Each time I saw this, my gaze would naturally be drawn higher, and I'd invariably see several boards fastened in a higher crotch, like a seat, with another couple apparently to serve as a back rest.

Of course I should have known. This area, in the south-central Texas hill country, has an awesome number of deer, whitetails, small of stature but making up for size by their astonishing abundance. I finally asked about the steps on the tree trunks.

The rancher grinned, "Why, that's how you climb to the deer stand up yonder."

"I didn't realize people here hunted deer from trees," I said.

He laughed. "Is there another way?"

Of course, he was kidding me. But later, when the season opened, I was invited to hunt on another ranch, and the owner took me out to a field that had grown up to wild sunflowers. Under the sunflower stalks, now dead and dry, grew a crop of winter oats and short green grass. Surrounding the field were pastures of woodland, live oak, Spanish oak, and Texas cedar. My host took my gun and nodded toward a big oak on the edge of the field.

"Up you go," he said. "Sit in that first crotch. You ought to have a buck in an hour."

I chuckle yet to recall that break-in experience. This tree had no steps and no boards for a seat or back or rifle rest. I had quite a time of it getting up to the first limb. Finally I made it and was handed my unloaded rifle. I got as comfortable as possible, which is to say horribly uncomfortable, and surveyed my hunting area. It was difficult to keep my mind on deer. The rough crotch of the tree was splitting me in two, chafing my backside in the process. Wherever I placed the rifle barrel

2

seemed certain to be wrong. My legs were cramped, and my back was cracked in the middle.

But suddenly I felt none of that. I was looking at a distant deer. No—two—no—three deer. A doe and two fawns. They had eased out of the woods and into the sunflowers to get at the oats and green grass. It was suddenly obvious to me why I had to be up in a tree, or at least up on a plane above the field. It would be impossible to see into the sunflower maze from ground level. From my position, however, I could see every movement.

By late afternoon, with the sun setting behind the timber, I could count 15 deer in that field. The startling part was that three of them were almost directly under me. They had come out of the woods and into the field, acting a bit uneasy but not sure what was wrong. Finally they moved away 30 yards and settled down. I dared not move. And then toward dusk the bucks appeared. Two were spikes, two were forkhorns. Several distant ones had more points, but I couldn't tell how many. But one, not an inch over 75 yards away, was as pretty a fat little 8-pointer as you could wish.

By some great good fortune, I had my rifle barrel on the right side of the limb. Slowly, slowly I eased my head down to the stock. The buck began to be uneasy. Some sixth sense told him things weren't just right. But that helped me, I suspect. The buck, with head up, stood absolutely still. The cross hair found his neck, and at the jolt of the rifle my first tree-stand buck was on the ground.

I confess that I had felt foolish and embarrassed while climbing the tree as the rancher watched. I also confess that I had felt—or tried to make myself feel—that this approach was somehow taking unfair advantage. Now I had mixed emotions. Certainly I wouldn't have had that deer if I'd stayed on the ground.

It was a short shot, granted. But the next time I collected one, which was the very next week and from a high, high seat in a tree (a stand with steps going up and a comfortable seat and backrest), it wasn't so easy.

That deer was in mixed timber and brush. It was also (as paced off later, as straight as I could walk through the cover) 180 yards. I remember that I tried to get a steady rest. The range was much too far to try offhand. Even when you have a rest, these small whitetails don't present any bulky target. The wind was blowing. The limb I rested the barrel against swayed. Leaves and branches kept weaving in front of my scope, and farther out some branches were inhibiting my view off and on. And when the scope's viewing field was clear, I couldn't keep the deer centered.

3

I kept taking in breath, holding, having to let go, then starting over. But at last came a lull. I shot. I couldn't tell where the bullet went, but the deer just perked up its ears and stood, wondering about the strange noise. I considered the possibility that my angle downward may have caused a high shot. That is one problem when you're shooting from a high stand. And the closer and higher the stand, the more exaggerated the problem is. But on the next shot, the buck was mine.

By now it had got through to me that this method was not always easy. It was by no means potting deer unfairly. It was, however, an advantage under various conditions. I quit fighting the idea and began to look around. Within a couple of years I had seen, and hunted from, high stands or seats of wide variety. Although I joked a lot about tree stands and the quirky designs—and full comforts—of some, it was mostly because this was all new to me. During the years since then, tree seats and portable high stands have come into wide use throughout the country, particularly across the South. But they also have spread to the West Coast and even up into Pennsylvania and the Northeast.

Tree stands and the like are not legal everywhere. So anyone considering a try at getting above deer should carefully check the laws. And even though a tree seat may be a legal hunting method, some states have stipulations about how it is to be built and whether or not it can be permanent. Pennsylvania has passed such a law. Some of the rules were pushed by people concerned about nails being driven into trees.

Some tree stands are available that are guaranteed not to harm the tree in which they're used. Among them are so-called self-climbing stands. One of these, available in several models and easily portable, is manufactured in Georgia and has come into high popularity. In Texas, where high stands have been in use for a long time, several firms manufacture unusual models. One, for example, is a steel tripod with steps on one of the steel-pipe legs, a swivel seat on top, and a railing around the seat for you to rest your gun on. These stands are carried by pickup truck out into a deer area, especially in the brush country of south Texas, and are placed in likely locations. The cactus and thornbrush is dense, and the main reason for using a high seat is that you can seldom find a place from which you can see a deer in such endless cover unless you look down into it.

Other designs, also on metal stilts, have a small boxlike coop at the top, with a seat, and observation and shooting ports. These are more comfortable than open stands in windy, chilly weather. In the brush country, I have also seen many old-time permanent high stands fashioned by setting a pole—of telephone-pole size—into the ground.

4

Wooden steps are nailed to the pole, and a platform and railing are built onto the pole 20 feet or more up. Deer get accustomed to such contraptions on their range and pay little attention to them.

During my first years of living in the hill country, I was intrigued by the numerous and ingenious designs of various stands. The simple tree seat I've described, made of boards nailed across a high crotch, and often with a backrest and a gun rest of more boards, was and still is one of the most common (with, of course, the pieces of two-by-four nailed to the trunk for steps). Although this sort of setup just isn't allowed nowadays on public lands, most ranches in the live-oak and Spanish-oak hill country of Texas have them. My own ranch had a number when we bought it, and my sons have built more. Some ancient seats obviously had been in trees on our place for many, many years, with only rotted remnants left. I doubt that the trees were injured.

Some of the permanent small buildings on high stilts are really masterpieces. On the Hi-R-U Ranch owned by George Ross near my home, I've hunted from high blinds that are entered by climbing a sturdy ladder and then going through a trap door in the floor. These blinds are large enough for two or three hunters. The interior is covered with dull-black fiberboard so there's no shine anywhere. The wall behind the hunter or hunters is solid and black, so no silhouettes show from the front. The front and both sides have sliding windows, to be used as shooting ports or to be closed for comfort, depending on wind direction. There are sandbags for windowsill rests, comfortable chairs, a bottle of fresh water, and even a roll of toilet paper.

In Texas, many ranchers who take paying deer hunters don't allow them to stray from a blind. This is a safety measure. The hunter is dropped off, say, at 3 P.M. and picked up at dark. Thus he puts in a fairly long sitting stretch, but in full comfort. At these blinds, and at many others in hill-country Texas, swaths are cut in the brush and trees in wheel-spoke fashion some distance out from the blind. So a hunter has a chance at deer that cross. The deer, thoroughly acquainted with the little high-stilt permanent buildings, are not inhibited. It is a fact, though, that they occasionally learn to look up at those windows (with which nontarget animals have probably had frightening experiences) and are ready to flee at the slightest scrape on the floor or visible inside movement.

The plushest high blinds I ever experienced were on a ranch owned at one time by Eddie Rickenbacker and his son, not far from Hunt, Texas. These were little clapboard-covered buildings tapering in slightly from the ground up, with a compartment at the top about six by eight feet. Hunters entered up an inside stairway. In the compartment, which had a big front port for looking and shooting, were comfortable chairs, a small butane heater, an old-fashioned chamber pot for emergencies—and a telephone. The phone was connected to headquarters and to several other blinds scattered over the ranch. A sheet on the wall listed the number of rings to be used to call each blind and headquarters. Hunters could check on each other to see how things were going, could get services as needed from the ranch headquarters, or could call in when they killed deer and wished to be picked up. The old tree seat had come a long way!

Although such accommodations may be carrying things a bit to the ridiculous side, high stands of whatever variety do give a hunter a substantial advantage, if he's the sort who can sit and wishes to. Deer may learn to look up at the seats when they catch a movement or possibly a scent. But as I noted earlier, deer aren't in the habit of peering upward into trees. The only regular dangers they know come at ground level. In addition—and probably because of ancient development to cope with ground-level dangers—the eyes of a deer are set for looking ahead. Its neck vertebrae are so put together that staring upward at a steep angle is difficult.

The permanent blind works well if you own land. You can select areas where deer habitually move. But generally the best rigs are the temporary tree seat and the portable "high sit," as it is sometimes called. A hunter using one of these is able to see down into cover and spot deer movement at surprising distances. He has a certain amount of comfort not usually achieved by sitting on the ground. He gets his scent well up above ground, and he is not nearly as likely to be spotted by a deer as he would be on its own level. Slight movements of the hunter are not so easily detected by the deer.

Scent, however, is not by any means always kept entirely from deer downwind of a hunter in a high stand. Much depends on how high the stand is, whether it's enclosed, and how far away the deer are. During my first seasons of spending some time in stands, I used most of my time observing the reactions of deer. I learned a lot. A deer might walk casually along on a calm day, come right under the tree seat or other stand, and never know the hunter was there. Incidentally, musk scent can be effective if it's daubed here and there near a high seat.

On a breezy day, in an enclosed high blind with windows on three sides, I found that deer seldom picked up my scent at a distance if I kept the downwind window closed. But if a breeze blew through—or when I sat on an unenclosed high seat—deer downwind easily picked up my scent. On a stiff breeze, they could pick it up 200 or 300 yards away, probably farther than if I'd been on the ground. At that distance the angle upward to the seat was so low that an alerted deer could (and often did) stare at me, or where I was. Conversely, a deer that came out of cover near the stand might not pick up scent even downwind. It blew past high over the animal's head.

An interesting slant on high stands, a tree seat, or a commercially built portable model is that any of them can be utilized advantageously in any type of cover. In Deep South swamp hunting, though such rigs are not much in use, they've been found most helpful when they were tried. Brush, as noted, is a perfect place for one, so you can see down into it. Curiously, a high seat spang in the open—as in a field along the edges of which deer forage—improves a hunter's chances.

In pine country, where most trees have straight trunks with few limbs down low, the portable metal seat that "climbs" is handy indeed. In mixed forest, the simple way—where it's legal—is to just climb to a crotch of a tree that has limbs to allow hand and foot holds. Usually a big tree can be found where fair comfort is possible, and even a backrest limb. A seat only six or eight feet above ground is still better than sitting at ground level. Getting higher up, of course, is even better.

Safety in such hunting can't be overemphasized. Your weapon, either bow and arrows or gun, should be pulled up by a light nylon cord or rope you carry for that purpose, after you're securely seated. Obviously a gun should be pulled up empty.

After you shoot a deer, keep your wits about you. Don't try in excitement to hurry down. The gun should be unloaded, arrows secured in a quiver, and the rope used again, this time to let the weapon down to ground. I have always made a point, when using a high seat other than a permanent enclosed blind, to leave my knife—unless it is a folding one—on the ground at the base of the tree or stand. Climb down carefully and as calmly as possible after a shot, to avoid a fall.

High stands are useful in numerous situations. For the habitual "sitter" they are exceedingly advantageous. But if you can't sit, then you shouldn't use one. You'll be too itchy and give yourself away. I can sit for half an hour, maybe even an hour. But I'm not the all-day kind. For other hunters who feel the same way, often a portable tree seat, or a semipermanent stand, or a series of several stands can be used to good advantage as a rest point between prowls.

To sum it up, the modern lightweight tree seats that can be slung over a shoulder and carried into the deer woods serve admirably. The distinctive advantage of these is that you can change locations as often as you wish, with little fuss and effort. If from one stand you continually see deer moving outside your range, and you decide there is a runway, or food, or water over there that is attracting them, you can simply switch position to your advantage during a brief lull in activity.

The heavier but still portable high seats, such as the metal-pipe tripods I've described that are made commercially, must be transported mostly by vehicle. In certain areas where there are no trees to climb or on which to use a self-climbing seat, these tripods are excellent. The cactus and brush of southern Texas is a classic situation that they suit. Other terrain, such as scrub timber, or sagebrush flats, or even such locations as huge cornfields in the plains states and small-farm regions of the Midwest where whitetails are especially shy and difficult to fool, are perfect for these and similar semipermanent high blinds.

Just be certain there's no regulation against placing one. On public lands, conceivably you might be required to move it after each day's hunt. With a pickup that's no tremendous chore. And, like the light tree seats, these heavier outfits can be repositioned as often as seems advantageous, without any physically overwhelming effort, as a season forces changes in deer habits or your study of the region locates better positions.

Regardless of the type of high stand you use, there is much to be said for the safety factor in this idea. In crowded areas, a hunter well up above ground is out of the general accident range of the careless shooter on the ground. He can't possibly be mistaken for a deer, either. In addition, he is always shooting downward, at varying angles depending on range of his target, so that his own shots are safe. And he's able to see deer much more often as "whole deer," not bits and parts that may be confused with other hunters.

In some places, of course, the high seat doesn't fit. A good example is the mountain country of much mule-deer range. I don't feel, as that Texas rancher told me kiddingly, that this is the only way to hunt deer. But it is a way that's helpful in numerous situations, particularly for whitetails. The view from a high place is usually a clear one, and the target seldom knows you have it.

WHAT'S THE BEST TIME

Early one fall I was in correspondence with a friend in Utah about a mule-deer hunt. He wrote to say that he wanted me to get a chance at a good head and that he'd keep a close watch and let me know exactly when to come. Could I get away on short notice?

What he wanted was for the *time* of my arrival to coincide with the *time* when weather, the rut, feeding conditions for the deer, and other factors all fell into such a lucky combination that my hunt would be almost certain to succeed.

The plan worked perfectly. Because of early snow, a collection of good bucks was down off the mountains. The bucks were compressed into a relatively small area of good feed, and they were running does. I rode out and spent a couple of days looking them over. And though it sounds perhaps more simple than it actually was, basically the hunt was a matter of selecting a deer. The buck I took was hog-fat from eating piñon nuts and weighed 215 pounds field-dressed.

I've heard a number of deer hunters claim that they don't really go out to kill a deer. They "just like to be out in the woods." Naturally I never believe this. Such a man is kidding himself, is trying to kid me, or isn't a deer hunter. I don't believe anyone ever went deer hunting without having at least some hope that before his hunt ended he would have his chance. He might be extremely selective about what deer he shot and might go home with an unfilled tag rather than take one he didn't want. But if the right one came along, he would begin panting.

Sometimes the right one comes along through plain luck. But Lady Luck isn't very dependable. So it behooves the hunter who is serious about taking home a good deer to set his stage so carefully that his chances will be the best he can possibly make them. With such staging, the need for luck will diminish and matters will be more in the control of the hunter. Nothing gives him quite so much control as *timing* his hunt with utmost care.

A few years ago I made a deer hunt in Arizona that was as big a fiasco as it's possible to arrange. To begin with, the area I'd selected had slowly become overrun with hunters and sliced up by Forest Service roads. When I arrived, I soon sized up the situation: if I was going to kill a decent deer, there'd have to be a lot of them to pick from, for there were a lot of pickers.

As hunters of mule deer know, in all the high country where heavy winter weather forces deer out, there are areas known as "summer range" and "winter range." The summer range in most areas at high altitudes is all but bereft of deer after heavy snows come. The deer can't stay because they would starve. They make what is called a "vertical migration": to low altitudes when heavy snow comes and back up in the spring. I was hunting on winter range, but the weather was balmy and beautiful. Many a mountain-country mule-deer hunter has had this experience.

However, in wholly wild country that is undisturbed by man (or only mildly disturbed), the winter mule-deer range does have at least a token summer population. A big-headed deer might choose to live there all summer. The reason for waiting to hunt lower-elevation winter range until mule deer have been driven down from above by heavy snows is purely one of odds—numbers of deer. Instead of being scattered from elevations of 1,000 to 10,000 feet, the deer on winter range are forced, so to speak, to bunch up.

All this, of course, is elementary. Any experienced mule-deer hunter in search of a good head in high country where migration to winter range occurs waits if at all possible for the big storms high up. What is not quite so elementary is that the winter range, as pointed out, can and does have good deer making their homes there all summer. Had I, on the Arizona bust, been alone in the region, or with only a scattering of hunters, I am quite sure I could have killed a respectable head. But the place was swarming with hunters and with cars combing the trails.

There were lots of does, dumb spikes, and giddy forkhorns. The few and scattered big gentlemen, however, had gone over the hill. In this case, the "hill" was the Grand Canyon. They had slipped down through the draws and lost themselves in the hideously difficult country below the lip. I came back from that hunt without having so much as fired my gun.

There were two ways I could have improved my chances. First of all, I had a choice between two hunts: an early one and a late one. The late hunt would have upped my odds. Normal weather would have pushed deer onto this winter range. The other way would have been to go just as late as possible in the first hunt. This approach would have given all the doe and spike hunters a chance to be limited out, packed up, and gone. The competition would have decreased and the disturbance would have subsided to some extent. Conditions wouldn't have been perfect by a long shot, but they would at least have been *somewhat* better. Poor timing cost me several hundred dollars and led to a lot of exasperation and no venison.

This experience pinpoints an angle that not one in a thousand deer hunters ever considers. Let's suppose that you must hunt deer in a region that has many other hunters. You, like most of the others, break your back to get there for opening day to get an even start. I'm not certain this is always wise. I can think of a certain forest road I know that, a week before opening, is lined one after the other with tents, trailers, and camps of one kind and another.

It's an excellent deer area. All summer the deer live in peace, with only an occasional trout fisherman to startle them. Then comes the fall invasion. Cars are roaring; people are shouting, chopping wood, making trips to a nearby village early and late, shooting those sidearms they all say they must carry for protection. All told, it is one hell-ripping hullabaloo. By the time opening morning has arrived and you've counted a hundred shots the first hour (even though only bucks are legal and there aren't over 40 in the general area) well, every deer that hasn't somehow stumbled into a hunter and got killed has got as much thick stuff behind it as it can.

Remember, these animals haven't been grossly disturbed for months. The first few days of pandemonium drive them nuts. But by the end of the first 10 days of a 2-week season, some of the hunters have worn themselves out and gone, and the deer that are still alive have started to get conditioned to the new circumstances.

The biggest, wisest old bucks are likely to be still living. And the late-season hunter who purposely times his hunt for the last few days has a good chance to collect one. For if he's smart enough to consider all this timing, he's probably a smart *hunter*, too. Just recall how often you've seen a real old buster brought out of the woods right at season's end. And how you've thought, "Gosh, he was there all the time—now why didn't *I* get him?!" Maybe your timing was wrong.

But let's take another look at weather and at the Western high-country to which so many thousands of deer hunters travel nowadays. When staging your hunt by the weather, there are two ways to be almost 100 percent sure of success.

● One depends entirely upon the *place* you've selected. If you can find a secluded place where no other hunters go, a place way, way up on a mesa somewhere, preferably above 8,000 feet, by all means go there for the opening of season, *if* the season in that region opens early.

As I write, I picture such a place in Colorado. It is federal land. But a ranch so cuts it off that getting into it is almost impossible unless you know how to go across the rancher's place and up a narrow trail to a mesa top. The top is at roughly the 9,500-foot elevation. It is a maze of shin oak, with pockets of beautiful aspen. Down the side draws are pine and other large trees. Grass is knee-high in the open places, and several thousand acres of country are almost as level as a field.

This is summer deer range. Deer are there by scores. They live all summer without any disturbance. They have innate caution, of course. But when they're surprised by the appearance of a man, some of them just stand momentarily to stare. Obviously they won't be here when the bad weather comes. But at the very beginning of season—and the earlier it opens the better—they're here. Weather is beautiful up here, given a normal season. The first time I was up there, my first sight of deer was of eight bucks in one bunch! Such a place as this, then, up *high,* is the place to be at the opening of an early season. But to make sure, if you're new to the region, it's well to check weather records and the long-range forecasts before you plan the hunt. If everything points toward open weather, you as good as have your buck.

● Exactly the opposite approach is possible quite often these days. Although many hunters are not aware of it, some states occasionally have what are known as "post" seasons. This means a season that opens for a short time after the regular deer season has closed. The purpose of post seasons is to harvest an oversupply of deer that would otherwise never be touched or a localized herd that's causing depredations on crops.

Let's say that a forbidding area of high mountains with topnotch summer deer range looms above an easily huntable valley or low pine forest. Further, the mountain area is just about impossible for the average hunter to get into. A few horseback hunters pack in. But the heavy population of deer up there is hardly touched. Meanwhile, down in the valley, hunters swarm during the regular season. But even if this season runs fairly late, only a portion of the deer are down from the high country. In order to really thin out the high-up deer and keep a healthy, stable herd, the need is for a large number of gunners to be able to get a crack at them. And so a post season is set.

Often these post seasons are not announced until shortly before they open. Surveys are made to determine the need. I think of one such season in a specified section of Colorado a few years ago when a limit of four bucks per person was set. That may never be possible again, but for that one time it was great. The time was December. Heavy snow had fallen even down where the deer were wintering. And there were just plain swarms of bucks. When two hunters can pass up 45 bucks in three days and still collect 8 between them, all with good heads—well, that is some deer hunting.

A letter to a game department along in early fall asking about post seasons, or early high-country hunts, might allow you to time such a hunt to your convenience. Keep in mind that the late season is cold hunting, generally in heavy snow. It requires good equipment and outfitting, warm clothing, and insulated boots. Vehicles must have four-wheel drive and snow tires if they are to be used for transport. Otherwise, it's horseback or slogging it out. Such hunting is not very comfortable, but it's almost invariably successful.

Weather has many other influences on the timing of a deer hunt. Some of these are not infallibly predictable, but I go by them when possible in my own hunting. One influence is the wetness or dryness of a certain period. I'm sure deer don't mind a little rain as much as hunters often do. In fact, during mists, light rains, and slow drizzles, deer—whitetails or mule deer—are often extremely active. The inclemency doesn't upset their routine. A hunter who's willing to be out in it may utilize it to immense advantage.

One fall in Texas when the whitetail and turkey season opened, I was trying for a turkey. I wanted to save my deer tags for another time and area. But because waiting out a turkey can be a long and sometimes dull proposition, I took up my usual hobby of watching the deer. Dawn of opening day had brought a heavy fog, which cleared somewhat about 8 A.M. and switched to mist, which soon changed to a light drizzle. Although I know better than to try chasing turkeys, I was chilly sitting, so I decided to prowl. Then, seeing a buck, I thought I'd stalk him just for fun.

That part of Texas is hilly and very rocky, with much brush and dead grass and other noisy items. When the country is dry, trying to make a stalk is ridiculous. Not even a deer can walk quietly then. But wet as all of it was that morning, and because the drip camouflaged minor sounds, stalking was easy. I could have shot two presentable bucks with my turkey gun. I've had similar situations occur in many places. The last deer I killed in the state where I grew up, Michigan, was done in because a light rain with pleasant temperature allowed me to move silently.

But there is the opposite side. Deer (all wildlife, for that matter) are like people to some extent: severe storms are disagreeable to them. They go where protection is greatest, which means into the densest cover, and they wait it out. A man generally doesn't want to be out in a deluge or a blizzard. And if he were out then, he'd have trouble getting to where the deer were. There is an old axiom among deer hunters that says, in effect: "Hunt when the deer are most active." This is a reasonable idea. When deer are active, your chance of seeing them (of their exposing themselves, which is always better than attempting to expose them) is enhanced.

And so it follows that a period of good weather immediately after a bad spate will produce animation among deer and a hot chance for a hunter. I saw an instance of this fairly recently in my adopted home state of Texas. Like most things in Texas, the rain that came that year at the beginning of deer season was giant size. The countryside was bogged. A few foolish hunters, and I was one, went through the motions for a bit. But it was no use. And besides, the deer, uncomfortable if not worse, weren't going through any motions.

As they say in Texas, however, "if you don't like the weather, wait a minute." Just when it looked as though the rain would never quit, the sky cleared. A week of simply sensational weather ensued. The deer acted as if they'd been called to a convention. The chance to feed, to be unhampered in their roaming after a period of partial confinement, seemed to exhilarate them. I have no doubt it really did. After all, animals must sense the delight of such a change just as we do. Bucks were cavorting on every hand, and it was not much of a trick to let one down. A hunter who can control his eagerness, wait out a bad period such as we had, then hit it hard the moment the break comes, is almost certain to be a believer in "hunt timing" from then on.

Time of day is also very important. Many hunters spend too much effort at the wrong times. I'm often one of those, mainly I suppose because it's hard for me to quit and because there is also the point that he who spends the most time at it by the laws of chance may get more opportunities. However, if hunting time is limited, then unquestionably—given normally good weather—the traditional early and late periods of the day have an edge.

I like the dawn time best, even though I hate getting up to meet it. The reasoning is this: at dawn, animals that have been active during the night are likely to be fairly calm and not quite as "jumpy" as those that have been in daytime hiding and are first stealing forth for evening activities. The active dawn deer is already on its feeding and roaming ground, not quite so keenly conscious of danger, because it has already looked and listened. The late-in-the-day deer does his listening and looking as he sneaks out to begin his evening.

There are exceptions to this line of reasoning. Various weather conditions may ruin a dawn. For example, if a weather prediction is for heavy ground fog at dawn, it doesn't make much difference to a hunter whether deer are active or not. Shots would be questionable. A prediction for a sudden midday weather change may also make hunt timing changes advisable. I've seen times in the West when a balmy day with absolutely no deer activity would suddenly be slashed by a spurt of chill wind and a fast temperature drop. A front had blown in.

I have always imagined that this sudden change could hardly help making deer restless. It makes *me* restless. I want to be stirring, although I don't know quite why. But I do know that deer aren't overly fond of hot or balmy fall days except for lazing around. And I also know that almost without exception the in-moving front with its gusty winds and falling temperature will put deer to bustling around. The demise of many a buck has hinged on this very situation, even though many times the hunter who did him in didn't realize it.

Once these varied situations are brought to mind, a hunter can begin to see how many of them there are. Obviously I cannot cover every such combination here. And, of course, there are exceptions to all of them. My point is simply that to give yourself every break, you can do worse than pay attention to the intricacies of hunt timing. If I had a choice between an excessively windy time—not a modest, brief, incoming front, but a period of truly windy weather lasting several days—and a time of calm or light breeze, I'd take the milder condition every time. All animals are more nervous during high winds. Logically so. They can't hear so well nor pinpoint the direction of danger. If my choice were between a hot fall day and a day after a severe night freeze, I'd take the day after the freeze. Deer with fall coats on aren't at all fond of warm weather.

Then comes the old business of the "full of the moon." Sounds pretty corny, I know, and many a modern hunter scoffs at the old-timer who just won't hunt until the dark of the moon. But let me tell you something about this situation. I'm no believer in the infallibility of the old native. He may have been wrong for 70 years, not right. But I do know some of the unarguable basics. The eyes of deer are fashioned to allow feeding in the dark, and their exceptional sense of smell is an assist.

Nonetheless, when no special weather is upsetting or other influences are interfering, deer will feed more heavily and will be more active when they can see well (simply because it's more convenient) than when they have to feel their way around. On moonlit nights, deer can see very well, just as we can. They roam around more and are up more than down at these times. Consequently, during these periods of bright moonlight, they don't require much "fuel" during the day to keep their engines running.

Conversely, when there's no moon, or only a sliver, or the moon sets very early, deer are, in general, much more active at dawn and dusk. A deer that hasn't traveled much during the night in pitch black will be up and scrounging at the first light of dawn. The animal may not necessarily be one bit more active during full daylight or—let's say—from 9 A.M. until 4 P.M. But from daylight until morning is well started, and again before full dark comes, the activities of deer will generally be more pronounced during moonless periods than during moonlit periods.

I'm not suggesting that you should refuse to hunt deer except "in the dark of the moon." What I mean is that your chances of killing a good deer may be better then—perhaps only one percent better. My hunting philosophy always has been: give yourself every break. If you can hunt during a "dark" period, by all means time your hunting to include this advantage.

Years ago I corresponded with John Alden Knight, the gentleman who originated the idea that tidal effect has much influence on the activities of wildlife. Basically the theory is that at the seashore we can see the effect of tidal pull, but that anywhere inland the effect is just as great although not so plainly evidenced to human eyes. Mr. Knight has been vindicated many hundreds of times by the studies of scientists who know a great deal about the marvelous "timing devices" of nature.

Originally John Knight's "Solunar Tables," as he called them, were set up to assist trout fishermen. There were, so Mr. Knight claimed, two periods of a day as a rule when trout were most active, and these he called the major feeding period and the minor feeding period. Later he enlarged his studies to include deer and grouse. I'm convinced that his conclusions, which were virtually the same for trout, were sound.

When I lived for a few years in northern Michigan, I used to set out to go trout fishing, usually about 2 or 3 in the afternoon. I always had to drive some miles through the woods to get to a chosen stream. I would always watch to see what the deer were doing. This, mind you, without checking Mr. Knight's tables, for I was going to go fishing anyway. If deer were up and moving—which my better sense told me they shouldn't be at this time of day—I would invariably find when I got to the stream that the trout were moving and feeding, too. On a number of occasions I did check the tables in these instances. Sure enough, they were right on the money.

I realize there are few halfway opinions about such things. Either you're a believer or you aren't. Again, I'm not insisting that you hunt deer by the famed Solunar Tables. But I will say that if I thought such a system would help me kill a good deer, I would at least see to it that I was out there trying during the times the tables said I should be, even though the major period of activity came that day at high noon and it was blowing a blizzard. In other words, it might happen that a major activity period will be in progress when you ordinarily would be resting in camp. It would be interesting at least to check the table, be on hand, and thus give yourself one more small timing advantage.

I should emphasize, however, that many conflicting influences are brought to bear upon wildlife. So the tables, or any of my suggestions here, or any of anyone's suggestions, may not work when you think they should. Some dominant influence not well enough understood by us humans may upset things. We can only do our best to consider all the angles.

In rough, hilly country it is a little understood fact that deer will be high up on one day, in the valleys the next. I have observed this phenomenon in Wyoming, Colorado, and New Mexico with mule deer. And in late years I've noticed it a great many times in hill-country Texas, where I now live and hunt whitetails each season. This puzzle has nothing whatever to do with food or shelter. I have sat on a flat with steep canyons sliding away on each side, and from 3 P.M. until too dark to shoot with a scope I saw not a movement, yet only the day before in the same spot I had seen a number of deer.

That happened one day during a recent season. At the ranch house that evening, I remarked that it sure had been a dull day. Two other hunters looked puzzled. Both had been stationed in valleys, and both had seen a dozen-odd deer. The very next day we were all in our same positions, and exactly the reverse occurred. I have no doubt that weather is mainly responsible. I would like to believe barometric pressure has some immense influence, and well it might. But the point is difficult to prove. Some researchers believe they have proved that it does not. Perhaps. Or perhaps their experiments have not been conducted with enough insight.

About one angle of hunt timing, however, there is no disagreement. Bucks in rut become both bold and addled, and they are more active at this time than at any other time of year. If there is any single slant on planning your hunt that can almost make it surefire, it is timing

This trophy buck is on the prod, so he's less wary than he normally is. Make sure you know the average timing of the rut in the region you plan to hunt, and make allowance from season to season for variations in weather.

it to coincide with the peak of the breeding season, if hunting season is open then. Some hunters are under the impression that a rutting buck is strong tasting and unpalatable. This is not true. A buck that has *finished* rutting is a sorry piece of venison. He is worn to a frazzle from chasing endless miles after does, from not eating, and from his lovemaking. But when a buck first begins the rut and is on into it while he's still virile and full of fight, his meat is just as good as it will ever get.

The timing of the rut varies a good bit depending on the latitude. In the Northern states, it is generally earlier than in the South and Southwest. But, of course, altitude is also an influence. High country is like another climatic zone. Also, weather—temperature—undoubtedly plays an important part, triggering the rut early or holding it up.

Given what can be considered a normal autumn, breeding time should be about as follows:

Mule deer, north: November
Mule deer, south: December
Blacktail deer, north: November
Blacktail deer, south: early as September
Whitetail deer, north: peak about November
Whitetail deer, south: peak about December

These dates are very general. In south Texas for example, where I hunt a great deal, and in northeastern Mexico, whitetails are rutting usually at peak late in December. Many times and in many places, you simply cannot come up with a deer (or at least only by dint of great effort) until the rut has begun. And then suddenly, from nowhere, here are the bucks.

I have found that the more abundant the does, as a rule the less "foolish" the bucks become. This is logical. No buck must try very hard to snare a mate. But in deer country where the population is scattered, healthy but not overabundant, a buck must hunt hard to find himself a willing doe, and believe me he can be foolish indeed about sticking with her. On several occasions I have seen two whitetail bucks after the same doe, and I observed what happened when one of them was shot. The other, seeming not to hear, kept right on with his pursuit!

One year a friend and I were hunting whitetails along the Mexican border. From atop a tank dam, we saw a buck running a doe round and round on a brushy hillside about 200 yards distant. We were totally without cover. The deer could hardly help seeing us. We fired, between us, five shots at the buck, missing him as he dodged among the scrub. Not until the fifth bullet zinged close and blew up in the dirt did he wake up. Even then he didn't bolt. He simply trotted off as though still undecided whether to give it up.

In this same area, where bucks are seldom seen at other times, they are annually in startling evidence during the rut. But then the same is true in many places. It is pretty obvious that a hunt timed for this period has every chance of success.

How can you time it? Fortunately, during seasons when weather is proper so that the rut is pronounced and does not fritter along, the peak of activity is sure to last a couple of weeks at least. By keeping your hunting dates as loose as possible, and keeping in contact with someone in the area where you'll hunt, you can have information passed along. As soon as bucks are observed with necks swelled and chasing around as though living in a dream world, by all means hasten to the spot.

It should be noted that the fighting between bucks, the fighting over does, and the stubborn chase after a doe is far more pronounced among whitetails than among mule deer. A rutting muley can be just as silly, but he doesn't seem as ardent or as high strung about it as is the whitetail. And sometimes several mule-deer bucks, all with swelled necks, will consort, bluffing now and then but not really fighting all-out. Their *activity* during this period is, nonetheless, at the year's peak. Afterward they become listless, settling down to a kind of family routine that is dull by comparison.

If you can time your hunt to the rising tide of the rutting season, your scheming will have been well spent. Even then, however, time of day, the weather, and all other influences bearing upon that big little word "time" will fit into the picture. It is just possible that neither how good a hunter you are nor how good the area you'll hunt is anywhere near as important as how carefully you have timed your hunt.

Pinpoint the Best Deer Areas

The most amazing wildlife phenomenon to occur in our generation, and the one least visualized or expected early in this century, is the growth of our deer herds and their unique adaptation in most places to exploding human population and progress. The annual accidental kill of deer struck by automobiles nowadays throughout the United States is greater than the entire national annual kill by hunters at the turn of the century!

It is quite obvious that something very special has been happening to our deer. They have not only adapted quite well to our civilization, but whitetails especially are thriving along with it. They even live in small woodlots and within city limits. When I was a boy growing up in southern Michigan, we had positively no deer there, yet there were thousands of acres of woods and brush. But in recent years southern Michigan has had a high deer kill on ever-growing herds, and some very large farm-raised whitetails are collected. In South Dakota's pheasant belt, deer so fat they can barely waddle are occasionally flushed from cornfields. Where I live, in Texas, it's so common to see 50 whitetails feeding in an oat patch any evening that we hardly bother to look. And the deer hardly bother to look up as cars whizz by. Texas has so many whitetails that some years the state hardly knows how to cope with them, even with any-deer hunts and an astonishing kill, of over 300,000.

Today deer are almost literally everywhere throughout the United States. Though there are trouble spots and more coming, deer are reasonably abundant to amazingly abundant almost everywhere. No one knows how many millions exist. Every state of the contiguous United States has hunting for deer. But now we arrive at a curious national statistic. Of the millions of hunters who annually go out to bag their venison, only about 20 percent succeed. To be sure, success in certain areas runs much higher—up to 50 percent or even more. These results are invariably in regions where herds have grown too

21

large and any-deer seasons are held with a crash program to bring the herd into line with the carrying capacity of its range. Even 50 percent is not really high, considering the number of deer.

But other regions—some entire states, in fact—show hunter success of only 5 to 12 percent.

Many reasons are offered by unsuccessful hunters to explain their lack of success. The most common one is that deer are scarce, which is hardly true. For some time now, it has seemed rather certain that while *deer* have adapted to *humans, hunters* have been slow to adapt to the new ways and living conditions of *deer*. Deer hunting is changing, has changed. Many hunters have failed to keep pace. While science has flooded the game-management field and has nurtured the deer and kept them abundant, the art of deer hunting is in many ways about where it was at the turn of the century.

Hunting By Statistics

Time was, for example, when no one really knew where the deer were. There were no ready references. Today game men know exactly. The sharp hunter checks statistics before planning his hunt. All state game departments gather kill figures annually. These show not just total kills but also (in most states) kills by counties or game-management units. They show how many bucks, how many antlerless deer. They show how many hunters and a final success percentage.

That success percentage is what counts. A high kill figure alone may simply mean crowded conditions. Crowded hunting is not only less safe; it also deprives the deer of an opportunity to react naturally. They get spooky. A small number of hunters but a high success rate indicates a good general area. That's where the deer are.

But be wary of total figures if you care what sort of deer you shoot. Deer may be abundant in a certain county or unit, and seasons may be for any deer. The possible result: a high success percentage. If you're a buck hunter, you probably don't want to go there. Overabundant deer often mean smaller deer, smaller racks. Large areas with lower deer populations and fewer hunters are another type of statistic for the trophy hunter to watch for. The lazy, inept hunters weed themselves out. The deer live longer and have time to grow those trophy racks.

You can even uncover statistics from game departments on studies that show the age of deer killed in various areas. If hunters are numerous, the kill consistently large, and the percentage high, the bucks invariably will be preponderantly young. The surveys will show this.

22

Such a place will be a reasonable one for the hunter who is just after meat. But the trophy hunter will avoid it. Look for a place that shows fewer hunters, fewer deer, and deer with a fair percentage of the bucks past five years old. If bucks are being killed off too fast, none live long enough to stand as real trophies. Check the statistics for the average age of bucks killed. A declining average age indicates declining trophy possibilities.

By checking such statistics for the past several seasons, you can get a good idea on where to hunt for the kind of deer you desire. You can also select a hunting spot this way with far greater chance of success, trophy or not. In Indiana, for example, hunting has been allowed for some years on the three large military installations in the state. These hunts have accounted for as much as half of Indiana's total deer kill.

Nowadays there are also all sorts of records compiled (by states, local hunt clubs, and the Boone & Crockett Club), that keep track of big deer. A careful study of any one state or on a national scale will show you that there is a definite pattern of "where the big ones come from." These may be county size or smaller. But few deer hunters bother to utilize this mass of helpful material.

Most game-department studies show that deer, like all other life, are a product of the soil. In some rocky regions, let's say, minerals are such that food quality remains high and deer show phenomenal growth, in both body and antlers. In certain other areas, correlations have been made showing definitely that on those soils, deer may be abundant but will almost never have perfect, or large, antlers. An average hunter would do okay here, but a dedicated trophy hunter is wasting his time.

Statistics also show very definitely at what season most deer are taken in a given locality—and often what percentage during that certain season are big bucks. To be sure, many states have a simple one-week or two-week season, but today special hunts are more and more numerous. Study the kill figures for these hunts, and you can select your hunt to take advantage of the secrets they tell.

Another statistic buried deep in deer studies and invariably overlooked by hunters is the timing of the rut, which is dealt with in detail in several other chapters. If a state has a brief deer season at a consistent time year after year, nothing much can be done about it. The rut either occurs then or it doesn't. But any deer-management biologist in any state can tell you precisely when the rut will occur at its most likely peak in various altitudes or latitudes of his state. Bucks are far easier to kill during the rut than at any other time. They will come to rattled antlers and often to a deer call. They follow does and act dazed and glassy-eyed and pay little attention to a hunter. The big bucks are often more vulnerable than the young ones because the big ones are more determined. Utilizing pinpoint rut-time statistics can put a trophy on your wall by helping you pick the right area as related to your hunt timing.

Utilizing a Stockman's Knowledge

Modern deer management by professionals has taught us—or will teach us if we will let it—many facts of direct application to hunting success. Much of this information arose from the accumulated knowledge of stockmen and cattle breeders. This claim may sound far-fetched, but it's true. It also reminds me of a poignant experience.

Several years ago I was hunting on a large Western ranch. The rancher, a well-schooled breeder of quality cattle, was showing a friend where to hunt for a big deer. The friend said, "I don't really want to hunt this area, because you killed the big buck out of it last year. Remember? You showed it to me and told me exactly where."

The rancher smiled and said, "But I didn't kill his progeny."

It is well known today that deer, like cattle, are individual creatures. Some physical specimens are better than others. A rancher buys a registered bull and culls his cows to keep the best physical specimens for breeding. Nature culls deer. But in some concentrated studies, biologists—on a specific study area—have purposely shot every buck that showed poor antler development and poor physical characteristics. It is astonishing how the true old "Bull of the Woods" passes along his good points to his offspring. I know a number of ranchers with large holdings who will tell you exactly where the best bucks will be. They have observed good "bulls" in these areas and know that when one is shot or dies a natural death it is very likely, because deer are not wide-ranging animals, that one of the offspring with like qualities will take its place. This is important—and seldom-used—modern deer lore.

Any pinpoint area where a good buck has been seen or killed is a good area to stick with to discover another, unless, of course, the place is severely overhunted. There are also certain characteristics of terrain in very special small spots that appeal to these larger animals. I know a certain small canyon in Wyoming that invariably has a big buck in it. These are undoubtedly progeny of some original old bull of great physical prowess. But the *place* has some attraction for a big deer and thus the "herd bull" (to which has fallen the task of preserving and passing along the seed) never leaves it. Hunters who seek these areas can bag a big buck every season.

Stockmen's knowledge of cattle, as deer biologists well know, can tell you many other things about deer. And this sort of knowledge is found not only on Western ranches; it is available just as precisely in northern Maine and southern Alabama. It is simply noticed more by ranchmen who know cattle and deer. For instance, a deer you glass that has white appearing antlers is not likely to be in the best health. Dark, mahogany-brown antlers indicate robust health. A deer with rough-looking hair should be passed up, if you have the opportunity to pass up several before selecting one. But a deer with sleek hair, an animal that seems to have been licking its sides, is a fat, prime deer. Cattle do the same thing.

The stockman knows too that domestic animals (especially sheep or goats, but cattle as well) react about the same as deer to weather conditions and time of day. Domestic animals are found over much of the United States in thousands of deer areas. If bands of sheep are feeding or cattle are on their feet grazing, it is very likely that deer are, too. The crafty hunter will utilize this knowledge to tell him how to hunt.

For example, old-fashioned hunters get into all sorts of arguments over whether it is best to stalk deer or sit on a stand. There is no such thing as "best" in this regard. Sitting on a stand while deer are lying down is ridiculous, a total waste of time, but taking a stand while deer are active may well be far better than moving. Livestock in the vicinity can help you decide which to do. And the stalk-or-stand argument is often easily settled by the simple expedient of observing domestic animals. A mixture of stalking and standing, properly timed, is by all odds the most successful combination.

Especially over vast areas of the Midwest and West, much hunting for deer is done in fairly open country where cattle may be seen. The modern hunter who follows stockman knowledge as I've suggested will avoid allowing feeding cattle to see him, just as cautiously as he will avoid giving away his presence to deer. Cattle invariably "point" anything strange in their domain. Deer watch the cattle uncannily. Perhaps you never knew this, but it is a fact. Thousands of deer have slipped away unseen because they saw some old cow "on point."

After your deer is down, a stockman, upon seeing you slice open the brisket, can tell you exactly how the meat should be used. If the deer is fat, and the fat is white, steaks, chops, and roasts will undoubtedly be tender. If the fat along the brisket—and elsewhere—is distinctly yellow, the venison is almost certain to be tough. But it is perfectly adequate as hamburger and sausage and, if roasted for long periods, as large roasts. Such bits of knowledge can be extremely useful to the modern deer hunter.

Reading Weather for Success

Just as mountains of scientific knowledge have been amassed about deer over the years that our herds have been exploding, so too have we learned much more about weather nowadays than was once known. Long-range general forecasts can be made with fair accuracy. These have important bearing on your deer hunt, yet most hunters still cling to only the rudimentary old-fashioned ideas. A hunter should use his knowledge of weather, long-range and short-range, to help himself succeed. In the previous chapter, I discussed weather as it relates to timing a deer hunt. Here are a few additional considerations.

Several years ago I was planning a hunt in a high area of Montana for mule deer. But in gathering information beforehand, I discovered that the place where I hoped to hunt had been hit by an extremely severe and extended series of blizzards during the late previous winter. Further checking showed a real debacle for the deer at that time. The die-off had been extensive. It would hardly pay to try such a place. Such information is nowadays easily at hand, yet many hunters fail to avail themselves of it and thus court disappointment.

Weather can influence your deer hunt in many ways. An early deer season in the East during a mild fall may mean that leaves are so dense in your chosen hunting area you can't hunt successfully. Perhaps you should wait to the last possible moment or go elsewhere. In the high-country West, an exceptionally dry summer and fall can be disastrous, at least until heavy snows come and drive deer down into concentrations at lower altitudes. The reason is that food becomes scarce in drought. Though deer may be doing well enough, they are scattered widely, searching for food as well as for water. An exceptionally wet fall in country strange to you may be just as disastrous unless you do some weather checking beforehand. I went to Utah one time without doing so and found every area of best hunting simply impassable because of the mud. The deer were there, but hunters couldn't get in.

Here's an additional fact about the rut: once you've found the general time of the rut's peak, check the fall weather pattern carefully. If the weather remains rather even (fairly mild, with no quick cold snaps) and continues so all season, there won't be any real peak to the rut. A few bucks will run all fall, competition may never become keen, and thus the rut won't mean much to you. You'd probably be wise

26

to switch tactics or places so you don't plan on the rut bringing you a buck.

But a fall that stays mild where you plan to hunt until just before rutting time and then suddenly offers crisp nights and still, cold mornings will have every buck going crazy at the same time. This concentration of breeding is the key to easily rattling up a buck or calling one, or simply sitting and shooting one that passes.

As I noted earlier, some herds of mule deer migrate vertically to their wintering grounds and become concentrated at low altitudes. Many a trophy that had never before seen a human has been collected en route to or while on winter range. Conversely, however, be sure you know your terrain when you start planning to scrag a big muley during migration to lower altitudes. Numerous areas of the West have no migration. The altitude is not great enough to necessitate seasonal movements. The foothills population is simply a stable one.

In the previous chapter I discussed moon phases. But suppose you must make your hunt during a bright-moon period. Well, then the moon is your clue to completely change hunting tactics or places. You can be rather sure that dawn and dusk will not see much activity. Taking a stand at those ordinarily good-stand times may not be worthwhile at all. Prowling will be better. But along about midday, select a good sitting place where you can watch the head of a draw, a brushy ridgeside, a stream bottom, or the edge of a woodland meadow. Deer bedded most of the morning will invariably get up and stir around a bit between 11 A.M. and 2 P.M. Many a big old buck will arise, walk a bit, pause to urinate or leave a pile of droppings, then rub his antlers on a bush and stroll off to seek another bed. An amazing number of deer are killed at midday during bright-moon days of the month.

In the whitetail country of Maine or Michigan, if you are to tough out a bad blizzard and prowl where you ordinarily wouldn't (for example in deep greenswamps), you can pick off a deer that never hears you coming and is bedded deep inside. But when the blizzard stops and the sun comes out, be sure you're along the edge of such a deep-swamp hiding place. Deer will come out of it from every direction to get out into feeding areas.

Mule-deer hunters often fail to take advantage of a place in which the weather will help. Mule deer love to feed along the open foothills. At daylight they will be there. If the day is chill and overcast, they may stay for some time and may even bed down there. But a day that feels pleasant to you is hot to a fat mule deer. The moment sun hits the valley or ridgeside, up go the deer to the rims. Invariably the deer will cross over to the shady side. There they will stay all day. Hunt the open until about 8 or 9 A.M. in such weather. Then climb over the rim and hunt the shady pockets. This is a way to get at short-range trophies you may never have suspected lived in such places.

Senses of Deer—Eyes and Ears

Years ago the effectiveness of deer senses was only conjecture. Today we have wonderfully complete knowledge. It is known, for example, that the poorest sense a deer has is sight. This is not to say a deer's vision isn't sharp. But a deer doesn't always know what it's seeing. Deer see movement instantly. But motionless shapes—though sometimes disturbing to deer— are difficult for the animals to correctly identify.

Deer see colors, if at all, weakly. Hunters still argue the point. There isn't any argument. The eyes of deer have few cone cells, the structures we all learned about in school as part of a human eye. The cones of the eye are the mechanisms that relay color images to the brain. Deer see most strongly varying shades of gray, from white through all the intermediates to black. You can use this knowledge to advantage, or confuse it to disadvantage. How you dress, for example, must be related to where you hunt.

As an exaggerated example, a white shirt worn in a dark-green woods is obviously an object that to a deer doesn't belong there. So is a yellow coat—if it moves. And the yellow coat, even immobile, may catch a deer's attention in a stand of conifers. This is not really a matter of color. It is rather a matter of intensity—or brightness. The yellow coat to the deer may not be yellow. It is almost white. A red coat, if fairly dark, may seem to the deer to be almost the same shade of gray as the timber.

If a deer spots a blob of too-bright or too-dark intensity in a domain it knows, it may stare. But if the blob stays put, the deer will usually get over its uneasiness and pay no attention—just as long as it gets no scent.

On the other hand, a well-camouflaged hunter, perhaps wearing full standard camo, with a camo net hung over bushes to conceal him, may spook deer because the net flops in the breeze. The deer knows every bush here, and the bushes don't flop that way. The deer doesn't know what is wrong, but a whitetail at least won't wait to find out.

What about the newer camouflage materials? Some of the camo reds are fine. The deer presumably see them as gray. But a too-bright yellow-orange camo suit, in most deer cover except possibly maples or aspens turned in fall, is an attention getter. The best camo clothing idea, if you're not hunting where by law you must wear red or blaze orange, is the sort that matches particular surroundings. I have, for example, a suit that is reversible, green mottled on one side, sand and brown on the other. In New England the green is fine if worn with required amounts of safety colors, but in much Southwestern desert country the reverse side is far better.

Certainly deer hear very well. But for many years hunters were mistaken about how deer *interpret* sounds. A rhythmic sound, for instance, is a real spooker. Steady footfalls are such a sound. Intermittent sounds—a step, a pause, two casual steps, pause, and so on, *very slowly*—often will not bother deer. Distant gunshots have little effect on deer. They have no way to know what the sound is. But stealthy sounds made by sneaking or prowling will instantly alert them. Mule deer will often come to investigate odd sounds; whitetails, with exception of occasional does, seldom, if ever, will. A low grunt or a kissing sound is a curiosity to a muley and quite often will not disturb a whitetail if the sound is not rhythmical. But a recognizable human voice is anathema. By now, most deer (even in wilderness areas) know human sounds and do not like them.

Scent

Although deer certainly are easily spooked by movements or other sights and by sounds, it is not at all uncommon to see a huge old whitetail stand to stare as a hunter stalks him, or as he hears a sound. But just let any deer *wind* something unusual and that ends it. In other words, deer translate all sights and sounds chiefly in terms of scent. If deer were suddenly denied use of this acute sense, every one of the animals would be dead in a few years. This is really the deer's only vitally important sense. You can kill a deer because of its curiosity over a sight or sound, but never because of curiosity over something it smells. A deer lives more by its nose than by any other sense.

Most hunters have only a very basic view of what all this means in relation to where and how they hunt. Sure you should hunt upwind. But the subject of scent is complex. You take a stand, let's say, and you stay put on a quiet day in a spot where you can't see far but where you know deer have been crossing. This setup is fine for perhaps an hour. But did you know that scent has an oozing quality? Expert archers, who must have deer close, never stay on a stand very long. A hunter's own scent spreads around too far.

One bow-hunter I know uses a high stand in a tree, in a state where this is legal, to avoid having his scent picked up by deer on the ground.

There is one tree stand he showed me, however, where he sees deer but can't get one close enough. The answer was not difficult to fathom. Tree stands or other high stands are not foolproof. In this instance, a deer close in might conceivably come in under the "umbrella of man smell." But at a distance, because of the way the terrain lies, man smell blows all over. I watched deer at 300 yards from this stand race away in terror. Their noses had told them to go. Another location carefully selected would have avoided the problem.

Some people smell stronger than others to a deer. This may not be a polite thing to say, but it's true. Find one hunter who in warm climes picks up numerous chigger and tick bites and find another hunter who is seldom so bothered, and you can bet that the one doing the scratching will be scented by deer far quicker than the other. Knowing these things can be helpful. But you must also use good sense. One friend who believes he's a tick attractor and deer spooker, ladles on aftershave lotion and the new male perfumes and deodorants to cover up the "man smell." Wow! The deer hunter who shaves and uses aftershave, or who uses deodorants or other "pleasant" modern odors may be driving deer away. The best insurance against having a deer quickly pick up your scent is a bath with some neutral, non-perfumed soap. But if you've been hunting with a "tick attractor" who wears smelly scents, better go it alone somewhere else.

Even clothing can have a strong enough odor to alert deer. I mean certain fabrics, the smells of which we get accustomed to. Once I knew a deer hunter who took clean clothing and buried it in leaves overnight before hunting. I won't sell him short. He invariably bagged a buck. This practice may not have been wholly responsible, but it may have helped.

Some hunters scoff at the idea that smoking on a deer stand does any harm. I try to stay away from smokers. Certainly no deer ever smelled tobacco smoke and thought to itself, "That's tobacco and a man must be near." But any smoke, to any wild animal, is a sign for danger. Instinctively to them smoke equals fire—forest fire—and that's danger. Smoke is an exceedingly strong scent and holds together well over broad areas. Tobacco smoke may not cause a deer to run, but it will by my own observations and experiments quickly *alert* a deer. That in itself may lose a hunter the contest!

Deer Personalities and Signs

Many hunters travel widely nowadays. Mule-deer hunters try whitetail hunting. Easterners flock West after mule deer. It is necessary to know the fundamental differences in these animals if you hope to be in the right place.

Whitetails are ever jumpy; mule deer are more placid. Mule deer may live in any of numerous types of terrain, from open sagebrush cut by coulees to dense forests with mountain parks. Whitetails are forest and brush animals, always of the edges. In areas where both deer roam (such as portions of Montana or some parts of Texas' Big Bend country), the mule deer may be in pockets of timber, but the whitetails always will. If there is no timber, the whitetails will be in the brush draws, but the muleys may be right out in the open.

A mule deer, when jumped in a draw, will probably run up the side. A whitetail will usually run along the bottom. A whitetail jumped on a ridge will hightail over the ridge and probably over several more. Mule deer will commonly race up the ridgetop, then pause to look back. If a mule deer runs over the ridge and you have the wind in your favor, you may stalk it and find that it stopped running the moment you were out of sight.

When you're looking for deer tracks, don't be misled. Deer wander much and leave many tracks. In hard earth that formerly was moist, old tracks may look fresh. Some hunters believe they can tell buck tracks from doe tracks. It's not easy. But it is true that tracks of older bucks are more rounded and that the buck drags his feet more as he walks. In rocky areas, though, discount the rounded-track theory completely. Deer there wear their hoofs down, so large rounded tracks may belong to an old doe as well as an old buck.

The abundance of droppings in any area is more important than the number of tracks. Droppings tell more accurately how many deer are present, what the composition of the herd is, and a great deal about what the animals are feeding on. Few hunters study this sign carefully enough.

Most hunters actually have little idea what deer eat. But biologists know. You can get copies of deer studies on any number of ranges coast to coast that will tell you the chief deer foods for that region. Deer eat a great variety of foods, and these differ widely state to state. If you know what they eat in the area you'll hunt, you have them pinned down just that much closer.

For buck hunters who are seeking a hunting spot, it is vital to look for rubs. These are made usually on trees or bushes of modest size, where bucks have rubbed their antlers vigorously. What most hunters fail to understand is that in any given terrain, bucks generally select certain varieties of rubbing saplings. In New York, it might be a small poplar or balsam. In the Southwest, it is quite likely to be a retama.

No one knows why. And, of course, this is not an infallible habit. But if you know the preferences for your area, you seek the places where those sapling varieties grow most profusely. A series of rubs is an absolute statement that a buck is somewhere within a square mile, probably much less, of where the rubs are.

If you find rubs, plus a buck scrape, you've got the old boy nailed down. A scrape is a pawed-out place on the ground. Usually there is a bush or tree limb over it at just the height a buck can reach with its nose. The buck paws the ground, urinates in the hollow, and nibbles at the limb above. The buck may make several scrapes in his bailiwick. Does visit them and urinate in them. Other bucks recognize them as keep-out signs. The buck that made them visits them time and again. A stand near one is as surefire as you can get.

Many volumes might be written on present-day knowledge of deer and how this information can help you to be in the proper place at the magic second. The deer hunter with the most knowledge is likely to be consistently the most successful. There is no iota of information that is worthless. Every bit can be applied toward success. For instance, it would be far better for a hunter going to strange deer country to plan a three-day preseason study period of the new terrain and a three-day hunt, than a helter-skelter six-day hunt.

Getting accustomed to the terrain beforehand, with no need to shoot anything, means a great deal. Deer look different in different cover or open areas. Range is more difficult to judge in open country than in forest. Strange areas puzzle a hunter. But to the deer that live there, every bush and rock and draw is home. A long and careful in-depth reconnaisance by the unhurried hunter may be the means of putting him at the exact spot to conclude his hunt in a round of fast excitement.

All of this, then, is deer hunting in the modern style. There is no need to be among that large unsuccessful percentage of deer hunters if you'll use the mass of information that is readily at hand.

CHOOSING A DEER RIFLE

During a hunt for mule deer one fall, I filled my tag early. Then the guide, with whom I'd hunted several times, asked if I'd mind helping him a bit. He'd had two hunters come into his camp unexpectedly, sent to him by a rancher who couldn't accommodate them. They were eager to hunt, and he was short-handed. I agreed to take one hunter out.

It was an exasperating experience. Not that the man wasn't pleasant enough. He was, in fact, too pleasant. It turned out that he was what is commonly called a gun nut, or gun buff, and a hot-eyed handloader to boot. Now I don't object to these hobbies, if a fellow is so inclined. But they have little to do with deer hunting.

My "client" chattered on endlessly about various loads. What did I think would happen if he ran up a cartridge for his wildcat caliber that had X number of grains of such and such powder and a bullet of X number of grains, with sectional density of so and so? I replied that if he hit the deer in the right place, the bullet would no doubt kill it. Well, what about—and on and on—and watch those bumps in the jeep or my stock will get scratched—what do you think of that rifle—isn't it a beaut?

I confess that to me a deer rifle is a tool. I like it to shoot precisely where I point it, and I don't want my scope knocked around, but I'm not much concerned about a stock scratch. I like a rifle that handles nicely, one that carries easily, one that (if I hold it steady) shoots to the same spot a couple of inches in diameter at a couple hundred yards or so. How it looks, and for that matter its caliber and what it is shooting—within reasonable limits—doesn't make very much difference to me. What I want it to do is to drop a deer, right now. Most of that dropping business, however, depends on the shot I accept and on where I place the bullet.

Well, we got the gentleman a deer. He wanted to shoot at a running buck, rear-end on, to show me what his marvelous piece could do. I insisted he forgo this ridiculous thought and finally got him on a buck standing broadside at 150 paces or so. And when he shot—with a rest that I also insisted he take—the deer went down. He was triumphant. That rifle and that load had performed superbly. By then I didn't want to do anything but get rid of him, so I didn't mention that a hundred other rifles and a hundred other loads would have done the same thing to the deer.

You might gather from my recitation of that incident that I am not a so-called gun nut. You'd be correct. Gun collecting, building, and fiddling-with are, admittedly, good hobbies. If you get all worked up over a 5,000-word article in one of the gun magazines about trigger guards, fine. But don't try to relate it to deer hunting.

Handloading I can understand as both a hobby and a means to putting together better loads for specific chores. But when you go shopping for a deer-hunting rifle, handloading isn't relevant. Standard factory loads will do fine. The fun of putting together an excellent combination is certainly a legitimate enjoyment. But I emphasize that it has little to do with the success, or lack of it, you have in deer hunting. In our modern world, there is already too much confusion for the beginner and even for an old hand. Besides, the ammo companies know very well what it takes to kill a deer, and they put the proper medicine on the shelves of hundreds of sporting-goods stores.

I have pointed out several times to aspiring deer hunters who are wondering what rifle to carry that a good place to start learning is to check state laws to see what is *not* legal. Countless numbers of deer have been popped by poachers using a .22 rimfire. That doesn't mean the .22 is a deer gun, and I know of no state where it is a legal arm. The .22 Magnum, with a hollow-point bullet, will easily kill a deer at short ranges, if you shoot it in the ear, and even if you shoot it in the ribs, although then you may have a chase. But it isn't a deer rifle either.

When I first settled in the hill country of Texas some years back, a number of hunters in my area were keen on the .222. The whitetails in that area are small, and many of them were, and are, shot from blinds—even baited ones—at close range. The .222 is a marvelously accurate little caliber. You can kill deer with it. You can also wound them regularly and never retrieve them.

At the other end of the spectrum are the big-magnum gentry. I've always suspected these hunters—remember, I'm speaking of deer, not moose, elk, and grizzlies, with which these heavy calibers do have a legitimate place—are at heart gun buffs and also the sort who like to blow hell out of things. I hunted one fall for mule deer with a man who carried a .300 Magnum. He was inordinately proud of what it could do. What it did was blow the whole front end of a nice buck to pulp. He hit it in the shoulder instead of in the ribs where he'd intended. It was an unnecessary amount of power for deer, it made a noise that hurt my head, and it kicked the bejabbers out of the hunter.

He seemed proud of the *damage* done. This is exactly the opposite of what I felt, and what any real hunter should feel. The goal should be, in caliber and load selection as well as in shot placement, to do as little damage as possible while dropping the deer instantly. The over-gunned deer hunters, I have long suspected, are more interested in the macho feeling of loud *bangs,* the feel of a tough recoil, and the splattering of the quarry than they are in seeing the moment of the shot as a climax to a proceeding in which craft has been the main ingredient, and the trophy and meat the reward of expertness.

Much has been learned over the past several decades about the necessary—and unnecessary—attributes of the deer rifle. There is no such thing as the one "perfect" deer rifle. Scads of them do a fine job. I'm happy that the days of the "old thutty-thutty" syndrome are about over. This is not to say the .30/30 is not a logical deer-rifle selection. It's a good deer caliber and has been one for many years. But reasons for claiming it as "the best" aren't true and never were.

A claim often made, particularly among Eastern hunters and especially in the Northeast by those who never hunt deer elsewhere, is that in their thick cover they must have a fast gun (they claim the lever action is the ticket) and open sights. These hunters say they must have a short gun, so they can snap off shots at running, or jumped, deer.

Well, a lot depends on how you've been brought up. A few years ago Deep South deer hunters claimed—as did their grandfathers—that you had to use buckshot and dogs if you wanted venison. Over the past two decades, however, more and more Southern deer hunters have got around to other places and have learned that a scoped, flat-shooting rifle can be used just about as effectively in their cover as anywhere else.

Snap shots with open sights at jumped deer are notoriously wasteful. You can hit a deer that way without ever realizing it. You can be more effective if you truly learn the craft of deer hunting. Forget about how many shots you can lever off in how many seconds. Instead, use your rifle for what a rifle is designed for—careful, pinpoint shooting. Let me point out that you don't need a big hole to shoot through. What you need is just a tiny hole among branches. A good scope can pick out that hole far better than it can be located with the eye alone and with open sights. Any truly expert deer hunter can get standing shots. Only the bumblers or the overeager need to accept jump shots.

The .30/30, nonetheless, is an all right choice, provided you keep in mind the basic limitations of its ballistics. For example, the 150-grain bullet has a muzzle energy of somewhat over 1,900 foot-pounds. Out at 100 yards, it has 1,360 foot-pounds. That's enough, granted. But I wouldn't want to settle for much less. The flatness is okay also out to 100 yards (at midrange it's only about an inch high if sighted-in for 100 yards). But beyond that range—which is a good average range, admittedly, for whitetails in wooded country—the energy falls off swiftly and the loop in the trajectory gets a lot higher. I certainly wouldn't sell this old caliber short to any deer hunter who'll keep his shots within or very little past 100 yards. I must say, however, that there are so many better calibers for deer hunting that I can't see any good reason to settle for the .30/30.

Now while we're right at that point, let's look for a moment at the so-called brush rifles. I have a friend who claims he whams right through the thickest brush and kills deer with no problems. It's a shame that anyone ever concocted the term "brush gun." If you want to know the plain truth, there isn't any such thing. It *is* possible to shoot through a sapling and kill a deer. I did it once, unintentionally, in the Great Lakes country while shooting at a whitetail that stood broadside among trees. The deer was almost against the sapling. I was shooting a .308 and probably jerked the trigger. The 180-grain bullet shattered the small tree. Because the deer was so close, the major hunk of the bullet passed on, decimating a rib and downing the deer instantly.

What does such an experience prove? Nothing except that I made a poor shot! What the brush-rifle enthusiasts claim is that an extra-heavy bullet (usually with a round nose and traveling at a relatively low speed) will just clop-clop right along through interference without deviating at all in its line of flight. Pure unadulterated nonsense!

In my rack is a .44 Magnum. It shoots a 240-grain bullet. Sure it'll kill a deer. Sure the bullet will go through some brush without breaking up. But then it won't go very far very accurately. A single twig will deflect it, just as a single twig will deflect the swift, small 80-grain .243 bullet.

In fact, *all* bullets are deflected by whatever they touch in flight. Some are deflected more erratically than others. The amount of deflection from the target depends on how far from the target the projectile is when it meets the interference. For example, you can shoot a lying-down antelope at 300 yards with a .243 and go through a clump of grass that's within six inches of its body and still kill it. But if you put the same bullet through a similar clump of grass only 20 yards out from your gun muzzle, there's no telling what tangent the bullet will follow. Only by long chance or miracle will it reach the target.

Bullet speed and shape do influence how much or how little interference is required to cause erratic flight. Even a "little bit" of deflection is too much. Again, a rifle is a weapon designed for pinpoint shooting, not for spraying lead around and hoping for a hit.

The old .35 Remington was a good rifle for short range. It, and the .44 Magnum and a few others have been dubbed "brush rifles" and touted as such. In my opinion, they aren't much as deer rifles. Not when so many better choices are available.

I hasten to emphasize that the fundamental idea of shooting through brush is an open invitation to serious trouble. If you believe you can wham away at any hazy movement or a figure screened by cover, and connect, you'll be inclined to wham away—and maybe collect a fellow hunter instead of a deer!

The whole "brush rifle" hokum should have been given a quick and unmourned burial long ago. It has almost died out, but it's still kept breathing by the few hunters left who stubbornly cling to the old malarkey about the proper rifle for the East and the proper rifle for the West. I always chuckle to hear this. I've heard it border to border and coast to coast. Some points in the "logic" exactly contradict each other.

The Eastern deer hunter, so the argument goes, needs a fast-swinging brush gun because he hunts in heavy cover. The Westerner—the Easterner says—needs a flat-shooting rifle with a fast bullet because he hunts in the wide-open spaces. What the hunters who say these things are proving is that they don't know this good old U.S.A. very well. A whole lot of Western hunters claim the short old .30/30 saddle gun, as they called it, is the last word for their country. Why, is never quite clear. Maybe the reason is that this rifle lies easy under your leg in a saddle scabbard. It is true that the West has a lot of wide-open country, some of it deer country. It is also true that if you dropped a New England deer hunter into some of the thick country of the West, he couldn't find his rear end with both hands.

The tangles of the west slope of the coastal mountains along the Pacific, for example, where the Columbian blacktail-deer is abundant, would stop a Maine whitetail in its tracks. The cactus and thornbrush of southern Texas and the Mexican border country, though not high above your head, is the reason rattlesnakes were invented. It takes a critter that supple to get through it. The mule-deer and whitetail country of northwestern Montana will match anything the East has. The shin-oak-blanketed slopes of the Rockies in Colorado and Utah can't even be pushed through on horseback.

It is true that wooded whitetail country often is dense. Yet there are opportunities—I've had my share in Maine, Michigan, Pennsylvania, and, yes, even in the Deep South, where supposedly a hunter can't see in or out—to accept shots at 100, 200, and even 300 yards. So there's no such thing as the Eastern and Western deer rifles. What I'm getting at is that because of the rifles built today and the ammunition to go with them, the last matter a hunter needs to consider in selecting a deer rifle is the character of the terrain where he'll do most of his hunting.

To some readers, my view may be akin to heresy. Ideas that are old and ingrained and passed down usually die hard. But if we didn't accept new ones, we'd still be using only the muzzleloader—which is fun and a challenge, but not recommended to the mass of deer hunters as the ultimate and all-round piece.

A most interesting view of rifle choices comes from looking backward at some of the standards. Every species of North American big game has been efficiently dispatched with the .30/06. I am not positive of it, but I believe the same is true for the .270. Millions of deer undoubtedly have been bagged by these standard calibers. They've been used and still are used by tens of thousands of hunters all over the continent.

This record should tell a deer hunter something important. If these calibers have hung on so strongly for so many years, are capable with one load or another of taking all big-game species, and are used every season all across the land to kill deer, then it would seem these would be a good place to start, a kind of standard from which to judge what will work well for you. If you're a one-rifle man, a choice of one of these, *or something roughly comparable,* would seem logical. You can use the gun to deer hunt every year, and you can make a foray after something larger with the same weapon, whenever you can afford the trip.

I don't mean that you should necessarily select either of those standard calibers. I mean simply that the .30/06 and the .270 are norms from which to make comparisons.

Start with two premises: 1) that energy out at the point of impact is what does the killing, and 2) that bullet speed is what controls trajectory. You may feel like disagreeing with these premises; maybe they don't fit with what you've heard from old-timers. But if you do agree with these points, the logical conclusion is that a fairly fast, flat-shooting load will be most efficient in the greatest number of situations.

Why limit yourself to 100-yard accurate shots and have to guess for shots farther out? Why not choose a rifle that you can sight-in at, say, 200 yards and not have to worry about being on target for in-between shots or shots somewhat longer? Get it fixed in your mind that, regardless of what you may have been told or somehow led to believe, a fast, flat-traveling bullet is actually better in cover than a slow, looping one, and a good scope beats open sights in every way. The scope gathers light in dim places and picks out the small holes that have no obstructions—something your eye can't do. And the flat-traveling bullet, always the most accurate kind, goes through the opening precisely. With such a combination, whether you live East, West, South, Southwest, or Northwest, whether you hunt open or heavy cover (if you learn to *hunt* deer, learn to hold steady, to shoot calmly, to accept no shots you don't like, and to place your shots precisely) you'll be hard to beat in the long haul.

Now look at a few basic ballistics. Bear in mind that you must answer the question: What is *required* to kill a deer? This means not wound-and-chase, but drop right now. Obviously bullet placement is a tremendously important factor. But by checking the standard calibers I mentioned a moment ago, you get an idea of what is widely known to do a thorough job.

The .30/06, 150-grain Pointed Soft Point Core-Lokt (Remington) bullet leaves the muzzle at 2,910 feet per second, and with 2,820 foot-pounds of energy. Out at 200 yards, velocity is 2,342 feet per second, energy 1,827 foot-pounds. In a rifle sighted-in at 200 yards, the bullet is only 1.8 inches high at 100 yards. The .270, with the same bullet style in the much-used 130-grain, leaves the muzzle at 3,110 feet per second, and with 2,791 foot-pounds of energy. At 200 yards, velocity is 2,554, and energy is 1,883. In a rifle sighted-in at 200 yards, midrange is 1.7 inches high.

These two calibers, and loadings, are adequately comparable. So if we can say (as we do know) that the .30/30 is an adequate deer caliber at modest ranges, and it has 1,360 foot-pounds of energy at 100 yards, then consider: the .30/06 and .270 have a huskily safe margin each with around 500 pounds more energy even out at *twice* the .30/30 ranges. Both the .270 and .30/06 reach out much better and shoot much flatter than the .30/30. You couldn't do better than to base your search for a suitable deer rifle on these considerations and figures.

My favorite for a number of years now, on both mule deer and whitetails, has been the extremely efficient .243. I know many hunters

Important points to consider in selecting a deer rifle are nice handling, easy carrying, and accuracy that will place shots in a two-inch circle at 200 yards. The caliber (within limits) and how the gun looks are among the least of your worries. This light .243 does a fine job for the author.

who use it, and I know some (mostly big-caliber enthusiasts) who don't think it's much of a deer rifle. All I know is that mine, in my hands and those of my sons, has brought down in our high-limit state close to 100 deer—whitetails and mule deer—without a single loss or one that got to its feet after hitting the turf. In my opinion that's a great record as well as a recommendation. The 6mm, almost identical in performance, is just as good a choice.

The performance figures on the .243 look like this: 100-grain Pointed Soft Point Core-Lokt (Remington); muzzle velocity 2,960 feet per second, muzzle energy 1,945 foot-pounds; at 200 yards, velocity 2,449, energy 1,332; sighted-in at 200 yards, midrange 1.9 inches high. At midrange the velocity is 2,697 and the energy 1,615. I like to carry this rifle. It is superbly accurate, and the recoil is inconsequential.

There are, of course, lots of other fine choices. I have hunted several years with three companions who all shoot the .25/06 on mule deer. It is in my view a sensational deer caliber. The velocity and energy, using exactly the same weight and type of bullet as I specified earlier, are somewhat higher than those of the .243 all the way across. If you use the newer 120-grain bullet the punch and the way it holds up are even better. Another caliber, the .308, is so closely comparable to the .30/06 that it easily fits as an excellent choice. All of these notes should give you a firm basis to know what you're looking for and for making a final selection.

Of course, there is the matter of action—lever, bolt, slide and auto. There is no use haranguing this subject too heartily. Too often it's like kicking somebody's dog. Some hunters like the lever, or the slide, or the auto because—they claim—"I can get off a series of shots faster with this than I can with any other." If there was ever a good reason for which *not* to select an action, that is it. Show me a deer hunter who prides himself on how fast he can pour lead through his barrel and I'll show you one I'll never hunt with, one likely to be dangerous and impulsive, and one who does more missing and wounding than gutting.

There is utterly no reason—unless perhaps when you're facing at close range a charging grizzly—for shooting a rifle swiftly, shot after shot. A rifle is meant to be aimed—carefully—at a selected target and at a carefully selected spot on the target. Choose a rifle that shoots accurately, learn to shoot the first shot at a deer that way, and it won't make any difference how fast you can get off the other several. Fast, repetitive shots seldom hit a deer anyway, except by chance. All arms makers—and target shooters—consider the bolt action the sturdiest, most trouble-free and accurate of the lot. That knowledge should help an open-minded hunter with his decision.

There's an old saying that the shooter is more important than the gun. It might need to be qualified sometimes, but it's close to the truth. As I said at the beginning of this chapter, poachers have killed, and still kill, hundreds of deer with a .22, by jacklighting, getting close, and accepting only a between-the-eyes placement. The careful, deliberate legal hunter, who accepts only the shots he knows he can make good with the gun he has in his hands, is the one who collects the most venison. Nonetheless, there are valid suggestions, which I hope I've made, for making the hunter at any stage of development a little bit more efficient. Selecting a proper deer rifle isn't any complicated matter. All it requires is a smattering of basic knowledge about what's available and what's required, plus a pinch or two of common sense.

What to Wear and What to Carry

It is true that most people are reluctant to grow old. But when you've attained what may be gently described as the downslope run past middle age, it's at times gratifying to be in a position of having a stance of appraisal for what is current and what preceded it. During my early deer-hunting days, I rousted around the woods in northern Michigan. No motorhomes, no pickup campers, no plush travel trailers were used as camps then. Although I lived right on the edge of the state forest where I hunted, I had the chance to look over countless camps of deer hunters who came from farther away. I also ate in many of these camps and stayed in quite a few.

Often as not, the camp was a big wall tent that had a ridgepole, side poles, and corner poles cut from poplar saplings on the spot. Today, of course, some city environmentalists who don't know a ridgepole from a manhole cover, and who don't realize that thinning out "popple" stands is good for the forest, would go into spasms over so much as driving a nail into a jackpine for a place to hang the lantern. The floor of the tent was the earth, cleaned free of snow, and the mattresses were piles of fresh straw that were brought in.

These were wonderful places. Everybody's vehicle got stuck a few times in the ancient logging trails, and everybody helped everybody else get unstuck. The smell of the stewpots was heavenly, even as you passed by along a trail where several camps were scattered. Coffee was always going, and anyone who paused to commend the bucks hung by their antlers from the meatpole outside the camp was welcome to a mug. Most times that coffee would cross your eyes and float an axe.

The rifles all these hunters carried had stocks that were never shiny or of fancy woods. They were old guns meant for deer killing, no petting and polishing. One part of the scene I most vividly recall is of hunters standing around outdoor campfires, warming themselves and lying to each other, whittling, and nipping a jug, and of how they looked.

42

Most of today's hunters in that northwoods environment, with deep snow and the temperature often below 10 degrees, never have experienced the exquisite suffering of an authentic deer camp. Today hunters climb into their mobile camps, remove their ski masks from tender faces, shuck out of their shiny, nylon-shelled blaze-orange down jackets, ease out of their insulated and often shiny, noisy-rustling jump suits, pull off their $60 lug-soled boots, switch on the generator unit that sends its ghastly clatter rattling through the timber, and touch off the electric coffee pot.

Perhaps somebody who saw the way it was and sees the way it is can be forgiven for thinking that the ultra-modern deer hunter at times looks and acts just plain ridiculous, and for suspecting that he may come packaged complete with a windup mechanism in his back that activates programmed status machinery. Even the way those deer hunters of the 1950s looked—the nostalgia of remembering is pleasant. The "Mackinaw" jackets were a kind of uniform. They were of 32-ounce wool, in red-and-black plaid, the red a dark shade. The pants, most of them, had a double seat and knees. You could sit your backside down in a snowbank for an hour straight and never get damp. You could walk in rain or melting snow and just shake it off when you came in.

And quiet! You could slip through the brush with scarcely a rustle, and when you walked and your arms whisked by your sides, or you paused to raise a binocular, there was not a whisper. Wool, without any question, is the best outer-garments material for deer hunting. But in all the cool-to-cold climes, the switch to noisy outer shells is about complete. Nylon windbreakers and various nylon and other synthetics for the outer coverings of down clothing—all are shiny and cast a glint of light, all are noisy when you walk, and all are abominable when you try to sit quietly. When you sit, you need to hear, to listen with dedicated concentration. The constant noise of hard-surfaced outer garments (or inner ones for that matter) is a hearing hurdle of high decibel.

Granted, in almost all deer areas today, at least on public lands, regulations state that you must wear so many square inches of blaze orange. Practically all blaze-orange garments are shiny and noisy. So we're stuck. It's not a matter of real color, so far as the deer are concerned. Deer see mostly in shades of gray. But the legal hues make too-light blobs against the darker woods. To a deer, they may look off-white, and the sheen is an eye-catcher.

If some hunters hadn't been so careless, or stupid, or some of each, safety colors wouldn't have been necessary. But they're here to stay, that's for sure. Where I live, in Texas (and hunt always on private lands in my state) the color of clothing is not a problem. We lock the gate and do as we please about dress. For years in mild climates, I have worn cotton or light wool shirts for deer hunting. Today, if I'm riding in a vehicle, cruising around, glassing, I wear the modern dress—a down jacket with noisy exterior. But I wear pants of wool or other quiet materials in a light weight.

On public lands, of course, it's necessary to use the safety color required by law. But my advice to any deer hunter is to wear quiet clothing over as much as possible of his body.

There are exceptions. For example, on a stand where you'll be peering across some distance and have reason to believe no deer will be close, use nylon or comparable materials that cover most down, if you can stand the whispering. But quiet clothing always allows you to hear better. If you're like me, when you can't hear you can't see your best. Maybe that's psychological, but I always get that feeling. Colors of outer garments don't make too much difference, as long as they are a shade that, when translated to gray, will blend fairly well with surroundings.

For example, a few years ago Woolrich—that fine old firm that has made wonderful woolens for the last century or more—brought out a handsome bright-yellow wool coat for hunters. I still have one. In the Rockies when the aspens have turned in early October, it's fine. But elsewhere, or when aspen leaves are fallen, it stands out as prominently as a white shirt. You must keep in mind that a deer, which lives for most all its life within a square mile of where it was born, knows every bush, rock, tree, and hummock with intimacy. At a distance, a man in a bright-yellow coat makes a vertical rectangle of a too-light hue. A shape so geometric seldom occurs in nature. It will catch the eye of a deer. And when the deer looks, it becomes curious. Curiosity is only one step from uneasiness and flight.

Camouflage outer clothing and hat or cap is undoubtedly the best choice for the modern deer hunter. Fortunately, nowadays it is possible to get camo jackets, pants, and caps in cold-weather as well as mild-climate models. Camo blends very well. Gloves should also be of camo material. For close stalks, and for sitting where deer may be able to spot you rather easily, a headnet—I carry one in a pocket always—is a good idea. The only difficulty with net is that it reduces your ability to see out. Nowadays you can get a net hung on an eyeglasses frame. It covers the part of your face exposed below cap brim and allows you to see.

If you don't mind the muss and fuss of putting on and taking off

44

makeup, camo stick greasepaints do a perfect job on your face and hands. Types of greasepaint now available aren't greasy and aren't difficult to remove. Not all deer hunters are aware that camo can be had in varying shades. A few years ago bowhunters launched the idea of red-and-black camouflage suits. Hunters saw them, deer didn't—or so went the theory. There is a wide choice of shades in camouflage cloth. The one that matches closest the vegetation and terrain you're in is obviously the best. I wear a sand-and-brown camo pattern on one jacket for grassy or desert locations in season when vegetation is gray to tan. It blends perfectly, whereas standard green camo makes you a blob to be instantly inspected by a curious deer.

Headgear doesn't get as much attention as it should. I suppose deer hunters are occasionally influenced by seeing photos of other hunters wearing Western hats. I've done it often for photos, I'll admit, because it looks natty. But trying to hide a nice pale-colored Stetson is on a par with trying to hide your face. I hunted recently with a fellow who wore one of those Aussie-type broad-brimmed camo hats—you know, with a leather band and chin strap and one side of the brim rakishly clipped to the side of the crown. He almost choked himself to death several times crawling through brush with that hat and having it pulled off.

Again the blaze-orange hurdle must be met. If you are required by law to wear a red or orange cap, that's that. If you don't have to do so for safety or the law, a common old camo cap or inverted-pot hat ditto is the best choice and the easiest to make inconspicuous and to wear. In cold weather, wool or fur-lined headgear of the same design works fine. The stocking cap has high vogue nowadays in the deer woods. It's warm and handy all right, but I like a brim not only to shade my eyes but also to help conceal the one part of my anatomy that's most terrifying to a deer. Everybody has a personal preference in underwear. Net is warm. Down usually—but not always—is too warm. Old-fashioned as it may sound, I think the wool or flannel longies with that fine and ancient device, the drop seat, still do a darned good job.

As for other clothing, again, it gets personal. I think a vest (down, wool, or leather) is the worst hunting garment ever invented. A vest, when you're exercising, keeps you warm in places you don't need the warmth. Then, when you're *not* exercising, the vest lets you get cold in the places where you need warmth the most.

Again looking at today and yesterday, I'm intrigued by the footwear many deer hunters settle on. Somehow the pull-on boot with low heel, partly copying a cowboy boot, grabbed a vast market some years ago.

I wear them, so I can knock them if I want to. I wear them many times because I hate the job of lacing boots. Nonetheless, pull-on boots are an abominable choice for much walking, particularly in steep and rocky terrain. They slip too much on your feet. They can cause serious mishaps or put you out of commission due to blisters. Regular leather-soled, pointy-toed cowboy boots I shouldn't even mention. If a deer hunter doesn't know better than that, he deserves to suffer.

Looking way back again to those old-time hunters—and this goes far back—the combination called "socks and rubbers" was probably the finest deer-hunting footgear for snow and cold that has come onto the scene even to this day. Lumberjacks and others wore these in the last century. In this century—along maybe in the 1920s or so—the idea was improved. The original was a heavy-felt boot—the sock—that was pulled on. Then a heavy low-cut rubber (with an oval top opening so it would stay snug) was forced on over the foot. Later on, the felt sock became a felt boot. It had a stiff leather sole, thick, and it laced up. These boots or shoes were, I'd guess, roughly 10-inchers. The entire upper was made of heavy felt. The same design in old-fashioned rubbers was pulled on over them.

I wore these even when traveling with snowshoes, which illustrates how firmly they stayed put. Snowshoe harnesses must hang tightly to your foot. The felt was all but impossible to wet through in snow. It "breathed" beautifully, and seemed as warm as down. It was also amazingly sturdy. I'll just say I never did wear out a pair. Of course, the rubber kept you dry in snow, and you could negotiate shallow water if need be. And when heavy frost was on, you were in good shape. The footgear was comfortable and quiet, and when you sat on a deer stand for an hour or two your feet, with wool socks on inside your boots, were toasty.

My reason for describing this old-time footgear is that the best in modern footwear for a cold-weather snow-country deer hunt should do what these felts and rubbers did. I don't suppose they're still available. At least I've not seen any in years. If you can find some and you don't mind side glances at how odd you look, by all means get 'em. But the leather-top, rubber-bottom pack (also an old-time idea, and now available with insulation and soft glove-leather interior) probably does about as well. The insulated rubber hunting boots also are warm and a reasonable choice if you need waterproof wear.

I've long been a fan of some of the waterproof leather boots. Perhaps there are many brands I don't know about, but Dunham Brothers started this idea years ago, and their boots really were and are waterproof. That kind of leather boot is a good idea for varied terrain.

If you're in a warm clime and there's a rain or a heavy dew, you're dry.

There's an endless array of good hunting boots nowadays, and most of the fairly expensive ones excellent. But the mountain-climber soles on some are just plain silly for average deer hunting. In heavy rocky going on the steeps they are all right, but I'm not a fan. Most of these awesomely heavy-looking backpacker designs are catalog stuff that grabs the dude's eye. And if you want to get into a mess, try soles with deep slashes in them—allegedly wonderful for nonskidding and for self-cleaning—on a grass-covered mountainside when it's muddy. You might as well have snowshoes, or banjos, on your feet. And you will in a few minutes—each glob at least a foot in diameter.

In dry country, I've worn six-inch boots, and sevens, a lot. But I'm not thoroughly sold. In thorn and snake country, they're no protection. Something higher is better. In places where rattlers are an authentic menace, the tremendously heavy and tall snake boots certainly do that job. But wearing such boots is like dragging a log chain around. If you worry about snakes, use regular hunting boots and add a pair of snap-around hard-plastic snake leggings, which cover the instep and reach almost to the knee. These leggings go on and off easily, are light, and can be worn only when you think you need them.

What Should You Carry?

When it comes to selecting what every deer hunter should carry, the very first item should be a good binocular. It has always amazed me how many deer hunters don't use one. Some hunters say, "I just scan things with my scope." If there's anything that infuriates me it's to be looked at through a scope. The rifle has got to be pointed right at me.

Using a scope instead of a binocular is first of all a dangerous practice. A fellow who thinks maybe he saw a deer move has that notion in his head. He has the gun up and aimed. It's just one click of a few nerve synapses to the trigger pull. By contrast, the same hunter using a binocular has time to consider, and he can't shoot you with it. Furthermore, a scope—which is a monocular—is not remotely as good a scanner as a two-eyed glass. A deer hunter can ease a binocular up in slow motion and look around carefully without attracting attention. The guy waving a long gun around is a good deer scarer but not much of a deer hunter. A gun is for shooting; the scope on it is a sight for bullet placement. That's all.

There are many choices of binocular. Although it's arguable, I believe that cheap glasses don't amount to much. I hear every year

Glassing is one of the most important facets of deer hunting, and a top-quality binocular (not a cheap one) is perhaps the best deer-hunting investment you can make.

about how marvelous this binocular or that one is, " . . . and it only costs a few dollars . . . ." I've never looked through one that could remotely match a top-quality glass. The good binocular can find you deer you'd never know were there. It is one of the best tools a hunter has, invaluable especially in poor light and for its light-gathering powers in dim, dense cover. A good one is a lifetime investment, so why not spend the egg money?

The best all-round binocular is probably the 7×35. The 8×30, and others in wide-angle, are reasonable choices. But it's hard to beat the easy carrying and handy use of the 7×35. The type of focusing is really not arguable. As between individual-eye focus and center focus with single eye adjustment, the individual-eye focus is far and away better. Each eyepiece should be marked in a plus-and-minus scale. So if, for instance, your perfect focus is left eye 1 and right -2, you memorize the numbers and can set your glass instantly when you uncase it, or after someone else has used it.

Speaking of what to carry, obviously you must carry your gun. That calls for a sling. A friend of mine says he'd as soon go hunting barefooted and with his pants off as to go without a sling on his gun. I agree. It's the best way to carry a gun and the safest way when you're with companions or alone. A sling eliminates the problem of what to do with your gun when you need both hands, such as for glassing or parting brush. When you pause to blow, you don't have to look for a place to lay the gun down or prop it up. And a sling is invaluable for steadying your aim when a solid rest isn't at hand.

It may seem silly to mention, but one carry item that hunters too often neglet is *plenty of ammunition.* Situations can arise—even getting lost—when an ample amount of ammunition, not just "a few cartridges," will save the day.

An additional fundamental item of equipment is a good knife. The fad of knifemaking nowadays and the millions of words written about knives serve only to confuse the average hunter. For knife collectors, those wild-looking designs are all right if that's what makes your adrenaline flow. But many of those knives are all but useless as deer-gutting implements. I've watched hunters carrying enormous knives almost as big as Mexican machetes. Others proudly wear a beautiful knife—but it turns out that it's a skinner, not a gutter. Others show up with fillet knives flopping on their belts, and you shudder because the knives are around in front, banging one side of the belly.

After using a great many knives, I have concluded that for the fellow who hunts deer a lot and doesn't want to be overencumbered, a sturdy jackknife of good quality and with a blade long enough to do the job is about the best choice. A small stone carried in pocket or day pack is invaluable for giving the blade a few strokes to keep its cutting edge businesslike.

What other items a hunter carries depends on the mode of hunting. In some places deer hunters cruise around in vehicles on ranch or forest trails. They pause to glass, finally make a stalk, and kill a deer, often within easy range of the transportation. These hunters can carry everything they need in the vehicle. For the walking hunter, about the only absolutely necessary additional items are a 15- or 20-foot length of light, stout nylon rope; a plastic bag to put liver and heart in if you save them; and a few wet wash pads in a small plastic bag, so you can scrub up after the gutting job—and put the used pads back into their bag for carrying out.

The farm-woodlot hunter needs nothing else. The stand hunter who goes straight to a chosen stand and stays there and then goes back to his vehicle, probably wants to take along a bite or two of food—jerky, raisins, candy, maybe even a couple of sandwiches. Perhaps, too, a thermos of coffee or hot tea. For far-afield foragers, I firmly believe in a small day pack of some sort. What goes into it depends on where and how you hunt. A compass is a must in any big-woods situation. A *good* compass. I like the cased pocket kind that can be set to mark routes going and coming with fine accuracy. Always remember, however, that a compass is worthless unless you know how to use it. Make it a point, if you hunt big timber, to bone up thoroughly on compass use *before* you need to use it. Even a few dry runs are helpful.

For close-in jaunts, a day pack can be simply a large game pocket in the back of a hunting coat. For longer ones, carrying a very small backpack, even of the economical Boy-scout canvas type, is the best way to go. A map is mandatory. This can be, for example, a detailed county map of the area you're hunting in, showing streams, trails, lakes, and roads. Or it can be the map of a state or national forest or of a section of such a forest. Or a topographic map, if you know how to read it. Even a good road map can help orient you in a pinch, in many not-too-wild situations.

Before any deer hunter goes into a big expanse of woods, he should be certain someone knows where he went, and how long he intends to be gone. I keep a basic pack ready all the time, to serve for all kinds of hunting and for fishing as well. It goes on my back, into a vehicle, or into a boat. In it are all the items already mentioned: rope, plastic bags, wet-wash pads, sharpening stone, extra ammo (for the gun to be used, be sure!), map, and compass.

A carefully thought-out first-aid kit is in my pack. The kit contains such items as first-aid creams, insect repellent, aspirin, Merthiolate, soap, bandages, adhesive, Q-tips, safety pins, snake-bite kit, and (for desert hunts) sun-screen lotion. Other items in the pack: matches in a waterproof container, a small packet of fire-starter cubes, a first-aid instruction booklet in a waterproof bag, clean handkerchiefs and one pair socks also in a plastic bag, a few staple food items that won't spoil, an extra jackknife, a few fish hooks and a roll of stout monofilament, heavy foil—folded flat—to cook with if need be, a spoon, and a few packets of salt in a waterproof container.

You can pick and choose as you like, but my little pack also contains: a spool of copper wire, some long leather laces, a light ground sheet, a big square of heavy plastic folded flat, a small flashlight with fresh batteries, one of those metal matches for striking sparks, a nylon-windbreaker shell that folds not much larger than a bandanna, a short fat candle, an extra-light nylon rain suit, and a little curved saw that folds its blade into a wooden handle and really works well, even on large limbs.

50

This may sound like a lot. Granted, you don't need it all for an afternoon in familiar territory. I take out—and always put back immediately when I come out and unload my gun—what I really won't need. The whole works weighs, with the light pack sack, believe it or not, just 10 pounds. Sure, that's quite a lot of extras to carry. As I've said, you don't need to take all of it all the time. But my main point is that with just that little pack I could, if need be, actually live in fair comfort for several days in an emergency. All it requires is a bit of ingenuity about how to use each item of equipment. The saw, for example, is sturdy and illimitably more efficient at cutting firewood or putting together a camp than is the all-but-useless traditional hatchet. And the saw requires far less energy in relation to results. The ground sheet and plastic sheet make a camp.

I learned years ago to take off my jacket in chill-to-cold weather when I'm walking. The jacket is often wool but sometimes is a down-underwear top worn beneath the light nylon-windbreaker shell. I could stuff the jacket into the pack. But I like the pack to be as small as possible, so I run the sleeves of the jacket together around my middle and tie the sleeves together in a simple knot in front. If the jacket material is inclined to slip, tie a leather lace around the sleeve knot.

The bulk of the jacket rides on your rear and isn't too awkward in brush. And, of course, you don't perspire so much. When you pause to rest, untie the jacket and slip it on. When I'm outfitted this way—and provided I have warm wool pants and waterproof boots—even in mighty chill country I could, if forced to, stay out overnight or for several nights without any debilitating discomfort. There's immense security in having this little makeshift home-away-from-home with you.

All of this, as I've emphasized, is for single-day big-country hunting. But I must warn the beginner, or the hunter who is easily turned around in strange territory, not to think that "big" means tens of thousands of acres. In my time I've helped hunt down lost men (an every-season occurrence when I lived in northern Michigan) who went into a forest that was cut every mile or so at the most by old roads and streams. In other words, these men got lost inside a square mile. That's 640 acres. When it's all woods, it can seem like a big expanse to an uneasy gent who can't find camp and who believes he has traveled several times as far as he really has.

I've purposely not mentioned drinking water until now. Most of the time, in most deer ranges, it isn't any real problem. Some hunters feel they need more than others. If you've any doubt, by all means carry a canteen. And in the desert country of the Southwest and a few other places, carrying a water supply on long hiking jaunts is a most important matter. It might be wise also to carry in a pack a bottle of purifying tablets, along with a heavy watertight plastic bag for a water container. For the average deer hunter, however, water isn't any real problem.

If you're uncertain about the purity of water where you'll hunt, pack some of your small backpack items into an empty quart-size tin can. Then you can stop and boil creek water in the can for 10 or 15 minutes to kill germs.

The main point to be made about what you wear and what you carry is that those items can make the difference between a pleasant hunt and a debacle. Sure, deer hunting almost inevitably involves some mild suffering. A fellow gets cold (or in some climes too hot), his feet hurt, his bones ache, he collects scratches and bruises and stumbles along nearly exhausted. Every deer hunter should learn to handle unavoidable suffering gracefully. But if you dress properly and take along a few extras proportionate in variety to the need of the day, you'll be in a better frame of mind for accepting a few mild discomforts.

You Can Call Me a Meat Hunter

On the opening morning of deer season, I entered the woods with the old excitement as usual frothing inside me. I selected a stand and began the tense wait, peering here and there, seeking the slightest movement that might mean "buck." And presently, here one came.

This was an eight-pointer with a very nice even rack. As it walked along, totally unaware of me and yet within easy shooting range of possibly 80 yards, another buck—this one a six-pointer, but with larger antlers than the other—stepped out of the cedars. The two bucks stood looking at each other. Both were good-size animals.

I didn't raise my gun. Instead I raised my binocular. For some minutes I studied the two deer. I was trying to decide if either was worth shooting for its meat.

Now I know scores of hunters who will snort when they read that statement. "Meat hunter!" they'll say. There is a term that has upon it almost the stigma of the criminal. Why? Certainly if I'd been jack-lighting a deer illegally just to collect any old hunk of meat, then the stigma would have been justified. But what I was looking for was a quality carcass of venison. These two bucks, I decided, were not in good shape at all. Their bodies and flanks had too many concavities and not enough convexities.

I won't deny that I felt the same emotion in seeing them come out that any big-game hunter faces at the appearance of game. It was all there. But over the decades of hunting, I had learned pretty well to discipline those emotions and channel them into paths of sensible decision. I shook a little bit as the deer walked away, but not for a moment did I regret my decision.

For several days after that, I was out each day, and I passed up in that time five more bucks as not "meat worthy." I then began, of course, to be disturbed over whether or not I'd get a deer I wanted. Any hunter is bound to feel that way. I wanted the hunting and I

53

wanted a deer. A dilemma of sorts. But I had my mind made up to go deerless unless I found what I desired.

The next week I was sitting one late afternoon watching a group of does and two dinky spikes. I looked at one spike rather closely. It was a good little deer, but it was too small. As I studied it, a movement off to the right caught my eye. When I turned my head, I knew I was looking at the deer I was going to shoot. A shot of adrenaline squirted into my bloodstream. My heart started thumping, and my hands trembled. The ancient thrill was just as great as if I were shooting at the world record. Here was a specific animal I had wanted and sought and waited for.

I raised the rifle carefully. Through the scope I saw an eight-point buck that was butter-fat. He was round in every muscle. He waddled. He was broadside. I thought I'd shoot him through the neck. But as I began my squeeze, he wheeled and made a little dart ahead. Only his rear was presented. I held my fire. This shot was unacceptable, even if I had to give him up. It would spoil too much meat, and that's what I was after. Would I have shot him in the skull if I'd been after his antlers? No.

Presently the buck heard some disturbing noise, raised his head, and arched his neck back over his right shoulder. I laid the cross hair on the neck and concluded my hunt.

Maybe you're not sure you agree with this kind of hunting. You may even be a little bit contemptuous. Meat hunter! But don't be too hasty. After many years of deer hunting and shooting, I sincerely believe that thinking of the meat leads to the most sporty and sporting kind of deer hunting. Not one hunter in ten thousand has ever thought of it that way, but I believe I can convince anyone who will listen.

First of all, I can well understand that the first-time hunter, or the boy after his first buck, can't ordinarily be expected to pick and choose. That's all right. But in my opinion, it's inexcusable for a mature, experienced hunter with a string of kills behind him to pick off just any old deer. The killing of deer by now should have become routine to him.

Think about it: what are the reasons for killing a deer?

All too many hunters nowadays seem to think that when they buy the license there's some unwritten law that places upon them the vital responsibility to fill it. What's so bad about winding up the season with an unfilled tag in your pocket? I had one at the end of a recent season in my two-buck area. I could have filled it numerous times. But if a hunter kills a deer just because he likes to *kill* something—and we have a few such hunters in the woods—then he's no sportsman. If he's determined to kill one just to take it home and show it around to prove to friends what a big sport he is, then his motive is degrading to himself and to hunting.

Primarily, the sportsman's reason for hunting any animal should be the *sport* involved. Filling the license should be only a thrilling climax to an otherwise enjoyable time out in the woods, *hunting.* What's so thrilling about accepting anything that comes along? If we're to culminate the hunt with the kill, then it follows that we ought to want, for some dignified and useful reason, the animal killed. It must be in some way *special.* What is it then that we want?

Three parts of a deer are useful in today's world (where such items as tendons and bone are not necessary to daily life). Those useful parts are the hide, the antlers, and the meat. I'm sure anyone would agree that killing a deer for just its hide would be a preposterous idea. It would be a whimsical and not very admirable thing to go after the whole animal just for the sake of a pair of gloves or part of a jacket. Many of us, to be sure, utilize the hide but only as a kind of extra little bonus, or we give hides away to institutions where they can serve charitable purposes. Neither use could possibly justify a kill.

Now what about the antlers? I won't condemn any hunter for shooting any deer, even in such a way that much meat is ruined, if the animal has enormous antlers or antlers with some especially desirable qualities. I'm not a hunter of record heads and couldn't care less about anything than the possession of a world-record head just for the sake of its *being* a world record. But I'd certainly shoot fast and accept any kind of shot if I had in my sights an extraordinary rack, or an exceptional nontypical one, or a freak head that would make a stunning trophy.

How many such deer are killed annually? Compared percentage-wise to the number of kills made, the real trophies are all but insignificant. Probably 900 or more out of every 1,000 deer taken annually fall into the category of so-so heads. The antlers of the spikes, the fork-horns, and the little sixes and eights are utterly worthless except to the animals whose sex they distinguish.

So what consideration have we got left? Meat. If we truly go big-game hunting for *sport,* and we kill not just to be killing or to brag, and we don't have a chance at a true trophy, then there's only one legitimate reason that will logically justify shooting: *meat.*

Antlerless deer are the classic example. Thousands are killed every season. Properly so. Successful deer management requires that a substantial number of does and fawns be taken each year to keep the herd from overpopulating its range. There should be no stigma whatever about settling for an antlerless deer. The sport involved is certainly comparable to the taking of a nontrophy buck. Game departments constantly stress the need to remove more does, and the need is real. However, antlerless deer are a prime example of the importance of the meat.

And now follow me closely. If you carelessly or impulsively shoot a so-so nontrophy animal in such a manner that you ruin a good share of the best meat, then you've done a really disgraceful and unsporting piece of business. And so we come right around the circle to the fullness of sport—and my contention—in meat hunting: selecting a top-quality meat animal to shoot at, or holding fire and accepting only those shots that save every bit of meat possible, add double handicaps and thus great sport to an already difficult quest.

Placing the Shot Properly

On a mule-deer hunt several years ago, I got my eye on an animal that I thought I wanted. The head was pretty fair: no record, but respectable. Since I already had two rather good mule-deer heads on my wall, I had little interest in the head for its own sake. The buck was exceptionally plump and looked virile, healthy, and young. It was walking away from me at an angle so narrow that the best I could possibly do would be to place the bullet under the back ribs. Such a shot ranges forward and certainly kills quickly. But it's an extremely delicate one. Shooting too wide to avoid the paunch will smash or graze a shoulder and possibly let the animal get away wounded. Holding too deep to make sure of a clean kill may take the paunch instead and blow up everything on forward.

As I considered what to do, the range got longer and longer. There was, of course, opportunity to take a tailbone shot. I have read many times how a deer hunter can make clean kills by holding for the base of the tail on a going-away animal. That's true enough. But anyone who takes this will be one of the greatest meat wasters of all. A bullet entering at the base of the tail may leave both hams prettily intact. But cut off a whole ham and roast it sometime and you'll find it strong and distasteful. Expansion of tissue as shock from the bullet travels outward forces masses of blood out between the layers of muscle. These masses show up when the layers are separated, especially after cooling.

Regardless of what anyone says, I maintain that shot-up or bloody meat can't possibly make good eating. One big reason so many persons believe they don't like big-game meat is that they've never had anything but poorly shot meat. And poorly shot meat usually becomes poorly tended meat. The fellow who shoots "at the whole animal" just to get it killed seldom knows or has regard for how to take care of the mess he collects.

Anyhow, at about 300 paces the buck finally stopped. After a little while he turned broadside. I got down and got as good a rest as I could. It wasn't as good as I wished. I put the cross hair on the animal's neck up behind the head. But I just couldn't have faith in making the shot at that small neck at that distance.

The next choice, because of the distance, was the rib cage. Here is an area where on a broadside shot only a very minor amount of waste occurs. But the shot must stay clear of the shoulders and be in the softest area of the ribs, yet far enough ahead to be sure to clear the paunch. At long distances, perfect placement isn't easy, but the shot does offer the largest clean-killing area of little meat, and thus offers the widest margin for holding error. I touched off at last and down went my deer. When I looked it over, I saw I had fortunately got the job done just right.

Can anyone deny that in collecting a perfect piece of meat I had also had more sport that I could have had by wild undisciplined shooting at a fleeing buck's rear end? Can anyone disagree with my thesis that by severely disciplined meat-shooting I gave myself a handicap that I could take pride in overcoming? This kill was one I could be justly proud of. Conversely, I have a friend who recently hunted for, and got, a mule-deer head that made the record book. He shot it badly so far as the meat was concerned. I can't argue over what part of the animal's anatomy he selected in order to collect it. He's a trophy hunter and had passed up many bucks (and also gone home without a deer several years) in order to select one he really wanted.

On many shots you may have to compromise. Maybe you won't get a chance at the rib cage. Unless a hunter is an exceptional shot, trying for the neck on a running shot is a poor idea. True, you may "kill clean or miss clean" as some hunters claim. You may also misjudge very badly and blow the whole backstrap, or saddle, right out of the animal. By sticking to the ribs on a broadside running shot, you have a good chance—assuming you know your own shooting habits and how you hold—to cause only minor meat damage. At the worst you'll ruin a shoulder or mess up the paunch. You take that chance if you elect to shoot.

I have never favored running shots, because of the chance of wounding an animal and perhaps never knowing it, and also because it is so routine to poorly place a bullet that way. I would, however, accept a running shot at a true trophy buck, if I wanted that specific one desperately. Then I'd be compromising between meat and antlers.

I must emphasize, though, that every deer hunter should make an honest appraisal of his own shooting ability. I know one deer hunter who is an amazing performer on running deer. He can just about call his placements when he has a broadside moving target. But if you know you do a poor job of such things, forgo the impulse to try. Likewise, if you don't believe you can make a neck shot good, and you have selected an animal you really want, then try for the ribs. Or be willing to gamble on a lethal hit or a clean miss.

The good meat-hunter shots are the really *sporting* shots. Just any old hit isn't good enough. In fact, if you're a good meat hunter, only a very few bullet placements are ever acceptable to you. Consider what limitations—and added sport—this kind of hunting gives you. You can take a neck shot, a broadside rib-cage shot, a head shot, a spine shot over and just behind the shoulders, or a frontal shot at the base of the neck (where on average-sized deer an opening only about as large as a baseball allows bullet entry into a vital interior area) without blowing up meat.

In other words, the entire rear half of the animal is denied to you, regardless of angle. And the greater share of the total square-inch area of the front half is also taboo. So you must either get into proper position to have an acceptable shot presented, or so contrive things that the animal will offer one that's acceptable. These limitations certainly separate the real hunters from the wild-eyed shooters.

Many times, the expert meat hunter must make a snap judgment on which shot to take, and whether or not the need to compromise has arisen. A classic example, although not concerned with deer, occurred to me one time in northern Ontario when I was moose hunting. A running moose burst from timber, hit the water, and continued running along shore. It was, in fact, plunging. When a moose runs this way in water a couple of feet deep and the range is a hundred yards, shooting at it from a canoe that's bobbing on waves isn't easy. Though it's easy enough to just hit the moose, placing a shot is difficult.

Because the animal was broadside, a neck shot under ordinary circumstances would have been the right one. A moose is big, and its neck is big: a good target when the animal is standing. But because the moose was plunging and the canoe was rising and falling, my snap judgment told me the neck wasn't the spot. Hair atop the neck is about 8 inches long. I could miss, get hair, and hit only the low meaty portion with a shot not immediately fatal.

58

Should I take the rib cage? No. When a standing animal that is not aware of the hunter is shot through the ribs, often it drops like a stone. But a fleeing animal, hopped up on the adrenaline in its bloodstream, often keeps right on running even when badly heart-shot. If the animal got back into dense timber, our chore of getting it out would be that much more difficult. If it plunged deeper or even started swimming out to deep water, we'd be in a real pickle.

I decided to shoot for the shoulder itself, to break the animal down right there. The bullet hit the big shoulder joint and went on to strike the tip of the heart. The animal stopped in midplunge and fell. I go over the details of this kill to point out that sometimes the meat hunter must purposely spoil some meat, as I did with that shoulder shot, in order to avoid worse circumstances. So he must consider thoroughly beforehand what to do under varied circumstances. His proper judgment must be instantly made.

Most good hunters dislike a head shot. It may ruin a trophy, and there's something psychologically distasteful about it. The neck shot, however, is one of the very best. It requires finesse and good shooting. The beauty of the neck shot is that it can be taken from numerous angles: (1) from above and directly behind, such as when the hunter is on a mountainside and the deer is below him; (2) from broadside; (3) from an angle, even though the animal has its head turned either way; and (4) from directly in front, when a deer's head is held high. On all deer, a bullet of weight and caliber big enough to do a proper job if placed elsewhere is just about certain to make an instantaneous kill if the animal is hit in the neck.

The frontal shot at the base of the neck, placing the bullet between the high forward portion of the shoulders and through that baseball-size opening into the lung-and-heart region, is also instantaneous. This shot requires exact placement, a good rest, and, obviously, a standing animal. The spine shot above and just behind the shoulders requires perhaps the most finesse of all.

I once shot a deer this way because the area just behind the shoulders was all of the animal I could get into the sights without having to go through brush. I wanted the deer, and I decided to try the shot. If done correctly, this shot ruins practically no meat at all. But you must know how thick the hair is, and you must get deep enough to break the backbone without getting way down deep into the shoulders.

When I shot, the animal crumpled. But when it was skinned out, we discovered that a placement possibly less than half an inch higher would only have pulled a little hair. My shot had barely scraped the top of the backbone with enough bullet energy to make a kill. This shot is chiefly useful in brush where no other acceptable portion is presented as a target.

From this discussion, you have probably inferred that of all hunters, the serious meat hunter is the *cleanest killer.* He doesn't shoot if he may shoot off a leg or smash up a ham. He learns first of all to shoot well and to discipline himself. And he learns something of far more importance that not one hunter in thousands ever thinks of. It's the best argument of all for being a confirmed meat hunter: the meat-saving shots are the most deadly shots; the meat-wasting shots are too often only wounding shots.

Indeed, the meat hunter knows well the meaning of that ancient bit of hunting advice: "It's the first shot that counts." He goes about his chore intending to use only one bullet, unless he misses entirely. Who dares call that unsporting? Some hunters go out not caring how many bullets they use, just so they somehow get the critter blasted to the ground. The good meat hunter often must give up shots and sometimes go meatless.

When Your Deer Is Down

There are probably as many favorite approaches to field-dressing a deer as there are rifle calibers. Some hunters make it complicated, some make it simple. Actually field-dressing isn't difficult for even the rank tyro. In keeping with the meat-saving theme, the basic approach should be to waste as little as possible.

Always approach a downed buck from the rear. Deer have been known to get up, and occasionally a hunter is hurt. Also, most hunters are excited after shooting a deer, so keep your safety wits.

After you're *certain* the deer is dead, unload your gun and prop or lay it safely nearby. If you're hunting in any state where a tag must be affixed, do it right now. It's easy to forget—to your possible chagrin and expense.

If the ground slants, get the deer's head uphill. Get it onto its back. If you're alone, prop rocks or sticks against the deer's sides to hold it on its back. If you have help, have your companion hold a leg to keep the deer belly up. A little trick I learned years ago is to bring the forelegs far forward, if you've killed a buck, and hook each under the corresponding antler. That step helps keep the deer in proper position.

Be sure your knife is sharp. It's worthwhile to carry a small sharpening stone to touch up the knife during field-dressing. Cut off the testicles of a buck or the udder of a doe. If you've shot a buck, take hold of the penis and cut the skin ahead of it and keep on cutting skin

60

Always approach a downed buck from the rear.

If the ground slants, get the deer's head uphill.

Cut skin ahead of penis, and keep cutting back toward rear.

In ream method, you cut around anus so that bowel and tubes to bladder are loose in cavity.

back toward the rear. Right where the tubes enter the anal opening, gently snip the bit of attaching cartilage. This procedure gives access to the anal opening. Now, if you prefer the "ream" method, slip the knife blade gingerly into the opening, holding it close to the bone and straight, and cut clear around. You'll probably have to first cut the skin surrounding the anus.

When you've made the cut clear around inside (using care not to puncture the bladder), you've loosened all attachment here. You can test this by a gentle tug on the penis and bowels together. To do this reaming chore properly, you need to raise the deer's rear end. A helper can do this simply by pulling the hind legs forward. If you're alone, prop up the hind end with a rock or a log. Incidentally, if the hairy gland on the inside of each hock is wet and smelly, slice skin well ahead of them and cut them off, so you don't inadvertently get musk on any meat. And avoid touching the glands so that you don't transfer any musk to the meat.

Now to the body cavity. From the point where you've cut the skin at the udder or penis, insert your knife blade with its cutting edge up; carefully slice the skin only, up to the rib cage. Now, with utmost care, make a small slit maybe one inch as the starter, in the muscle at the lower abdomen area. Insert two fingers of your left hand there (if you're right-handed), and, with the blade's cutting edge up, gingerly slice the deer's muscle between your fingers as you work forward to open the abdomen. Your left fingers (and hand as the opening grows) should press down on the bowels and then the paunch so that you don't puncture them.

If you must drag your deer some distance, or you intend to have the head mounted, continue the cut only to the forward limit of the brisket. To do this, observe the white sternum bone (breast bone), which shows at the lower end of the rib cage. Insert your knife, cutting edge up, straddle the deer, and cut just to one side of the sternum, with ripping strokes. Be very careful not to hurt yourself or a helper. This cut opens the rib cage. If no mounting is planned, and little dragging, continue the cut clear up the neck so that you can remove the entire windpipe.

Either way, cut off the windpipe as far up as possible. Now you can pull out windpipe, heart, and lungs from the cavity. Slit the diaphragm on both sides of the cavity. It separates the heart-lung area from the paunch and bowels. Once the diaphragm is cut—be careful not to slit the paunch in process—you can roll the deer onto its side and roll and pull out all the entrails. Then grasp the bowel low down inside and

Cut skin first and then muscle up belly to sternum (breast bone). Note white sternum bone showing at lower end of rib cage.

63

Roll deer onto its side, and pull out all entrails.

Grasp bowel low down inside, and pull forward to remove bladder, anus, and so on.

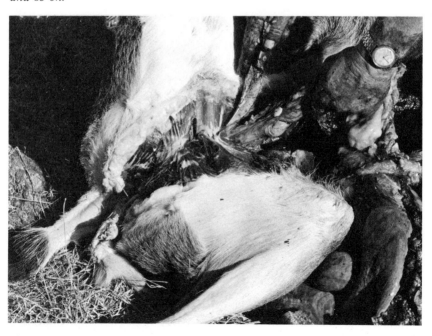

firmly but gently pull forward. The bladder, anus, penis, and attached parts will all come through the opening to be discarded. The liver, heart, and kidneys if you eat them, go into the plastic bag you should have for that purpose in a pocket.

Many hunters don't use the "ream" method at the anus. They prefer to split the pelvic shield or bone that protects the anal cavity. There is a kind of seam in its center that you can feel. Feel both inside and out. A heavy knife (or if you must, a small hatchet) can cut beside this seam, through the bony area. Once the cut is made, place one foot on the inside of each hind leg of the deer, lean down and grasp the tail, and give a sharp upward jerk. The bone will split, laying open the anal cavity. Now you can pull the bladder, gut, and penis up through it. Finally, either roll the deer over or (if it's small) lift it by the forelegs so to empty accumulated blood from the body cavity.

It's not always possible to skin a deer immediately. But if you can get the animal hung up and skinned while it's still warm, the chore is much easier. Some hunters hang a deer head-down, claiming (without authenticity) that head-up hanging allows blood to run through the veins into the hams and ruin them. It's true that hanging head-down—that is, by slitting the gambrels and hanging the deer with its

If you prefer splitting pelvis, use this trick to split the cavity open. Stand on hind legs of deer, seize tail, pull sharply upward.

65

After entrails are removed, deer is tipped onto its side to drain out blood. Some turn it completely over to drain. If two hunters are present, buck can be lifted by antlers to drain excess blood out rear cavity.

hind legs well separated—makes skinning easier, simply because the carcass doesn't turn as you work. Either way, the skinning procedure is similar.

If you hang a deer head-up, first slit the skin from knee joint to chest inside each front leg. Then cut clear around the neck. Now begin to peel the skin downward from the neck, working it loose with your knife blade as necessary. When you get the skin down to the front legs, peel it down each leg to the knee. A small bone saw is handy here. Simply saw off the meatless hocks. If you don't have a saw, cut into the joint with your knife, twist the leg to break the joint free, and cut off the lower leg.

Now use your knife to loosen the skin on each side of the brisket.

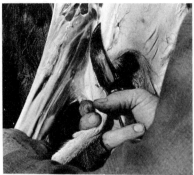

Above: Work loose the skin of each foreleg (previously slit inside from knee to chest), and then pull as shown.

Left: Here's the skinning of a deer that's hung by its head (simply reverse all steps if you prefer to hang deer by its rear gambrels). Cut around neck and work skin downward.

A strong pull at the rear (with blade assistance here and there) will now peel the skin downward over the body.

Then slit the skin inside the hams, peel the hide clear down to the tailbone, cut that, and keep on peeling. Loosen the hide inside the hams with your blade if need be. Now cut off the hind hocks, and the job is complete.

There are so many ways to cut up a deer that there is little point in giving endlessly detailed instructions. Most deer are taken to processing plants nowadays. If you want to do a fast basic job on your own, here's how.

After the skin is off and the deer is still hanging (let's say still head-up), slice deeply inside each foreleg, meanwhile pulling the leg away from the body, and cut free the whole leg and shoulder. There is no big shoulder joint—just muscle to cut. Place the shoulders in plastic bags to be cut as desired later, at a butcher shop or at home.

If you have a saw, and a clean place to work, cut across the backbone barely above the hams, so both hams come off in one piece. Now set them on a board or block, and saw down the center to separate them.

If you don't have a saw, slice deeply with your knife up each side

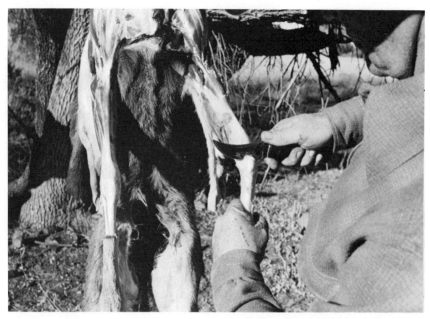

After cutting skin loose from foreleg at knee joint, cut into joint as shown, twist shank, and then cut it free for discard.

Slit inside hams, peel hide down, and cut off tail.

You can get a good start on cutting up deer while it's still hanging. Cut deeply inside foreleg and remove each shoulder. No cutting of joint required here.

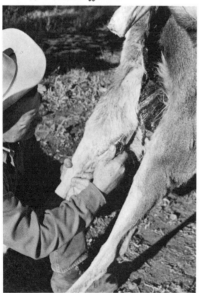

Neat trick for removing ham in three steps without using a saw: 1) slit from top down between ham and body; 2) slit forcefully upward beside tail; 3) seize ham as shown here and force it sharply upward toward inside of body. This motion snaps the joint, and then ham can be cut away whole.

of the tailbone (the end of the backbone). Now make a deep cut inside each ham, seize the ham shank, brace your other hand against the back, and bring the ham sharply up toward the body cavity. The spot where the haunch joins the back will crack, and you can cut the individual ham off. These also are bagged to be cut for roasts or steaks later.

You now have two choices.

- One is to bone out the backstraps. To do so, slit down the back from shoulder to ham area closely on each side of the backbone. Then make a cut across at the shoulder end, and use your knife to slowly work the individual loins loose, each one whole. These make fine fillets. If you do this, now go inside the body cavity and remove the small "tenders" from low in the back. All that's left hanging are the neck, the ribs, and the backbone. Saw the ribs off each side. Split each rib slab in the center so it will fold for packing. The usual procedure is to whack the slab of ribs across its center with a hatchet or saw. This procedure breaks the rib bones about halfway along their length but leaves the connecting tissue. Then you can fold one half of the rib slab onto or atop the other, making a compact chunk. Cut the neck from the head so

Bone out backstraps (one on either side) by cuts along backbone as shown.

the neck can later be boned out for a roast or used for sausage, hamburger, or chili meat.

- Your other choice is to have chops instead of boneless backstraps. After the hams are removed, saw crosswise at the base of the neck and you have rib cage and loin in one big chunk. With saw or hatchet, remove the ribs close to the loin, as is done in butcher shops. The loin can be cut into wing chops, or sawed down through the middle and then into single chops, or cut in two crosswise for saddle roasts. On a large deer, you should cut away the flank meat below the ribs and use it for ground meat. You may also wish to use the rib meat and the shanks for this purpose.

At any rate, this is a quick and simple way to get the meat ready to take home, or even to cut it up at home, with no waste. If you have been a good "meat hunter" and selected the deer and the shot you wanted, you'll discover that your sport, enjoyment, and challenge are enhanced. And the eating will be excellent.

How Good Are Deer Calls and Deer Scents?

As a result of doing a substantial amount of experimentation in the use of calls for deer, I have come to the conclusion that this is one area of deer hunting lore that could use a lot more research. And I now believe that calls have far greater possibilities than have so far been realized.

Certainly a great deal is already known about various techniques of outwitting deer, so it can't be said that hunters desperately need an additional method in order to succeed. Yet deer calling offers a challenge that greatly appeals to me.

By "calling" I mean the hunter's utterance of sounds, ordinarily by using a mouth-blown call. Rattling up bucks by the use of loose antlers is obviously a method of attracting deer by sound. But that's another approach entirely and is covered in detail in another chapter.

One factor that has held back mass interest in deer calls is that deer are generally considered nonvocal creatures. Tens of thousands of deer hunters have roamed the ranges since colonial days, and only a scattering of them have ever heard a deer utter a vocal sound. I admit that in some four decades of deer hunting, and of observing and photographing deer outside hunting seasons, I have seldom heard them make sounds.

Where I live, in the hill country of Texas, we have what is believed to be the largest population of whitetails anywhere on the continent. My home place has 27 acres of woods and 2 ponds, and we have deer in the yard around the year and resident in our wooded area. Some miles away on our ranch—a large acreage completely wild and quite remote—I have spent days on end watching deer while I hunted or just prowled. If deer "talked" a lot, certainly I'd hear them.

I vividly recall some sounds I've heard deer make. One season up in the Great Lakes region, I was sitting on a stand in the forest and suddenly heard a plaintive, quite loud bleat, repeated over and over. Presently a fawn of the year, probably one already weaned but still

71

following its mother around, came into view. It called over and over as it wandered past. I presumed that either someone had shot the doe, or else the young deer had become separated. That is one of the few times I can recall having heard the bleat of a whitetail.

On another occasion I was still-hunting with a companion in the Pigeon River Forest in northern Michigan. The forest was rather dense, and as we prowled along we glimpsed movement. We hauled up and watched. A doe came out into view at close range. The way she flopped her ears and looked behind, we knew a rutting buck must be pursuing her. Indeed, in a few seconds he appeared, nose down to her track. I eased up my rifle and shot the buck. It was not an instant kill. The doe ran, and the downed buck let out a bawl of a kind I've never heard since. It was almost like a snarling growl, but pitched higher. It seemed to us—both my partner and I were positive of what we heard—to be a sound more of rage than of pain.

Just once the buck uttered the sound, unable to get up and run off. Later, on two other occasions, I heard wounded deer squall in a wild bleat. I cannot believe this is a common occurrence; it certainly is seldom noted. A buck in rut does grunt at times when following a doe. This I've heard a number of times. The sound is usually a series— throaty and deep, coarse and grating, but not very loud—*argh, argh, argh.*

Friends in mule-deer country who are around fawns in spring and early summer have told me the young deer are often fairly vocal, bleating quietly, and sometimes not so quietly, to the does. A number of naturalists and a few hunters, myself among them, have heard fawns caught by predators, or deer hung in a fence, bleat repeatedly in fright or anguish. But not all do. A very few hunters claim to have dealt with bucks that fairly bellowed at them when wounded. Overall, however, it is doubtful that deer (during hunting season, at least) utter many vocal sounds.

Most detailed natural-history books that are authentic list the vocal utterances of both whitetails and mule deer as bleats and grunts. Just about everyone knows, of course, that deer snort and "whistle" through their noses. But these are hardly vocal sounds. Some hunters claim fawns often bleat like lambs or goat kids, that adult deer do likewise but in coarser tones like adult sheep, and that all deer when hurt or caught vent vocal anguish. It might be easy for a reader to infer that a hunter anywhere on populous deer range would commonly hear these sounds. But since no one commonly hears such sounds, it must be assumed that deer don't often make them.

And yet deer certainly react to sounds. Several summers back I hunkered down in a patch of brush with the Burnham brothers, the noted animal-call makers. This was whitetail country. One man blew a call, and the three of us were all but run over by two does racing in to the sound from different directions.

How should we have interpreted this action? That's the key question. Admittedly, the call worked. But this was before hunting season, during the season when fawns were still nursing. Were the does coming to what they thought was the call of a fawn? Did they think the fawn was in trouble? Or was this simply a natural reaction to come running, like any mother when a youngster calls? Or did they come to the sound simply out of curiosity?

From a hunting standpoint, it wouldn't make much difference, just so it works. But would it work when fawns were grown? And was it only does that would respond, or would bucks also come to the call?

In some counties of Texas, a state where the citizens are mighty darned independent and individualist, deer calls of any kind for use in hunting are illegal. The reason is that years ago—when deer were in precarious supply and hunted year-round by poachers and poor hard-scrabble country people who considered them a prime source of staple food—a great many people had discovered that in spring and summer the does would run to a fawn-squall imitation. Supposedly so many deer were killed this way that finally the call was made illegal. The law is still on the books.

What is generally sold as a "deer call" nowadays is fundamentally a modification of the predator call. It is a barrel with a reed (or "squealer") inserted, and you blow it. The standard predator call is high-pitched and presumably imitates the death screams of a rabbit caught by a predator. A lower tuning—often advertised as a low-pitched predator call—imitates the lower-pitched and coarser cry of a jackrabbit.

Now, of course, wildlife calls of varied kinds appeal to different emotions. Ducks and geese respond because they are gregarious and believe companions are calling them down from flight. In addition, they undoubtedly interpret the calls of those supposed companions on the ground to mean "good food and safety here." Predator calls are directed at the killer instinct of the meat eaters, who believe the sound means an easy kill. And, of course, there's the related feeling of hunger. But such a call also may be an appeal to greed. Many a predator comes to a call when its belly is bulging. Feast and famine is the life-style of predators. They never miss an opportunity to gorge.

An elk bugle appeals to the sex urge. It imitates the sound of a bull elk that's proclaiming his macho qualities and daring other bulls to

As this hunter sounds off on a deer call, a big buck sneaks silently out of brush. Calls sometimes work surprisingly well on mule deer.

fight him for his harem. Antler rattling has a similar appeal to buck deer. But deer aren't buglers like elk, or even harem gatherers. Deer, of course, are vegetarians and so not attracted by any call that says "easy meat." And deer don't have the emphatic gregarious instincts of waterfowl. All in all, deer can be a perplexing problem. They seemingly must be appealed to by a sound that may arouse either curiosity or the instinctive protective urge toward young.

Yet there is probably more useful information that can be discovered. Deer calls and results need much further research. I have a friend in northern Arizona who has demonstrated something interesting on many occasions: he can go into an area where mule deer are abundant and soon have them just about running him down, bucks and does together or separately. How? Simply by squalling on a standard predator call. He has demonstrated this knack not just in summer, when both whitetails and mule deer come to a call rather regularly, but also in fall and winter.

One puzzle for people who've fiddled with deer calls is that results are generally not predictable everywhere. The reason, however, well may be that no two callers go at it in the same way. You must use judgment and be patient. If you want a natural response, you must be sure that deer in the vicinity can hear the call and yet aren't aware of you. One friend in a northern state swears he has killed a number of big whitetail bucks with the help of a call. He hides and utters a single blat. Then he waits a minute or two and repeats. He carries a stick, and in between calls he whacks it on the ground once or twice, like a deer stomping its foot.

Deer do this apparently when uncertain, or puzzled, possibly hoping to get a reaction from whatever it is they think has disturbed the scene. My friend says that every now and then he has had a buck sneak in for a look, and this hunter has collected it. I think those deer have reacted out of curiosity. I must emphasize again that from all my own experiences and those of others I've collected all across the nation, the sum is that reactions are erratic. But it just may be the *callers*, not the deer, who are erratic. Perhaps we callers need to learn more. For example, it is conceivable that precise pitch is more important than we know.

In my own experience, I have used deer calls chiefly to appeal to what I at least interpret as two opposed emotions: (1) curiosity, which brings them toward a call; and (2) fright, which sends them fleeing. The point is, both approaches work, because both get deer into the open. So, I suppose both could be termed "calling" even though the one puts them in reverse.

Probably one more appeal should be noted. As I've said, in summer the does come quite readily to the simulated bleat of a fawn. The instinct is strong. I'd say that in areas that have doe seasons, a low bleat (not too loud) to imitate a young deer either just anxious or in distress should do big business.

It may be that the presumed curiosity appeal is a mixture of curiosity and the protective instinct. One year I spent several days with Jim Barbee, a man from Fort Stockton, Texas, who during deer season is a professional long-experienced and successful mule-deer guide. We both wanted to do some scouting of the territory for the hunting season soon coming up, and I wanted to get some photos. Our expedition was to a vast west Texas ranch where Jim would guide his hunters later on. It is a stunning expanse of wild mountains some miles north of the Big Bend country and in the vicinity of Alpine.

It was legal in that county to use a mouth-blown deer call, but not any electronic device. In the experience of everyone I know who has tried deer calling, mule deer (perhaps because they are more gregarious and placid and in general less spooky than whitetails) respond more consistently. Jim and I soon had this proved time and again.

One striking experience occurred during the middle of the day when we were sure the deer would be bedded down. We climbed out on a ledge that overlooked a steep, narrow canyon. This canyon had ample cover: mottes of various low trees along the ledge-cut sides and grass, rocks, and scrub in the bottom. The canyon was probably about 150 yards wide, and we could look both across it and up it to the head, where a jumble of enormous boulders with pathways among them could take a deer out to the mesa at that end.

Jim and I lay on the flat ledge, partially screened by rocks, and he blew the call. He blew loud, because this was a big sweep of country and also the air currents in such mountains are whimsical. Jim blew a number of bleats or squalls. The sound, whatever it simulated, was certain to be interpreted by any kind of wildlife as one of anguish. We had selected this spot because it was the type of place where a number of mule deer might congregate to rest during midday. Sure enough, within seconds a big doe stepped out of brush below us, stood in the open, and stared in the general direction of the sound.

I kept glassing steadily. The deer moved closer, flopped her ears, and seemed genuinely mesmerized as well as disturbed. In a short time Jim blew another series. The doe walked still closer toward us, although, of course, well below. Then, as I scanned the shaded side of the canyon, I began to see more deer. Two other does came out into the open. Then from another spot came three. Jim nudged me and gestured up-canyon. Atop a rock toward the head a good buck had appeared. He stared intently toward us.

Now Jim blew only one or two bleats, not so loud, waited several minutes, and repeated. Within possibly 20 minutes, we had assembled a regular herd of deer. Fourteen does were in sight, strung up the canyon, and we saw one small buck and the big buck. The big buck would have been a long shot, but possible. The small one was in easy range, as were all the does. Finally there was literally a single-file string of nine additional deer all traipsing down-canyon toward the sound, all in plain sight. The others we couldn't tell about because they moved in cover.

What we wanted now to know was the reaction to continued calling. I mentally predicted that the deer would become disturbed, at least to the point where uneasiness dominated curiosity. That prediction was correct. Jim purposely continued to raise a racket with his call. Finally, the big buck disappeared and was not seen again. One doe and then another turned away. They didn't flee in wild fright. They were puzzled, but they'd decided maybe ours wasn't a legitimate enterprise. They trotted single file up the canyon, a beautiful sight as they hopped agilely atop and over boulder after boulder and at last disappeared in the jumbled header.

What did the deer think that the sound was? Nobody can say. They first showed strong curiosity, strong enough to make them leave their beds and have a look and move *toward,* rather than away from, the sound. But when it persisted, it frightened them at least enough to run them off.

That was just one of a series of interesting incidents we had during the several days. One afternoon we drove a four-wheel-drive rig far up atop the mountains, left it, and walked half a mile to where the huge and rough mesa dropped to a desert flat. The rugged slope was in shadow, the perfect bedding ground, and there were innumerable places for deer to hide. It was, we figured, a good spot for bucks because they could see for miles out and down, and from above nothing could possibly get down the first perpendicular drop to bother them.

First we glassed the entire area meticulously. We saw nothing. Jim began with the call. We rested and watched for five minutes. He tried again. It was better than half an hour before we saw our first deer. It was an excellent buck, far below, standing between two enormous boulders and staring in our direction. It had, we guessed, arisen from its bed. Mule deer will stay put if they think they're unseen. In the full hour we spent up on the rim, while Jim called and both of us glassed, not a deer fled the place. We had eight deer, all bucks, in sight at various times.

At last one started running—down and away, of course. In mountain country like that, the clatter of a deer running on rock can be heard for several hundred yards. We picked up the distant animals by sound and then zeroed in with our glasses. All eight were moving at the same time.

Here again, the animals had first evidenced curiosity. But persistent calling had made them decide something was amiss, and they ran. Because of the terrain, it would have been practically impossible to get near the deer from below without their being aware. But had it been possible to get within range, I'd wager every buck would have arisen for a look, moved even closer to the sound, and presented a shot.

During the preseason scouting, I kept a rough count of deer that definitely reacted to the call. It was somewhere in the forties. What Jim and I deduced, the more we experimented, was that too much is too much, as in most other kinds of wildlife calling. To produce a positive reaction, a little calling is all that's needed. From other experiences, this notion is well proved. Mule deer especially can be brought in—bucks as well as does—but the pitch must be proper, the sound not too continuous, and the waits between long enough. Conversely,

A sudden blast on a deer call makes this whitetail pause long enough in a small opening for the hunter to collect him.

if the object is simply to roust out hidden or bedded deer, then a lot of calling with few pauses will do it.

Whitetails in my experience react, in general, the same as mule deer, except that they take fright much more easily. A few years ago I discovered by accident that in thick cover you can put every whitetail to flight by calling. I was sitting on a high knoll in the undulating thornbrush and cactus country near the Mexican border, intent on calling in a coyote with a standard-pitch predator call. For anyone who hasn't seen this region, I must explain that it's a mass of cover broken only by roughly bulldozed ranch roads or trails and by stock ponds (tanks). You can't see very far into the cover on the level. But some of it is rolling, and from a high vantage point—never so very high—you can see a large area and look down into the cover.

This was in deer season, and in that county deer calling was legal. Anyway, I wasn't after a deer, having already taken a good buck. At any rate, after a few loud squalls I saw a deer. I raised my binocular. It was a real buster of a buck, and it stood peering out of a welter of brush at a range of possibly 200 yards. At the next few squalls, it turned wildly and went bounding off. Near me another thicket exploded, and far across the flat below another. I had put five whitetails out of cover in the area over which I could observe them. They all ran on over the low ridges and disappeared.

In other states I've witnessed small groups of hunters using predator calls and deer calls to push whitetails out of dense cover. So this is another side, calling in reverse perhaps. But there is still more. In three different and widely separated states, and widely differing kinds of cover, I have stopped a moving buck—on one occasion dead in its tracks because I shot it—by using a call to get its attention.

This can be an important use of a call. For example, on one of those occasions I was sitting on a stand and saw a deer move in heavy brush. Finally it came out but was walking swiftly—not frightened or aware of me, but simply going wherever it had in mind to go. Another patch of heavy cover was only a few yards ahead. If the deer got into that, I'd never see it again. Everyone has heard about the trick of whistling at a deer to stop it. Sometimes it works. But in hard-hunted country, more often a whistle scares the bejabbers out of the animal, particularly if it's a buck.

I hadn't time for anything but a snap shot, and I don't like to accept those. I raised the call and went *baaah,* short and sharp. The buck stopped with a jerk and swiveled its head to stare. In the next couple of seconds it was on the ground. My theory of the reaction in such instances is that the call—not a predator call but a lower-pitched deer call—is a sound that may occur, and probably does now and then, in the woods. The instant impression the deer gets is that another deer is present. It instinctively takes a look. You won't stop a buck for long this way, but it doesn't take long to collect a standing target.

In searching around among available deer calls, and also in old literature and ads, I discovered that not very many deer calls have ever been manufactured. At least two that were advertised some years back claimed to be designed to imitate sounds made by Indians in Alaska to call deer. Well, maybe, maybe not. I'm not easy to sell on those recipes for success alleged to be copies of practices of ancient peoples. Whether Indians called scads of deer in Alaska or not I don't know. But the calls made sounds to imitate the blatt, or bleat if you wish, of a fawn or a doe.

There is no reason, incidentally, why this sound—if it is supposed to have anything to do with the sex urge—should appeal to a buck at any time except during the rut. And it is doubtful that sex appeal is involved. Does are no more vocal—probably not as much so—during the rut than at other times. One of a pair of calls marketed a few years ago supposedly made sounds of anguish and the other was billed as a love call. These, and the few others now available, are based on the bleat of a deer. But by blowing louder and modulating the cry, any of them can be turned into sounds of anguish—a deer injured or in trouble with a predator. As I said in the beginning, it is doubtful that these sounds are heard often but certain that they are heard occasionally.

So now what about scents? I don't mean to be too skeptical, but any writer who accepts the claims of every outdoorsman he talks to and who accepts all advertising without questioning authenticity isn't much of a reporter. He'll have long legs—from having them pulled so much. Make no mistake: scents—of which a number are marketed today—are valuable in deer hunting. But, I have seen at least one or two advertised as "calls," and I think such a claim is going a bit too far.

Some scents have what I consider a pleasant smell, some quite the opposite. Most scents have as the chief purpose the masking of human odors. Scent makers take two tacks here. One is a mask that is pleasant to the nose of the hunter and presumably smells good to a deer. The other—skunk essence, for example—is so strong it is horrible to use, and you can be sure of avoiding crowds if you use it. Still another idea—possibly the best of all—is a scent based on the musk odor of deer from secretions of the glands on the hind legs and also from glands at the inside corner of the eye. The musk scents presumably appeal to deer as a whiff of their own kind. At the same time, these scents cover up human odor.

There are numerous well-authenticated instances, especially among bow hunters who are avid scent users because they must get close, of bucks following a scent trail laid down by a hunter. This scent, of course, is of the musk variety. Buck reactions are best during the rut.

Most intriguing to me is the idea of using both the sound of a call and the smell of a scent to fool deer. Let's suppose that you're stalking a deer and you're wearing a heavy dose of deer-musk scent. You're also carrying a call. You spook a deer, and it runs around to get on your downwind side. You blow a short blast on the call. The moving deer, picking up the musky odor and hearing the call, hauls up and gives you a chance.

One scent maker confided to me his favorite method. "You select a good spot," he said, "and place deer-musk scent on several bushes.

It overpowers your scent, and it smells to a deer like other deer. Then you go off a short distance and keep watch. When you see a deer, blatt at it two or three times, quietly and sparingly. Scent and sound working together are often very effective."

As all deer hunters know from scent advertising, the smell of apples has been used a great deal by scent purveyors. There is nothing wrong with using this scent—if you just don't take too much to heart some of the malarky that is occasionally peddled with it. Probably the scent of apples does not disturb deer in any region. And probably it does act as a mask for human odors. But I raise an eyebrow at claims that deer love this smell because one of their favorite foods is apples. Usually the claim goes farther, that deer are accustomed to eating apples on the ground in abandoned apple orchards.

Well, I have discovered old apple plantings right out in the woods in locations as far separated as Maine and Michigan. In these instances, presumably the trees grew from plantings or from cores tossed out at lumber camps. Indeed, deer were fond of apples when a good growing season presented them with fruit. But a fellow who can find an abandoned apple orchard in the south Texas brush country (renowned for its trophy whitetails) or in the mountains in Montana will have to search longer than he has time for. The plain fact is that the great majority of deer have never smelled an apple.

Despite some overenthusiastic advertising, deer scents are unquestionably worth trying. The masking of human odors is certainly valuable. The musk scents do definitely sometimes attract deer, especially during the rut. One manufacturer markets a soap that is said to clean you up so you don't smell like a human but more like a deer. Beware, however, of wearing such a scent—an attractant presumably, not a mask—when you're prowling after deer. Such a scent is simply a way of calling attention to yourself and your location. I doubt that scents can be classed as "deer calls." But scents may well be one more little edge in the difficult game of deer hunting, so I certainly wouldn't scoff at them.

One year while I was making a film about antler-rattling for whitetails, Wally Chamness, then a representative for Marlin and an expert shot and hunter, carried in a jar fresh musk glands cut from the legs of deer killed by hunters at the ranch where we were operating. When we selected a stand, he'd get out a couple of these stout-smelling swatches of hide and hang them on bushes on the downwind side. "Rattled" bucks coming in will circle if there's any breeze at all, and they'll come in from downwind—or else run off. Wally's theory was that the deer would pick up the authentic musk scent and that it would overwhelm ours. We were extremely successful. How great a part the scent played, if any, is impossible to judge.

Most call-experienced deer hunters follow roughly the same rules as those who don't use a call: they believe the early hours of daylight are the prime ones and that a quiet morning is best. They caution against incessant calling. In fact, a friend who is an expert turkey caller and who has also had some deer-calling success tells me the same rules apply: (1) call sparingly; (2) if you glimpse a deer moving toward the sound, clam up; (3) don't expect every deer that is intrigued to come running, because like turkeys some tear in and some sneak along; and (4) you must be patient.

To those rules I'd add that taking a position higher than where you presume the deer are—as Jim Barbee and I did—is best. Then it's easy for you to see the deer but difficult for them to see you, because deer don't do much looking up. I'd also add that the scent–sound combinations just may be the key to the highest success.

How much faith you eventually put in deer calling unquestionably will depend on your personal results or lack of them. Even though I am, as I've noted, skeptical in my trade of almost any related experience, I must admit that the stacks of letters from users that call makers and scent makers keep on file are impressive. I've had the opportunity to look at many. They come from all over the nation. A substantial number, of course, scoff at the product the writer fell for and claim they've been had. Many more tell grand tales of amazing success. Some of those undoubtedly are just tall tales. Lots of letter-prone people love to exaggerate. But some must have happened. If the use of calls and scents raises your chances of success even a percentage point or two, it would be hard to argue down.

Sure Way to Give Yourself An Edge

Can you imagine the thrill of glassing an open mountain slope in bright fall sunshine shortly after dawn and counting 14 mule-deer bucks, all 8 and 10 pointers, scattered on it and feeding placidly? Several seasons ago two friends and I witnessed just such a gathering.

We had arrived in our hunting area five days before the deer season opened. Odd as it may sound, we were planning on doing our concentrated "hunting" *before* season. That would leave us only a couple of days to actually bag our bucks before we'd have to leave. But from past experience all of us had come to believe that the most important part of the hunt, for either mule deer or whitetail, is the preseason operation. That is, the deer enthusiast who is willing to gamble on allotting no more than half a vacation trip to conventional hunting and the other half to quiet preseason study of the area will seldom need more than the first few hours of opening day to take his pick of the lot.

I had checked out the region earlier, by studying the game-department kill figures for several past seasons, which is important. Deer were obviously plentiful. And I had gathered figures on the percentage of the final total that were bucks, also an important consideration. But the first move my two friends and I made was not to go scouting deer but rather scouting spots where the afternoon-before-opening influx of hunters would almost certainly set up camps. Official forest and other camp sites would draw swarms. Areas near water sources would also be favored.

The first day we mapped the surefire camping spots and then worked back in on rough trails far enough away so that the majority of hunters wouldn't get into that country until a day or so after shooting began. We purposely shied from obvious water sources, even away from easy camp spots. Deer know scores of small watering places and are seldom absolutely bound to those easily located. In addition, we purposely passed up places that would seem to many modestly experienced hunters like the best deer range imaginable. We

Surprising as it may seem, a sizable recreational vehicle makes a fine deer camp. It's quiet, produces no smoke, requires no noisy wood chopping, and never has audible voices if you're careful to remain silent outdoors.

You can often measure potential of an area by the number of does and fawns you see. If they're not especially spooky—like these mule deer does lying placidly in shade as I took their picture—undoubtedly some prime bucks are somewhere around, and not unduly pressured.

wanted to find some secluded ridges back in that looked more barren but that had ample food. Scads of such locations fool hunters but not deer!

We had with us a short-wheelbase four-wheel-drive rig and also a large recreational vehicle in which we'd camp. We could thus make a dry camp even in an unappealing place. It may sound wacky to say, but a full-comforts recreational vehicle is a most inconspicuous camp. We stashed this one in a narrow hideaway dry canyon that had rock walls and no deer sign. When you live in such a camp, there's no campfire smoke, no noise of voices around camp, no wood chopping. If you come and go quietly, the sounds are all inside the RV. Deer a few hundred yards away seldom know the camp is there.

Next day we began our scouting. Not obtrusively. We stayed on the trails with the four-wheel-drive rig, used the spotting scope often, and did no walking. A walking man frightens even a wilderness deer, but a vehicle that is not noisy seldom bothers deer much. We were pretty sure that the deer in this area had not been disturbed all year. They could be near the trails as well as far away from them. What we intended to do was get our bucks all "selected"—I'm serious!—and then wind up the season swiftly when it opened.

We looked over scores of deer. And then came that early morning when we spotted bucks on the slope. The first buck we picked up with binoculars. Then we got out the spotting scope. We made a sneak a hundred yards closer, still probably 500 yards from the deer. Then, from a small copse of cedar, we scrutinized that slope with binoculars and spotting scope and were all just simply awed. Fourteen bucks! Every one was well worth taking, and at least a couple were mounting-size racks.

There was a series of low ridges here, with spotty cedar and piñon and some low brush. We withdrew. I said, "You can bet those bucks all live right in these ridges. If we check them out this afternoon late and they're here again, we don't need to look any further." We did check, and sure enough, toward dusk they were all out again.

From then on, we left the place alone. We scouted other places just in case we'd find something better. We lazed around camp. Two days later we made another check. We didn't see all 14 bucks, but we did count 10.

The afternoon before opening day, our plot came close to blowing up. A pickup loaded with especially noisy hunters somehow stumbled upon our camp. They stopped. "Finding any deer?" one asked.

I didn't lie. "Nothing much right around here. Maybe we picked wrong."

"What's the country like up ahead?" He waved in the direction of our distant ridges.

Again I didn't lie. "Just a bunch of dry ridges." They turned around and went back.

Before dawn next morning, we'd made our move. We were hunkered in a patch of juniper well in range across the face of the slope. By 7:30, every last deer of the 14 that apparently ran together was in sight. We checked them out and made our choices. In seconds the hunt was concluded.

Now, of course, the action doesn't always go just like this. That hunt was a classic. But in today's world of deer hunting (when a lot of people get into the woods for opening day), I find it simply delightful to do my "hunting" in the pleasant way, before season, enjoy myself thoroughly for a few days of scouting, taking deer photos and just "smelling the country," then take my buck quickly and turn the area over to the crowds.

A big factor in the success of my method is the basic deer personality. Most deer, if left undisturbed, live and feed in a small area all year long—except where high-country snow in the West forces vertical late-fall downward movements. Mule deer especially are exceedingly gregarious creatures. It is not at all uncommon in good mule-deer country to see mixed groups of 5 to 40 does, bucks, and fawns. Whitetails that are young and antlerless will commonly consort in groups, although the bucks are not as clubby.

I have always presumed that the mule deer, an animal of the mountains and Southwestern deserts and foothills, gains some of its naiveté from its wilderness or near-wilderness habitats. To be sure, whitetails also were wilderness animals in early days. But they adapt to civilization far better than mule deer do. Muleys never have the same total wildness of the whitetail nor its adaptability. Yet I don't mean to imply that the mule deer is stupid.

The best way to explain the differences between whitetails and mule deer is as follows. Even in farm and woodlot country of the Eastern United States trophy whitetail bucks may live practically underfoot and never be seen. They're crafty. Disturb such deer (or whitetails anywhere) and they don't move far. They're simply so wily and adept at hiding that they stay out of sight. Yet before-season study can locate their hideouts.

But now consider that group of mule-deer bucks we saw on those ridges. First of all, seeing half a dozen or more muley bucks together is not at all unusual. In mountains and Southwestern foothills, most mule deer are not right on the fringes of settlement, as thousands of whitetails are elsewhere. There aren't as many people where mule deer live. Their country is big. Certainly whitetails may live in vast expanses too. But mountains, even to a man in them, have a different atmosphere. Bigness. Most mule deer, when disturbed, won't race crazily away. They'll bound over the ridge and then imagine the danger is gone. But when groups of mule deer living in close harmony (as all those big bucks were) are unduly disturbed, they'll just move back and move back, over the first ridge, the second, the third—and you won't see them again until long after the disturbance has ceased. Their hiding places aren't purposely as secretive as those of the thick-habitat whitetail. Most of their country is simply conducive to "getting lost in it."

86

When the hunters come, this disappearing act is what many mule deer do. A few small deer and some does may hang around. But when the human deluge flows in, the good mule bucks just move off, and the whitetails slip into their secret sanctuaries. Surveys show that at least 95 percent of deer hunters hit the hunting areas of their choice either on opening morning, the day before, or else on into the season. This record is understandable. Today most hunters travel some distance to their grounds. A fellow has only so much time. He doesn't want to waste any of it getting there early. He wants *hunting* time. But is the preseason time "wasted"? Hardly! If you know how to go about it, that *is* the hunting time, the most valuable part.

A few years ago I hunted one fall in eastern Wyoming in an area that has both species of deer. We arrived at a hot location the afternoon before season. We got our tent camp set up. Two other groups put up camps the same day not far from us. A rancher had told us that the valley next to us up the trail was swarming with deer. By evening, several other vehicles came in. They ran up and down the road, and some of their members scouted the valley up ahead. Next dawn not a deer was there. Too much noise and disturbance. I doubt that the deer were very frightened. They just didn't like it. The good whitetails hid out, and the big mule deer went up the mountain. Before anybody found them from there on, he had to go way up on top. In an area such as the one where our 14 bucks were, all the deer had to do was drift back about three ridges. It doesn't take many ridges to discourage most hunters in big country like that.

I think probably the adjective that best describes any deer is simply "shy." Not wildly spooky. A whitetail that runs off with flag waving isn't terrified, it's just uneasy about anything other than solitude. The first day of season, if pressed, whitetails retire to nearby secluded places, away from the clamor and disturbance. During the second day, hunters crowd harder and the deer become more shy. The harder the pressure and the harder the hunters work, the farther the whitetails are likely to drift (or the more cleverly they contrive to hide).

If you plan on arriving some days early, often there won't be a soul around. As I've noted, scout for camping places and get away from the good ones, the obvious ones. A smart thing to do if you possibly can carry enough water is to make a dry camp. Or spot a water source at one of the obvious spots where others will go, and come out every couple of days for water if need be. If things go right you'll hunt only one day anyway!

Most hunters are wary of dry camps. They also believe deer won't be in the "arid" spots. Nonsense! In normal years, few deer have water problems. They know where enough of it is. Food is more important. But often excellent food is available and hunters don't realize it, because they haven't boned up on what deer eat in that area.

One fall in west Texas I hunted some skimpy, unappealing hills that didn't seem to have enough food for a goat. But my first look showed much lechuguilla that the mule deer had been digging at on the slopes. Driving a trail and glassing up, as we came into cedar country a bit higher, I noticed a different shade of green up above. The binocular easily showed that it was piñon. Not a great deal of west Texas is high enough for piñon. But where it is and in a year when the nut crop is excellent, mule deer grow fantastically fat on this food. We checked, and sure enough: we found not only abundant nuts but also abundant deer in the piñon.

I once had a similar experience in Arizona, discovering a great deal of mountain mahogany and also an unusual crop of juniper berries in the same region. These are local forage eagerly taken by both kinds of deer, and the deer were there—coues (a smaller version of the whitetail), and desert mule deer—although the country didn't look like what an eager visiting deer hunter might think of as prime hunting country.

How you do your scouting is important. Don't disturb deer unless you absolutely must. If they haven't been disturbed, they'll be visible from vehicle trails. Try these first. If deer go bounding away at breakneck speed, every one of them, you'd better find a new spot. Such deer have been disturbed, possibly by human neighbors or poachers.

Vehicles that move along at modest speed and that are not noisy don't bother deer much. If deer stand at least momentarily to stare and then just trot off, or bound to a ridge top and stop to look, you're okay. They haven't been bothered. Unless it's necessary because of terrain, don't stop to glass and stare back. Go right on by. If you find a single big buck in a specific spot, he may be there or nearby day after day. If several bucks—particularly mule deer—are together, you can just bet they'll be in the area somewhere from then on until they're run off. If you must stop to look at a deer, don't shut the motor off. For some reason a deer that will stand while a vehicle stops to look at it will invariably run soon after the motor sound dies. It's an abrupt change, and something about it seems to spell trouble. Incidentally, though many hunters use topless four-wheel-drives for reconnoitering, an enclosed vehicle disturbs deer far less.

If you don't see deer from vehicle trails, then you have to get back in farther. In whitetail country, try to take a position where you can glass a lot of terrain and thus walk as little as possible. Granted, in some areas this can't be done. A canoe trip down a stream may make a fine scouting trip that gets into people-less country. Use ingenuity and caution. Do your best at this stage not to go poking into what look like perfect hiding places for a big old buck. No old trophy likes to have his favorite lie-up spot discovered.

In proper country, especially in the West, in both whitetail and mule deer-ranges, horsebacking is a good way to go. Horses will certainly spook deer, but not as badly as a man on foot. Don't just ride aimlessly, barging into every pocket and draw. Ride beneath a rim not sky-lighted. Dismount and glass from thickets. Tie your horse and walk to a ridgetop and—screened by cover—look into the next valley. In other words, make yourself inconspicuous. And when you find what you want, don't hang around unless wind and cover and the entire situation is such that you won't be detected. Leave the place alone for a day or two. Then come back if you've found a trophy, and stay with it all day if necessary. Distantly, of course. That way you'll have a check on the deer's daily routine, and your chances of a quick collection will be excellent.

Scouting for mule deer requires that you know what signs to look for. Tracks are obvious, but in much deer country they may not show up plainly. And sometimes it's difficult to tell the age of tracks. Where high country is available to mule deer, it's important to make certain you're not scouting the winter range of the deer—unless you're there during a winter season, when they've come down from up on top. In early fall, a foothill area that has quite a few old shed antlers in it and a lot of deer droppings that are old and dry is virtually certain to be a winter range, probably with few or no resident deer at this season.

Droppings that are reasonably fresh are a clear indication that deer are present. I noted this point in an earlier chapter. Biologists often do deer population-density studies by counting piles of droppings and marking each with a can of spray paint, then continuing counts as time goes on. This routine may sound mildly amusing, but it's a sure indication. One fall some years back, I started a New Mexico hunt in an area where I saw no droppings at all during my first day of scouting. This place had been recommended to me by people who still insisted deer were plentiful. I just couldn't believe it. As it turned out, in five days nobody got a shot at a deer or even saw one. Make certain when checking for droppings, however, whether sheep are using the area. You could be misled.

In open foothills and any fairly open deer country, the deer are more easily seen at a distance than they are in forested regions. But their daily habits during periods of normally good weather will be roughly the same. In fall, deer become fat. They're lazy and dislike heat. If the weather is warm, they may be out at dawn but not for long. They commonly drink at this time, then head for cool spots to spend much of the day.

Points that run out on the shady side of a ridge should be very carefully studied. Old trophy bucks lie up there. They can see out over the valley, and they get a cool breeze. The base of rimrocks offers excellent bedding spots for mule deer. You have to check very meticulously with your glass, but often a long search will pay off in your spotting antlers. A big buck bedded in such a place probably lives right here and will be on the same slope day after day.

In open country of sagebrush foothills or rather barren hills with spotty juniper or similar cover anywhere from Montana to west Texas, newcomers are often puzzled about where to look for bedded mule deer. It's really no puzzle. They commonly lie down on a breezy slope beneath any bit of vegetation that gives shade. I've seen them stay for hours beside a Spanish bayonet or a small juniper. If there's grass or low bushes, all you'll see are the antlers. So it pays to look closely.

Whitetails seldom pick such spots to rest and be cool. On our own small ranch in Texas, we often find them on warm days lying under a rock ledge that drips water along the creek. They may also lie in mature forest, far back, and on a ridge, where a breeze blows and where they can see through the timber. But of all the fine places for the whitetail, the finest in any rolling woodlands with small draws that reach up from creek bottoms are draws that have some brush but also have tall shade above. A big buck may spend all day at the head of such a draw, then move down toward dusk.

Weather can severely upset your scouting. I like early-fall hunting when it's available because that time of year is so pleasant. At this season in mule-deer range, however, an early storm can pile snow into the area. These first storms upset deer routines drastically. I've seen times when not a track showed in the fresh snow, not a deer moved anywhere. Later in winter, a storm wouldn't bother the animals so much. They get accustomed to storms. Also, they've lost weight and must forage. But the first abrupt change is uncomfortable, and the muleys just disappear. The best thing to do is stay in camp and wait it out.

Several years ago on one of my hunts, a sudden snowstorm howled in. We drove some and walked some, saw hardly any tracks and not a single deer. A bitter wind was whistling even though the snow had ceased. We went back to camp and took our ease for another day. That next morning dawned crisp, bright, and still. That afternoon, as the area warmed, we cruised around again. We counted over a hundred deer! They just seemed to have popped out of the ground. So don't let an early storm discourage you. Immediately after it has blown through, scouting or hunting will be better than ever.

Deer wander considerably over the slopes, ridgetops, and flats of their home bailiwicks, but they're inclined to make and follow distinct trails. They're much like cattle, snake-tracking up or down a ridge or along a bottom. By glassing the slopes in open areas, you can pick out these trails. In whitetail woods you can discover sections of them without following them far. Quite often they lead to water. They are made, remember, because the deer have a specific objective. Try to deduce from the terrain what that goal is. It might make a perfect ambush. When you see trails, it's a good idea to check them carefully. Are cattle making those trails rather than deer? Tracks and droppings will tell the story.

A heavily used deer trail that goes to a favorite watering place is well worth watching. Set up a hiding place in view of the trail and stay with it a day. If you see the buck you want, you'll get a line on his habits. But don't hide near the waterhole. All animals are much more shy coming close to their watering place than they are on the trails some distance from it. Game animals know—through long experience—that danger lurks at watering places, concentration points for so many creatures.

It has often amused me to hear hunters say that an area has "just a lot of does and fawns." If there is one thing I measure potential by more than any other it's how many does and fawns I see in any new area. Now it is possible that you could get into a heavily pressured place where the good bucks have systematically been taken year after year until few trophy bucks are available. Most times, however, swarms of does and fawns that are not very spooky indicate that somewhere around are plenty of prime bucks that also may not be more than normally spooky. Where else do the fawns come from?

But you may not see the bucks in the same places that you see groups of does. Big bucks tend to like areas somewhat different from where most antlerless deer hang out. Small bucks may hang around with antlerless deer, but the big bucks will spend most of their time elsewhere.

Because mule-deer bucks of a general age and size group so often band together, you may have to do an extra amount of scouting to locate the big ones. In other words, the ridge where a group feeds and beds this week or month may be the only place over a square mile or so where that many bucks are located. The problem is much like hunting bands of mountain sheep. All (or most) of the big mule-deer bucks in an area of a dozen ridges may be ganged up in a single basin. Undisturbed and placid, they move very little.

Individual whitetail trophy bucks, by contrast, are usually loners. And they're more scattered, and far more secretive.

Some very large, old mule-deer bucks are also loners. They're likely to be high up, except during times of heavy snow. In the Southwest desert mountains, these big fellows will select a certain canyon that is secluded and stay on its slopes and in its brushy side draws weeks at a time. One fall I spent a full week before season scouting mule deer in the Big Bend country of west Texas. A partner and I got so we knew practically every 10-pointer along the ranch trails we cruised and on the slopes we horsebacked and glassed. We actually had our deer picked out several days before opening.

The ranch owner, Gage Holland, had spotted a buck he wanted his wife to have a chance at. To illustrate how surefire such a scheme can work, he told me he'd take me back to the place and show me the deer. That sounds preposterous. But we went back in on an exceedingly rough trail to the mouth of a small canyon that butted into the side of a mountain. Then we walked in a short distance along toward sundown and hunkered there glassing the canyon and slopes carefully.

Presently the big deer appeared, strolling down from the brush at the head of the canyon, without concern and unaware of us. We moved out. But at dawn the next day, Gage and his wife were there and gathered in the old buster. My partner and I met them about 9 A.M. By then we had our 10 pointers, too. A big whitetail, if you can scout out his private little hangout, is just as predictable when undisturbed.

That hunt when we took the 10-pointers was a great one. Like many I've had, it was especially enjoyable because we had our "hunting" all done long before the shooting started. While the opening-day crowd was scurrying around wondering which way to go and where, we were loading our trophies and heading home.

Indeed, the most pleasant deer hunting is when you have the forest, mountain, or desert all to yourself. The deer have long forgotten last year's flurry. The deer woods sounds the way a deer range should, which is to say it is nearly silent. That's the time when hunting is very literally by craft. And why carry a gun for a week when by proper preseason "hunting" you need it for only a few minutes?

SECRETS OF WARM-WEATHER SUCCESS

For quite a number of years, I've been hunting whitetail deer every season in country that is without snow and commonly has days during deer season that are at the least balmy and at times are downright hot. This experience has been a great education, particularly because for a good many years previous I had hunted whitetails every fall in the North, the snow belt.

How well I recall the way everyone looked forward to cold weather and a good snow for deer season in northern Michigan, where I lived for a number of years. It was just about impossible, everyone claimed, to operate successfully without a "tracking snow" and cold weather. But I also recall several seasons when the weatherman pitched a big curve to deer hunters. Deer season opened with the woods dry, no snow, days like September instead of November, and the rut not started. Talk about messed up! Hunters wandered around aimlessly, in frustration, not knowing what to do.

During an unseasonably warm hunt in Texas recently, it suddenly occured to me that warm-weather whitetail hunting anywhere has many special problems connected with it. Throughout all of the Mid-south, South, and Southwest, most whitetail hunters never have a "tracking snow" or any other snow. And the weather affects the deer in ways that change the hunting drastically from what it is in areas that have more emphatic seasonal changes. In the North, however, the warm-weather influence and problems are even more pronounced when they occur. And so the problem is not just a regional one. The difficulties of warm-weather whitetail hunting occur annually in the mild and warm zones, and from time to time in the Northern states. So it's a good idea for all hunters to recognize what the problems are and to know how to overcome them.

One of the most important areas of learning concerns the rut. Many whitetail hunters claim that the first severe frosts turn bucks into crazed creatures with greatly diminished wariness. This claim has a lot of truth in it. But the trouble with such flat statements is that there are many variations. Without any doubt, the easiest time to kill a buck is during the rut. But whitetail hunters should understand that the rut is not always a sharply defined circumstance that ends in a few days or a couple of weeks. During some seasons, to be sure, weather makes the rut quite concentrated. Those crisp, or cold, still nights enhance the urge, and suddenly most of the bucks are following does. In an average deer season, however, whitetails may breed over a period of some weeks. In Texas, I've observed rutting bucks in September and in the same season have seen a few still avidly running does in January. The rut is generally briefer in the North, but not necessarily as short as some hunters surmise.

A temperature drop certainly does affect the rut. Sometimes the drop can be a matter of only a few degrees, and the effect may be wholly unsuspected by frustrated hunters. For example, one fall I was hunting in northern Michigan during shirtsleeve weather. Leaves were down, the woods noisy. Prowling was all but useless. Deer were bedded all day in cool spots, and there wasn't the slightest sign of rutting. Any concentration of breeding had obviously been held back by the summerlike weather.

Before deer season, I'd done some scouting and had discovered a low ridge adjacent to a trout stream. Several prominent buck rubs were evident over a modest area. Small balsams had been denuded of branches and the bark skinned off. Obviously a buck lived here. I took a stand overlooking the general region and spent a disconsolate afternoon half dozing while a gentle southwest breeze pleasantly drifted over me. Not so much as a red squirrel or a jay moved.

Next morning I was back shortly after dawn. Something about the weather was different. I even felt an excitement and more enthusiasm. The air wasn't chilly. But presently I was aware that the breeze had turned. It had quickened a bit and was now from the northwest. I guessed that the temperature was only 5 to 10 degrees lower, a piddling drop, really, from the summerlike high. But I had not been on the stand half an hour before a doe appeared. She trotted into a small opening and kept flopping her ears back and looking behind her. Now that behavior was a sure sign that a buck in rut was following her. I couldn't believe it, not in this balmy weather. Not until the doe moved on across the small clearing did the buck step out into full view, and I immediately concluded my hunt.

At least 10 years after that, I was hunting one fall in south Texas in early December. The so-called brush country there was a total waste of time. Days were in the 80s and searing 90s. Nothing stirred.

But on the very last day of my stay, I got up at daylight and tested the breeze. It was from the north, a complete switch from past days. That breeze had the barest hint of coolness in it. A friend and I checked the temperature: exactly a 10-degree drop. Still warm—but "not quite as." We got right out into the brush. Deer were popping up everywhere, and everywhere bucks were chasing does.

I was reminded then of the Michigan experience. The peak of the rut in both cases had been held back because of warm weather. The fall was getting on. The moment the slightest drop in temperature and turnaround of breeze began, the message was evident to the deer: now or never.

The lesson to be learned is that those severe frosts are not *always* necessary. A north or northwest wind, which has changed quickly from a southerly direction, and a drop of a few degrees can (even though it may not materialize into any drastic change to low temperature) trigger an active rut late in season when mild weather has held it back or discouraged any peak activity. This is one of the most important lessons for warm-weather whitetail hunters to learn, regardless of the latitude in which they hunt.

Something the Northern hunter who gets caught in a warm deer season can learn from his Southern counterpart is that tracking snow is nowhere near as important as he has always supposed. The fact is that more whitetails by far are killed in snowless country simply because there is more of it. So you're not out of business when you're out of snow.

Snow, however, does give you two tracking advantages: (1) it easily shows fresh tracks, and (2) it allows you to track a wounded and bleeding deer with ease.

Nonetheless, deer tracks are not very important to your success. A single doe and two following yearlings can make enough tracks in snow in one night to look as if a dozen deer had been in an area. Further, though many readers may be ready to argue the point, it is virtually impossible for anyone to distinguish the track of a buck from that of a good-size doe. I've watched a few track experts trail "an old mossy-horn of a buck" and come up on a big old doe with hoofs worn down! The warm-weather hunter who will look for droppings and forget tracks is the one who'll be able to judge most accurately the abundance or scarcity of deer.

Now, of course, warm-country whitetail hunters, just like the Northerners who want snow, are always eager for cold or at least cool weather. Most hunters in both regions think of "hunting season" as cool to cold. And when winter arrives, North or South, it is a fact that

Tracks are not so important as some hunters like to believe. Furthermore, tracks can be hard to find in warm weather except in dry washes, such as the one shown here, or in mud.

deer do change their habits. These winter habits are what the average hunter envisions as "how deer act during hunting season." But if hunting season comes along before winter arrives, the hunter gets confused because "the deer aren't acting like they're supposed to." The fact is that they're acting precisely the way they're supposed to—in warm weather.

When the air gets extremely cold, deer in the North will move deep into greenswamps and other heavy cover; deer in the South will gain the protection of dense cedar brakes, brushy thickets, or the sides of draws and canyons that cut off bitter winds. They may not be active right at dawn, but as soon as the sun warms a slope, they will come out to feed on it. If the cold continues all day, they commonly will find bedding spots out of the wind, yet where a warming sun seeps through.

The warm-weather hunter, puzzled about what the deer are up to, simply must reverse all this lore. It is the way of nature that deer grow fat in fall—if food is available to fatten them. This is not a phenomenon of only Northern climes. Growing fat is not entirely for protection against cold. In the South, deer fatten in fall because they know instinctively that as winter progresses, even though the weather may not be cold, food will become progressively scarcer. The growing season is over, and the pickings become slim. Fat deer are as susceptible to heat as are fat men. They don't like it, and they won't move or feed in it unless they absolutely must.

During the entire day, with few exceptions, whitetails will stay under cover in the coolest places they can find when weather is warm. They may be out as dawn breaks. But whereas they might stay out until 10 A.M. in cool to cold weather, when it's unseasonably warm in any latitude they'll disappear the moment the sun is up. At evening they may not show at all until after dark. But *where* they lie up all day will differ drastically from place to place, according to terrain and various habitat features.

For example, I've watched hunters new to the so-called brush country of south Texas hunt all day, sweating away, trying to jump deer in exactly the places they're least likely to be. This country is a mass of seemingly endless thornbrush and cactus. It contains some stunning whitetails of trophy proportions. Much of the brush country is rolling. There are low ridges, and dry-wash "creek" bottoms (creeks only when it rains, which is seldom) with dense vegetation. The tallest, heaviest brush invariably grows along these washes because that's where the preponderance of the scarce water is most of the time when any water is present.

So, a naive hunter thinks because it's hot he'll fool the deer and hunt the cool ridgetops. He's wrong. When it's hot there is *no* really cool place in the brush country. But on the ridges the brush is lower, and the sun beats down unmercifully. In the bottoms, under the tallest vegetation, there may be little breeze, but there is escape from the sun. A clever stalker who is quick with a rifle and who will put his nose into the breeze, if any, and gingerly prowl those washes on warm or hot days will be right where the big deer are and will jump them. He may or may not be adept enough to get a shot, but at least he's where the deer are bedded. Any desert whitetail hunting is the same.

Now move up to the hill country where I live. It is similar to many other expanses of Southern and Midsouthern whitetail country: well-forested hills and steep canyons with creeks, dry or otherwise. If there is a flowing creek, with porous rock bluffs along it that drip water from springs within the rock, deer may lie in shade in such spots. But in most of this country the canyons and creek bottoms are downright hot in warm weather. No breeze gets in. Even flowing water is so heated in open creeks that it has no cooling effect. Almost without fail, most deer will be up on the ridges in warm weather. In an open-understory cedar brake, for example, on a ridge or bluff top, any breeze sweeps through, and the dense cedar crowns offer shade. These are the coolest spots in the whole region. Deer bed down in them and even feed within them. So you have to appraise your terrain and the vegetative cover and relate it to daytime comfort for the animals.

Now then, almost all Southern and Southwestern whitetail habitats of this variety have either pines or cedars, plus oaks and hardwoods. Any observant hunter soon realizes that wherever hardwoods grow, they drop their leaves in fall and that if there's no rain, you just can't walk on dry leaves, no matter how slowly, and get up on a deer. The only exception would be during a stiff breeze to cover sound. But in the brakes of mature cedar that are open underneath, and in the pines, you can prowl quietly. Sure, it takes finesse. But most of all it requires *patience.* My sons and I have walked up on bedded deer in such places when it is warm—but we take an hour to move 300 or 400 yards. If you practice restraint, you can kill bucks this way.

So now we move up to the North country. Typical might be the Great Lakes region, where poplar and white birch and maple are interspersed with varied conifers. There are ridges and hollows, and there are stream bottoms with alders and blackhaw along their courses. It is all but impossible to move quietly on the ridges. Dry leaves from poplar and other deciduous trees crackle and pop, even when there's a fair breeze. But most of the time when the weather is warm, the deer won't be there anyway. The creeks and such here are of trout stream quality—that means *cold water.* An alder thicket, dense and shady, with a second story of haw or maybe even tamarack, and with conifers lining the bottom just off the bank, is the coolest place in these woods. I have watched deer lie right on the bank, in deep shade, with the coolness from the swift stream laving them. Thus, rather curiously, deer here in the snow country during hot spells in fall will often be in the same places, relatively, as those in the searing cactus country down on the Mexican border.

This swift-stream country offers a tremendous advantage to the hunter in warm weather. He knows the deer will be bedded. If he's astute, he also knows that a rushing stream is noisy. It can often "cover his tracks" and allow him, with what small breeze may be present, to walk right up on his quarry. One fall a few years ago I hunted in Maine, one of the last places a hunter would expect warm weather during deer season. But things did turn out that way. I wound up hunting just such a stream course as I'm describing here, and I

98

made my greatest effort during midday because I was positive deer would be bedded then. As it happened, I didn't kill a deer, but I did find several. They were just a little bit too quick for me, and the stream noise covered their flush as well as my sounds until it was too late. But one of our party, hunting exactly this way, took a beautiful buck in its bed.

Experience convinces me that the snow-country hunter often gets the idea that Southern or mild-climate hunters don't have half the problems he does if he hits unseasonably balmy hunting weather. And I know well from what I've observed that the nonsnow hunter thinks the Northern hunter has it easy, regardless. The plain fact is that whitetail hunting *anywhere* during warm or hot weather presents practically identical problems. This is not a localized situation. If a hunter is well-traveled, he knows that utterly bitter weather, comparatively, can occur in north Florida, Alabama, Georgia, even south Texas and southeast Arizona during deer season. All of the South does have winter, at least now and then. The degree is different from the North, but drastic changes anywhere will switch a deer's routine in the Deep South the same as in the North.

Thus, when what we may call "summer" continues abnormally past what would ordinarily be the season for summer, deer simply continue their summer habits rather than switching to what might be termed "hunting-season habits," which are based on cool to cold weather.

A prime influence upon whitetail habits as summer or Indian summer slides on into crisp fall and then winter—is food. Chill weather, frosts, and snow inhibit or stop entirely the natural production of warm-weather deer foods. I'd like to cite an example that has nothing to do with deer but succinctly illustrates the point. Prairie chickens, in short supply nowadays, feed all summer on grasshoppers and what biologists call "soft foods." They continue the same way into fall, and this pattern keeps them scattered. If warm weather persists during the brief seasons in the few states that still have prairie chickens, like Oklahoma, the kill is low. But if early frosts kill the insects and the soft green foods, then the chickens are forced to concentrate in grain and seed fields, and hunting is better. Almost exactly the same sort of thing happens in the world of the whitetail deer.

It is common in southern areas to find oak trees loaded with acorns at the opening of a warm deer season. Only a scattering of them have fallen. The rest remain on the tree. Deer relish acorns. But if they can't get this food, they won't be under the oaks. And anyway, they won't need the acorns yet. They'll still be eating the green foods available. Somewhere back in early deer research, the idea was disseminated among hunters that whitetails are entirely browsers, that they eat almost no green grass or other soft green foods. Like many such flat-out "facts," this one—without qualification—is utter nonsense.

I remember a balmy fall in northern Michigan after a very late spring and early summer. Growing seasons were running behind schedule. When deer season opened, woods openings had endless patches of bright green clover. Even some wild fruits were still available though shriveled. And I remember patches of mushrooms here and there in the woods, and the shoots of poplar in cut-over areas still with juicy leaves. Deer were taking all of these foods. Living for them was easy. There were even abundant apples, ripe and unfrosted, in a few old orchards back in the woods. With a friend, I hunted the clover patches, the apple trees, and even patches of wild strawberry plants. The deer were avidly eating all these, and one buck I saw dressed had a paunch stuffed with clover.

In a similar instance where I now live in Texas, nobody was seeing deer. Everybody was complaining about the weather. I discovered that on our ranch the tall cedar brakes had much green grass still growing underneath. We also discovered that this was what the deer were eating. They hardly came out of the cover at all except for water at night. There was no reason to. So we slowly prowled these areas, and we got our deer.

Of course, a hunter must bone up on what deer eat in his territory. It is easy to be fooled, because whitetails will obviously take what is most abundantly available and palatable. In my area, ranchers plant small fields of winter oats purposely for deer. These fields remain green all fall. If you want to see the theory that whitetails are strictly browsers knocked into a cocked hat, have a look at such a sprouting oat field sometime. Morning and evening, every deer in the area will be on it, gorging away.

In other words, deer take advantage of what's available. Of course, they're chiefly browsers much of the time, but not always. Warm weather, when softer green foods grow, is really a bonanza time for deer. Later, in the North, they'll be much interested in maple twigs, wintergreen berries and leaves, yellow-birch twigs, black cherry, dogwood, sumac, and, among the conifers, particularly white cedar. They'll eat these because they have to. But they'll take soft foods with these as long as possible. If weather has been cool enough to drop a good acorn crop, deer anywhere that oaks grow will gobble them up from the ground. If weather then turns warm, watch certain big oaks that have unusual acorn crops. Check beneath them for deer signs. But

100

watch them very early and very late or on overcast days, times of most comfort for the animals to be out.

So far as foods are concerned, warm deer seasons tend to scatter the quarry. Greater food variety is available. Deer are not so forcefully tied to specific foods. But a hunter who makes it a point to know what the deer eat in his area (and which items they find most palatable) can sort things out to his advantage.

Regardless of where deer live, they usually have little difficulty finding water. Certainly water is plentiful all across the Northern ranges of whitetails and their Deep South ranges. But water can occasionally be scarce in places like Texas and other dry states such as those on the plains. And, when an extra-warm deer season occurs, it often produces drought conditions that further deplete the water supply. In addition, deer need more water during warm weather. Studies have shown that in winter where snow is available, deer make little attempt to utilize open water. But without snow, and with weather warm, a deer that weighs, let's say, 150 pounds on the hoof will require from 3 to 4½ quarts of water daily. (The ratio is 2 to 3 quarts for every 100 pounds of weight.)

Thus, watering places and routes to and from them to bedding or feeding places will be important hunting spots in warm seasons. The scarcer the watering sites, the more use they'll get. Whitetails commonly use a lakeshore heavily during these times. One fall I photographed deer coming at dusk to both feed and water from rock ledges above a lake. The ledges were on the shady side and facing the breeze. There was lush green food at the lakeshore, and a cool breeze, and, of course, plentiful water. But the only times the deer appeared (they may have been there at night) were right at dusk and at earliest dawn.

On two occasions, once in a lake and once on a stream, I have seen whitetails feed in a manner that, it is claimed, they never do—like moose. There was a wide-bladed aquatic grass beneath the surface, and the deer thrust their heads under to get it. Both these occurrences were during deer season, in extra-warm weather, one in the North and one in the South. Cool water and moist green food made a great combination.

One warm-weather influence upon whitetails that is seldom considered by hunters is the discomfort caused by insects. Deer flies, hordes of gnats, mosquitoes, and other flying insects often cause deer to select places for bedding or travel that they might not ordinarily choose. In humid swamplands of the South, I have watched a big buck stand in or travel along an opening or channel. Here the best breeze blows, helping to disperse insects, and he can wade and splash to help drive them away. Last fall I even watched deer running across a marshland, splashing water high. They had not been disturbed; they were trying to rid themselves of swarms of biting insects.

Insect exasperation will sometimes influence whitetails to select spots for hiding that are not to their greatest safety. A couple of years ago I glassed a buck that was swinging its head and swishing its tail along an edge of timber. Then I watched it race across the meadow opening to a very small, dense thicket of shin oak. I was able to get close because the buck was so disturbed by flies that it paid me little heed. It stood in the thick, stiff shin-oak shrubs, rubbing against them, using them to drive the flies away. I collected that buck and learned one more bit of warm-weather lore.

If you observe carefully, you'll note that a warm fall does not produce heavy, gray winter coats on whitetails. If summerlike weather persists, the coat will be thin; sometimes the animals may retain their reddish summer coats. Although this summer coat is cooler, it does allow insects to distract them severely.

Because whitetails range over such a vast expanse of the continent, and thus have colonized such a variety of terrains, few hard-and-fast rules can be laid down that will apply to every situation. For instance, I have observed an interesting habit among deer that live in dry country that has fair cover but has ridgetops that are unforested and have only scattered thickets of modest size. These thickets are shady, shutting out direct sun. They're also cool because any stirring breeze passes through. They are also likely to be somewhat removed from insect swarms. In warm weather, deer will bed down in these places. It's not always easy for them to see out for any distance. And considering themselves totally hidden—which they are—they will lie as snug as quail when a hunter passes by. Hunting such thickets and disturbing them thoroughly will occasionally jump a good buck right into the open—but always on the opposite side of the thicket. In a situation like this, two hunters operate better than one.

In wholly arid country that has ridges or mountains, exactly the opposite habits are evident. The barren ridges furnish no cover. A mule deer might lie up there beneath a single bush or even just on a shady rock ledge. But not a whitetail; it must have more cover. In such terrain, whitetails are forced to go to the canyon bottoms. It is here that the brush grows and here that they will invariably hide. On many hot days there's no breeze in such country, or at least only faint stirrings. But canyons will always have thermal currents, and deer use them to scent danger. As a rule, thermal currents move up-canyon after the sun comes up and begins to warm the air. But late in the afternoon, as the air cools even slightly, the movement will be downhill. Therefore a sharp hunter will head into the thermals by hunting downward in the morning, even if there is no readily detectable breeze, and then reverse his course and walk uphill in the afternoon.

Thermal currents occur in any latitude where you find ridges and valleys. When the woods are dry and without breeze and walking isn't feasible, then the only way to hunt is to take a stand. The times will be very early and very late. But the stand you take should be selected with air currents in mind. If you want to watch a ridge and a valley, sit up high and look down in the morning; sit below and look up in the afternoon. That's the procedure only when you can detect no breeze direction. The same principle works well on watering deer. In general, they'll come down to water as soon as they get up from their beds in late afternoon and therefore will be moving toward you.

If you're like me, sitting is the hardest part of deer hunting. I can stand it for half an hour, but then I've got to move. When weather is warm and the deer country is noisy to move in, you can prowl if you'll simply forgo aimless wandering and stick to well-worn trails. The warm part of any deer season is most likely to be the first part. Before deer season opens, the animals have been disturbed very little for months. Later in the season, they may shy from old log roads, vehicle trails, and stock trails. But earlier, where a good feeding spot, bedding place, or watering location is beside or near such a trail, a deer is as likely to be there as anywhere. Stick to the trails when walking. They'll be quieter underfoot. And if you select your course to take you through good territory, you have an excellent chance of scoring.

All of the suggestions here are the cream skimmed from what experience in both the North and South has taught me over a number of years. Nowadays I seldom get to snow country for whitetails. But so far as hunt success is concerned, warm weather no longer disconcerts me. Regardless of where you live and hunt, just remember that deer will be deer. When it's unseasonably warm, the animals will be reacting to that kind of weather. If you do likewise, you won't feel aimless. And while you're working up a sweat, you'll have just as good a chance of putting a fine head on the wall as you would if you were shivering.

Look Where the Deer Food Is

One year a friend and I were on a mule-deer hunt in rather open mountain country. As we rode along in a jeep, looking over our hunting ground, he told me he thought he'd hunt a certain range of hills we saw.

"It looks real good to me," he said.

It did look like good deer range. In fact, practically all of the region did. But an odd thought struck me: *Why* had he suddenly picked out that certain range of hills? I asked him. The best he could do was to say it just looked the way he thought an excellent piece of deer country should look. He had, he further explained, a hunch.

As we discussed it, I kept thinking that a tremendous number of deer hunters set about the business of collecting their venison in this same haphazard fashion. It doesn't seem to me that this is good enough. A deer has reasons—not hunches—for being where it is. Certain specific factors tie deer to the land. I don't believe that my horoscope for any hunting day has ever pointed me to a buck. And I don't believe the so-called "hunch" has ever killed a deer. Thousands of hunters bumble into a buck and kill it. Thousands more, by dint of much anguish and labor, somehow manage to get a deer on the ground. Then there are those hunters who go about it, in any expanse of hunting country, in a far more logical and scientific way. These are the hunters who usually get the job done with surety and dispatch.

To point it up, let me tell you about that fall's hunt. The gentleman who had a hunch about that nice-looking range of hills drove into it, after dropping me off at a spot I wanted to hunt. He walked those hills off and on for three days. During that time, he sighted two does and a fawn. And the odd thing is, those hills still looked good to him. He was hesitant to quit. Yet all he had to do was observe that the low cover he hunted was almost entirely creosote brush. There was some juniper, but not much. There were no rimrocks or other good bedding

104

places, and it was—as far as we could discover later—a range without water. Since nothing eats creosote brush, and there was little comfort and no water here, there was really no sound reason for deer to be here. And they knew it!

Thousands of spots look just dandy to a hunter. But, unfortunately, hunters and deer don't judge a dwelling place alike. Many a hunter who tries to "think like a deer" winds up just thinking like a man who *thinks* he's thinking deer thoughts. The relationship of deer to their habitat is an extremely vital matter, both to the deer and to the hunter who would collect one. Once you understand this, you're practically on your way to the locker plant and the taxidermist.

If I were to set up one general rule of more importance than any other in deer hunting, it would be: *Hunt where the feed is.*

The basics required by any animal are food, safety, and comfort. Consider for a moment the last two. The safety factor, as deer and civilization become more and more intertwined, is changing. Many a deer must find what it deems adequate safety within sight of city or village, possibly in somebody's backyard. I live three miles from the outer limits of a town of 20,000. At night or at dawn, I often count half a dozen deer in my yard. No hunter would expect to hunt a deer out in the middle of a big meadow in broad daylight near a town. But in wilderness or near-wilderness areas, safety is invariably present for the deer. Or, to put it another way, almost any hunter will be hunting territory where a deer will certainly have cover enough of one kind or another to feel safe. Otherwise, it wouldn't hang around.

Comfort is something a little more complicated. And success can certainly be unalterably attached to your understanding of comfort. One of the best examples has to do with temperature. Deer definitely do not like hot weather. They may also think the day is "hot" when actually, to you, it feels quite cool. When a mule deer, for example, is fat and has put on his fall coat, he thoroughly enjoys frosty weather. In mountainous country, he'll have spent his entire summer as high up as he can get and still find ample food. The low valleys may have great abundance and beautiful cover, but the deer won't be there.

In a region of lower snowless mountains, mule deer may lie out on the cool, low flats during the night. But shortly after dawn they'll walk up to the highest rims. They'll get on the shady side of these and there they'll stay until late in the afternoon. On many days when, to your way of thinking, the weather is lovely and even exhilarating out in the sun, days on which you'd be chilly if you went over and sat under a rock on the shady side of a rim, big fat mule deer will doze in supreme

105

comfort all day in a rocky cranny in deepest shade. So, you can't think in terms of *your* comfort. You must consider what's comfortable to the deer.

Or consider the whitetail. It happens I hunt two kinds of whitetail country in my home area. One is the Texas hill country, which is rocky and covered with cedar, live oak, and shin oak. During mild days you can just bet the deer will lie back in the dense cedar, up on the ridges. Here is shade and cold breeze. Only early and late—or on crisp or cool overcast days—will they move out. My other whitetail country in Texas is along the border, in the cactus and low thornbrush. Here and there run dense-brushed dry creek bottoms. On warm (or hot) days, this is where the deer stay. Why? Because these bottoms are the only places where the deer can stay both safely and comfortably.

In like manner, deer in the Great Lakes region or in New England will lie up on the cool ridges when weather is warm or even mild. In a swirling blizzard, they'll get down into the cedar swamps and dense alder thickets where the wind is hardly felt at all. It does not seem to me that it takes much more than good sense for a hunter to catch on to what is and isn't comfortable for a deer and to plot his hunting accordingly. The comfort fundamentals are quite simple and succinct.

Water source is obviously a consideration. However, it is seldom as important as most hunters believe. Obviously, a deer needs to drink water. But a deer has far sharper and more detailed knowledge of where any water is than any hunter has. In what may seem to you a waterless area, the deer may have a secret watering hole. It's good business, to be sure, for you to locate a creek crossing or a waterhole in a region that is rather arid. Certainly all wildlife will frequent it. But bear in mind that deer aren't even born in totally waterless regions of great size. In fact, there are few such areas that hunters will get to anyway.

Nature automatically arranges that a deer will be where its liquid requirement can be filled. But, unlike the hunter, the deer in an extremely arid region is well acclimated and adjusted. It need not necessarily drink every day. It may get most of its daily water requirement from certain plants, such as prickly pear cactus pads. Besides, a deer doesn't mind traveling a long way to get water, though in most deer territory he won't need to. Watercourses are excellent places to hunt, but they are usually so because of other elements having nothing directly to do with water—those of cover, comfort, and food.

Now we come to food. Remember three things: 1) water seldom is a problem, 2) safety for a deer is a matter of keeping out of sight (not difficult for a deer, which nowadays has few predatory enemies except man), and 3) comfort is available in some form wherever the deer happens to be. So food becomes the deer's most important consideration. Every day of the year, every day of the deer season, food is the deer's one great big *must.* Place a deer in a wonderfully safe and comfortable spot that has lots of water but is barren of food or has no suitable food and you have instantly eliminated the possibility of the deer's staying there. It must move out.

Simple enough so far. Now go one step further. Ask the next 10 deer hunters you meet what deer feed on. You'll be surprised at the high percentage who don't know. That's only half of it. Ask the hunters what deer eat specifically *where they hunt.* Very few hunters can answer correctly and confidently. It isn't even good enough to be able to say, "Well, in Wisconsin our deer eat this, and that, and that." Sure they do. But Wisconsin, and every other deer state, has scores of widely differing areas. In a region of all hardwoods, the deer obviously don't eat what they eat in a region of conifers and low brush. So if you select a specific corner of a specific county in which to do your deer hunting, the deer *right there* perhaps don't feed on the same things that seem to be manna to other deer a few townships away.

Consider what happens when you go out of state to do your deer hunting. Tens of thousands of hunters nowadays travel far for a deer. If you live in Illinois and you go to Wyoming for a mule deer, you can be darned sure the trophy awaiting you isn't munching the same grub the whitetails eat in your home state, or even the same food as the buck you shot last year in northern Michigan. Nor will the muley you go after eat the same menu in the open sage country west of Gillette, Wyoming, that another mule deer lives on in the tall timber outside Pinedale.

Deer, when left to their own devices, are not wide-ranging animals. Excepting migrations from summer to winter range and back, plus a certain amount of extra traveling bucks do when in rut, an area of a couple of square miles contains most deer all their lives. Of course, a deer might be driven out by continual harassment. But otherwise the only thing that will move it from its general birthplace (which, remember, must have contained all the necessities or else the deer wouldn't have been born there) is a lack of adequate food. During a drought that decimates the food supply, most deer die rather than move.

Furthermore, deer are reasonably sedentary unless rather violently disturbed. They don't want to go far to eat. They like to bed down near their feeding places. We say the "deer are moving today," when actually what we mean is that they are on their feet browsing—excepting, of course, the times when they move because of the rut. On scores of occasions, I've spent most of a day observing a single group of deer. It's most interesting to see how small a piece of country will contain them, provided they have the necessities.

One fall, for instance, I had located a group of seven bucks in the Big Bend country of west Texas. They were a handsome lot. Another hunter was with me. We spotted these bucks just after daylight. We watched them for some time. We had no intention of shooting. We just wanted to see what they'd do. This is open country, and we could watch them as long as we chose. They browsed around quite late that morning, I presume because the air was rather chilly. Then they drifted from sight into a small canyon that led to a higher area of big rocks. There we lost them. I imagine they bedded down.

We came back in midafternoon and picked them up high on the hillside. They were working down onto the lower ridges. By 4:30 they were right back where we'd seen them in the morning. We again left them and went on. But at dusk we returned the same way. All seven bucks were about 200 yards from where we'd left them. We mentioned them to the ranch owner. He said: "Yes, I know the group. They've been there together all year."

The first question that will come to every hunter's mind is: "How can I find out what the deer are eating where I'm hunting?"

No chapter of this length can tell you *all* the things deer eat in *all* parts of the United States. The list is tremendous. One reason that deer have been able to spread into practically every corner of the country is that their "grub list" is so varied. Many of the items are things a hunter would least suspect. Many others don't appear every year but are eaten with great relish when they do.

For example, during one season in my home area, hunters complained of seeing few deer. This situation was easily explained by the fact that we had a bumper crop of acorns. The live oaks, the Spanish oaks, the blackjacks, and the burr oaks all bore a fine crop. Deer love acorns and grow very fat on them. That year it was hardly necessary for a deer to get out of its bed in order to fill up on them. The previous season we'd had practically no acorns. Deer had to move around to browse and so were more in evidence.

Another excellent example occurred one fall when I hunted mule deer in Utah. In the region of this hunt, near Kanab, piñon are abundant. That fall there was a fabulous crop of piñon nuts. I've never seen deer fatter. I stood for hours beneath low-growing piñon while waiting for a buck to appear. As I waited I picked the nuts from the cones and ate the sweet white meats, getting just enough pitch with them to give a wonderful flavor. It wasn't difficult to understand why

In areas where oak trees are abundant, deer don't have to move out of the oaks when the acorn crop is heavy. Here a buck in the oaks is taken by surprise.

the deer were after them. But it would be a foolish hunter indeed who hunted the piñons only, or the oaks only, without bothering to observe the state of the nut crop *that season.*

Always keep in mind that the deer on any range eat what's available. But they eat it in the order in which they relish it most. If the season has in general been a good growing season, the preference of the deer will be for the richest, tastiest, most succulent growth available. If the season has been poor—dry perhaps—certain favorite foods just won't be available. So then the deer will turn to the next best, just as we would if we found our preferred foods scarce but "bacon and beans" abundant.

In severe times, deer will eat many foods they won't touch at other times. This behavior can fool a hunter. A friend of mine in Michigan one winter saw deer eating jackpine. He lived in Detroit, made periodic trips into northern Michigan, and this time was on a bobcat hunt in the dead of winter. He was reminding himself that next year he'd hunt the jackpines because he actually saw deer eating this forage.

The plain truth is that deer will starve eating jackpine. They were on a starvation diet right then. They were eating it because they had nothing else. This was a desperate measure. During deer season, the whole situation would be changed. Not a deer would be eating jackpine.

Comparable phenomena occur in the West, where deer may have to resort to browsing continuously on sagebrush. There's an oil in sage that inhibits assimilation of various nutrients. Deer can eat sage and starve. You'd hardly be wise to hunt the sage flats in fall just because deer, during the crucial part of the winter, must resort to picking at nothing but sagebrush.

In the Great Lakes country, whitetails often browse on cedar. But in the West where mountain juniper grows—often confused with cedar by visitors—these treelike shrubs are exceedingly strong of taste. However, this variety during a good fall is loaded with bluish berries. Often the limbs get so loaded that the ground all around the base of the tree is blue from fallen berries. I've seen deer absolutely stuffed with these mountain-juniper berries. Yet they don't care especially about browsing the twigs unless forced. In much of the West, the shrub called mountain mahogany is a prime deer food. You can just about bet that ridges with mountain mahogany in abundance will have deer likewise.

You can systematically learn what foods the deer like best in any region. Sometimes, though, the task is tricky. Where I hunt in the borderland brush country, the terrain is an endless rolling welter of thornbrush and cactus. A newcomer surely would think deer would starve here. Actually, the whitetails grow very large and healthy. What do they eat? A variety of the brush as well as grasses and mesquite beans. One of their favorites is a feathery leaved shrub that has only tiny thorns, so tiny in fact that they are quite innocuous. This is huajilla (wa-HE-ah). One 2,500-acre ranch pasture I always like to hunt near Laredo is densely covered over much of its area with this bush. That piece of country invariably has a number of enormous bucks in residence.

In the west Texas Big Bend country where I hunt mule deer, several hundred miles west from Webb County, where Laredo is situated, there's very little juniper or cedar, no huajilla, and none of the other shrubs and plants with which I am familiar as deer food. But here in these open mountains, I have learned, the mule deer grow fat on such oddments as lechuguilla, a low-growing member of the century-plant family. Find an area covered with lechuguilla, and you'll almost certainly find deer. Many other plants are eaten there, too. I offer this information only as an example of how, right in my home state, I go from oak stands in the hill country to huajilla in the brush country to lechuguilla in Big Bend.

Good sense should tell a hunter a lot about where he is likely to find deer feeding. I recall years in the Great Lakes country when the black-cherry trees in my bailiwick were loaded until their branches hung low. Deer stuffed themselves on these cherries. I recall hunting in spots that had been cut over by pulp cutters after poplar logs. Where the trees had been lopped every which way, we saw good deer cover and a welter of young poplar shoots pushing up. It was a dead cinch that deer would be using such a place. Maple, willow, dogwood, grape, witch hazel, elderberry, blueberry, wild rose, and many other foods rate high on the whitetail diet in wooded Northern areas. If areas have good green grass in fall, or an alfalfa field at the edge of a woods, or a place where fall mushrooms grow in great numbers, these may be the very places that will draw deer from a large area. I've seen deer feed avidly on puffballs in a woods-edge meadow.

When snow is on the ground, these same whitetails will prowl for basswood shoots and twigs of birch, maple, willow, and many other trees. I've often seen deer paw down through snow to get at large beds of wintergreen or sweet fern. But you might remember that in dense maples, for example, wintergreen doesn't ordinarily grow. The deer will eat maple twigs and even crib the sweet bark. The wintergreen is more often found in mixed forests of poplar and birch and balsam. So it's handy for you to know a little botany along with your zoology.

In the West, how often you've heard successful hunters tell of working the "quakey" patches in the high draws for mule deer. They mean the aspen stands. The reason the deer like these areas is that aspen is a favorite mule-deer food and usually one of the most abundant. The shin-oak stretches on the big mesas also invariably hold deer, because this is good browse and sometimes heavy with acorns. Manzanita, mountain ash, willow, Oregon grape, serviceberry, cliff rose—there are scores of items that deer eat.

It may begin to sound like a puzzle. How will you know what the prime food is at any given time and place? A serious hunter won't have too much difficulty tracking down the answer. There is not a deer state today whose game department hasn't done careful deer studies. The biologists know exactly what the deer eat in every portion of their range. Many of the original study reports are available in pamphlet form from the department. Many others can be made available to you to study, if you go to a regional headquarters and ask.

Through the local game warden, you can often get in touch with a resident biologist for that district. He will know precisely what the deer feed on in his area, and what they're most likely to be feeding on during that deer season, that is, what wild "crop" has been most productive. Many a game warden will also be very well informed on the same subject.

If you can't seem to find pinpoint information, get from your game department or from the state where you'll be hunting a list of deer foods for the state. Then take the trouble to bone up a bit (that's what libraries are for) so that you can recognize the various plants, shrubs, and trees. The next step is obvious: when you get on the hunting ground, take a careful look. Discover what, among the items deer like best, is abundant there that season. You'll be well on your way to success.

I think of an experience that points up the whole idea very sharply. One fall I was cruising around in the Pigeon River State Forest in northern Michigan just prior to deer season. It had been a warm, open fall, and there was no prospect of snow for opening day. The deer would obviously be scattered, and apparently they'd have an abundance and great variety of forage. During lumbering days a half century or more ago, there were many small settlements—lumber camps—back in the forest here, and many a lumberjack had pitched out an apple core. From some of the seeds, apple trees had grown. In some places a number of these trees are still in evidence way back in the woods. They occasionally, but not each season, bear a good crop.

I stumbled upon one of these backwoods "orchards." In a little clearing beside a cedar and alder swale, six or eight scrub apple trees had branches that bent low. The grass was beaten down flat. There were deer droppings and bedding spots everywhere. As fast as apples fell, the deer got them. Deer of the entire locality might be browsing far and wide on a great variety of fare. But these apples were simply irresistible for dessert. This little windfall had tied a number of deer to this specific place. As it happened, I couldn't get to that wild orchard on opening day, but I sent a friend. With one shot he corroborated my thinking that invariably the quickest way to a buck's steaks is through his stomach!

Twists and Wrinkles

for Different Covers

The deer of North America were eminently successful eons ago in colonizing widely varying types of cover. Whitetails range from the woodlands of the East to dense swamps of the South to the cactus and thornbrush of Southwestern deserts. Mule deer are at home in aspens and conifers of the high Western mountains and also thrive in both the sagebrush foothills and the desert.

Time was when the average deer hunter never got far from home. He learned his hunting territory in fine detail and stuck with it season after season. Some hunters still do. But hosts of other deer hunters nowadays travel widely, ever trying new terrains. That experience quickens the spirit. But many hunters find themselves utterly perplexed. In a habitat totally unlike the one you're intimately acquainted with, where will the deer be and how should you hunt?

I was brought up in the Great Lakes region, which many hunters would call "typical" whitetail country, even though there really isn't any such thing. The basic terrain type in my native area is closely akin to that of New England and much of the Northeast. About 25 years ago, however, I found myself spang in the middle of a seemingly endless sweep of desert along the Mexican border. No tall trees grew there, and only a tangle of thorny bushes and prickly pear clumps offered cover. I could hardly believe whitetail deer could live there. Soon, however, I discovered that some of the continent's largest whitetails called this area home. I had to rearrange my thinking entirely to find success here.

My first Western mule-deer hunting was done in what I'd still call "typical" mule-deer country—the forests and mountain meadows of the Rockies. But my next mule-deer trip took me into country between Gillette and Buffalo, Wyoming, where hardly a tree of consequence grew anywhere. The land consisted of rolling, barren hills with shale outcrops, and deeply eroded gullies, plus some farmlands. Again, it

113

Mule deer, as long as they have slopes, can live in a surprisingly wide variety of areas, whether forests or—as here—desert. The subspecies of desert mule deer is at home in such terrain as this.

was difficult for me to see this as deer country. But in it I collected the largest mule deer I have ever taken.

No question about it: cover types that are strange to you *do* present puzzles. But a deer is a deer, wherever it lives. That's the big lesson that hunting many states has taught me. The habits of whitetails and mule deer are different. So are their fundamental personalities. Yet all deer require the same basics:

- Food
- Water
- Comfort
- Safety

114

All you have to do is look a strange place over and ask yourself: Where, in this place, will the deer of the species I'm after find acceptable amounts of those four basics?

A hunter who will pursue that line of thinking with fair intelligence can hunt anywhere with a reasonable chance of success. Often he can go into a totally new terrain and have it figured out in half a day.

There are, of course, infinite subtle differences in habitats only a few miles apart, but at rock bottom all deer habitats—cover types—can be narrowed down to a modest number, each with certain general and exceedingly fundamental characteristics:

- Vegetation
- Amount of moisture
- Topography

Keep those three elements in mind, plus *food, water, comfort,* and *safety.* These ingredients are the substance by which any new habitat is judged. Out of my own experience with whitetails from New England to Texas, and with mule deer border to border over the West, here are tips for the most common cover types that should help orient you toward hanging venison on the camp meatpole.

Whitetails

Mixed Woodlands

This is what many hunters envision as typical habitat—partly hardwoods, partly conifers—and it includes most of the Northeast and the Great Lakes area and down to the Midsouth. This is the cover that most average whitetail hunters know best. Water, comfort, and safety are practically never problems. Food is highly varied. However, some special foods (such as apples in an abandoned orchard, a stand of beech heavy with mast, and especially a slashing where poplar pulpwood has been cut and new shoots have come up or tops are still on the ground) offer perfect opportunities for stand hunting.

If you discover no special food concentrations, then patiently staying on a stand that overlooks a forest opening, a saddle in a ridge, or a stream crossing is one of the most successful approaches. Most of this terrain is in snow country. So finding deer concentrations by tracks is fairly easy, and something of the makeup of the groups can also be read from tracks. Most buck rubs in this country will be on small, rough conifers such as balsam. Be alert for these. When the forest is wet, your slow walking, especially where you can watch "edges," often pays off. Mixed woodlands generally are the least puzzling of all whitetail covers. Incidentally, hunting whitetails in the West in places like eastern Washington, Oregon, upper Idaho, and eastern Wyoming belongs in this category of cover types.

Farm Fields and Woodlots

Whitetails thrive mightily nowadays in thousands of pockets in farm country, from cornfields and brushy creek bottoms in Iowa to the woodlots of Pennsylvania and southern Michigan. Here again, both water and food seldom are problems for the animals. The big hurdle for these deer is to find safe havens for resting. Such places may be scarce. Old bucks will be awesomely wary.

There are several keys to success here, and you're almost certain of big, fat deer. Use your binocular long and carefully. That advice might seem more applicable to wilderness. But it's even more important here because you should never wander around trying to locate the safety hideout. If you spook a big buck out of it, he may change habits entirely. He's living, remember, on the brittle edge of civilization.

It's not difficult to spot by binocular the few most secretive places a big buck might select. And you can dope out the route or routes he'll take going to and from there. Plan on a fairly long shot, from a vantage point as far from the resting places as possible. Hunt very early and very late. Some woodlot deer seldom feed except at night and in low-light periods. In this situation, however, never overlook a good feature that may tie deer to a spot. A patch of winter oats bordering the cover of a brushy creek bottom or woodlot is a perfect example.

Drives can be extremely successful when you hunt woodlots and farm fields. The deer are limited in where they can go. But don't drive except as a last resort. A single drive can force uneasy deer to abandon their routines.

Southern Pines with Scattered Undergrowth

Much Southern cover fits this general category. The apparent sameness of it throughout puzzles many a visitor. Deer can be anywhere. Food is usually highly varied, so it doesn't often tie groups of deer down to any one spot. Although water may not be a problem, it may be unevenly distributed. Thus small ponds or lakes with moderately open shores are sometimes magnets. Also, because of the sameness over large areas, any opening tends to draw deer.

In the pines, there are invariably places where old abandoned houses or other buildings stand, with a field or two, and good edge cover. A stand where you can observe the entire edge, even a stand

116

from beside or in an old building, is virtually surefire for presenting shots.

Where it is legal—and in most states it is—the tree stand is becoming more and more effective for such cover. Straight pine trunks, many branchless for some distance above ground, are easy to climb, especially so with the popular self-climbing seats that don't mar trees. From such a vantage point, your ability to see among pines is excellent. You can see down into any undergrowth. A tree stand at the edge of an opening, or at the junction of well-used deer trails, is a fine ambush.

Southern Bottomland Hardwoods and Swamps

Hunting deer with dogs was born in these places, and it's still carried on. The moist bottoms and the swamps are among the densest and most difficult whitetail terrain on the continent to dope out. Walking quietly in them is virtually impossible. You can't see very far, and often you can't shoot very far. Water and possible lie-up spots for deer are on every hand. Food is scattered over the entire tract.

Many hunters who decry deer hunting with dogs have never understood that the dogs don't run the deer full tilt. Any dog that acts that way won't be used long. Dogs are selected for slow pace. The idea is to just keep the deer moving but not to run them out of the country. Many hunters still use shotguns with buckshot for this hunting. There are really only two successful ways to hunt this type of cover:

- One is the drive, using either dogs or hunter-drivers. Other hunters are placed on stands a safe distance apart. Success is likely to be best if the group is large. The thick cover inhibits deer to some extent, too. They get accustomed to using trails over and over. So stands along trails that have fresh and ample sign, or where two trails cross, are good locations.
- The second method is for the lone hunter. He should very carefully scout a swamp edge and look for watery trails leading in. Almost every Southern hardwood bottom or swamp has small hummocks or dry islands scattered within it. These invariably are safety havens for deer. You can bet a well-used trail leading into a swamp through bog or water will point to such a spot. Don't disturb it. Make your setup in a tree stand or a ground stand nearby on the perimeter. Then you can watch for deer coming and going.

117

In the South, whitetails live in bottomland hardwoods, and often deep in bordering swamps. This buck is in Louisiana.

Open Country and Plains

There really is no such thing as wholly open country serving as whitetail habitat. But there are millions of acres of midcontinent plains that, at first glance, look to a deer hunter from east of the Mississippi as if no whitetail could ever live there. Portions of north and panhandle Texas, more of middle Oklahoma and on up across parts of Kansas, Nebraska, the Dakotas, and even on across some of eastern Montana and into the Prairie Provinces of Canada offer this sometimes puzzling but often excellent whitetail terrain.

A lot of this region is rather dry. Water is the key. Not just for drinking, but also because beside water is where the cover grows. In fact, the stream courses—without fail—are where the deer are. Most of the available forage grows along the streams. Practically all of the comfort and safety havens are there, too. I'm not necessarily talking about only large rivers. But the large river courses have made possible a sustained existence and expansion of the whitetail over all of this vast domain.

The deer may not always be abundant. But most are big and have fine heads. These deer are really rather easily huntable, even though you might be frustrated on the first try. I hunted once in Nebraska in an area that simply looked wide-open clear to the horizon. But a friend from the vicinity pointed out to me a small creek that meandered for some miles across the open plains. Its course was plainly indicated by willows and other brush, and by heavy weed growth where farm machinery couldn't maneuver on the snug bends. In several miles, we jumped eight deer.

Three hunters working such a creek bottom have a setup tailored for success. One hunter stays in the brush and doesn't do any shooting. The two others take opposite sides, off a bit and ahead. Granted, running shots are the rule in this situation, but also quite commonly a deer will burst out, duck back, and stand, wondering what's going on. Along larger rivers, drives sometimes work well, but more often stand-hunting or very slow prowling does better. In plains whitetail hunting, all you have to do is look for flowing streams and their edges. That's where the deer are. Everything they need is there.

Desert Scrub

Desert whitetail hunting is almost entirely in Texas and across the border in portions of Mexico. The Coues deer (Arizona whitetail) hardly belongs in this category. It lives chiefly up in the oak, grass, and juniper zone—well above the desert floor. Its cover is more like mixed woodlands. But desert whitetail hunting in southern Texas and parts of western Texas is among the most intriguing and difficult found anywhere, and to a visitor the most perplexing.

The so-called Texas "brush country" below San Antonio is the prime area. Here an undulating sea of thornbrush and cactus spreads away endlessly. Forage is of infinite variety, scattered hither and yon. Deer can't be tied to it. Here the magnets are water and what serve for openings. The water is in the form of dug ponds (or tanks, as they are called) for cattle. A stand on the fringes of a tank will show you deer, if you're willing to stay with it. There are two kinds of openings.

- One is what locals call a prickly-pear flat, interspersed with low thornbrush, that can be observed from a high knoll. These low places are natural deer crossings. Again, a stand is indicated. Walking aimlessly in desert country is useless.
- The other openings are the grid of narrow ranch trails, many bulldozed through the brush by seismograph crews searching for oil. Here again, you sit and wait, preferably on a high spot from which you can observe valleys on either side. Deer constantly cross these trails. They must do so whenever they move much.

119

If you're a patient, slow, and quiet prowler, then the places to try are not on the ridges but where a visitor would least suspect: in the so-called creek bottoms. Only when it rains are they wet. But the heaviest vegetation grows here. These are the safety spots where the big bucks lie up. If you're good at the sneak and at short fast shots, you can take a trophy from these thorn-jungle washes.

Mule Deer

High-Country Conifers

The dark recesses in spruce and pine furnish safety and comfort to mule deer. But these places do not offer much deer forage. A stranger to the mountains might think he should plunge into the coniferous timber. In general, this move is a waste of time. You can't operate quietly in it or even see very well to get a shot. The deer you jump are gone in a trice. Further, if a deer is by luck killed in such a jackstraw crisscross of standing and down timber, it's all but impossible for you to get it out.

When you're hunting this type of cover, the slopes and valleys between dark-timber stands are the places. And you should watch them early and late. It is here that most of the deer do their feeding, here that the best shots will be presented, and here that a big buck is accessible for dressing and packing out.

Quaking Aspen

"Quakey" stands are commonly interspersed with strips of conifers in most of the mule-deer range. Generally these stretches of quaking aspen are cut up by mountain meadows of various sizes. Mingled also with the aspen are clumps of varied forage shrubs, from mountain mahogany to wild rose and others. It is all but impossible for anybody to walk quietly during deer season among aspen because of down leaves. Even in snow the cover is open enough as a rule for deer to be gone before you have a chance to shoot.

Here, however, the small meadows on the slopes are the key to success for two kinds of hunting. Mule deer appear at the edges of these meadows just at dusk and are usually in or along the meadow edges also at dawn. A well-chosen stand overlooking a meadow, with perhaps a small stream in the valley, has undone more good mule-deer bucks than perhaps any other approach.

Careful appraisal of a complex of small meadows and quakey stands also allows many a successful drive. A series of aspen patches along a slope, with small meadows in between, is virtually perfect. Deer pushed out of one aspen patch race across the meadow to the next.

120

Noisy walking of the drivers helps. Many a good buck will pause to look back before entering the next aspen strip. Shooters properly placed can easily collect such a buck.

Foothills: Juniper, Piñon, and Sage

To the tyro these expanses don't look like hotspots, but they're among the best. Food, except in good piñon-nut years, is not abundant, but the rocky bluffs (below which gnarled juniper melts into sage), plus the piñon clumps and the expanses of sage are marvelous lying-up places for mule deer. And often, in locations where winter migrations to lower altitudes will concentrate the animals, these places are the prime wintering grounds.

Your careful glassing during midday often reveals the dark antlers of a big buck bedded in heavy sage. Among the grotesque shapes of old junipers at the foot of a rock bluff, where boulders are jumbled, there are innumerable places for deer to hide and rest. These deer are seldom spotted with glasses, but a drive here can often lead to success, even with only two hunters. The driver must get right into the cedar clumps and the rock crevices. Three hunters working a draw, one in the bottom, two on the rims, do much better.

A lone hunter should use his binocular long and hard in these

Foothills like these are some of the top mule-deer areas, places where piñon, juniper, and sage offer scattered cover in fairly open areas.

covers. And he should also find the nearest water source and the best foraging places. With patience, a hunter who watches from a stand above such a draw can locate the well-used trails that deer follow to and from lie-up, food, and water. Best hours for watching such trails: from dawn to first full light and from 4 P.M. until dusk.

Shin Oak or Oak Brush

Mule-deer range in the Rockies is, in many places on slopes, practically solid with dense clumps of low-growing oaks. Few other trees are in sight. With leaves on or off, the low-growing oaks offer wonderful deer cover as well as food: both browse and (during bearing years) acorns. Many muleys stay in the oak brush all day, bedding and browsing, leaving only to move downslope for a drink.

First-time hunters in the steep Western country commonly go above the oak brush, which doesn't look very appealing to them, making for the higher-up aspen stands. But the brush is good both before and after snow. It is always, however, a tough problem. In Utah, for example, I've hunted such cover on horseback when I had to give up. Couldn't get through. The going is noisy anyway and hard to spot deer in.

A lone hunter should stay well hidden in the valley and incessantly glass the brush of a slope. Often mule deer move very little in it as they feed. Sometimes one deer stands interminably. But now and then you can spot a good one and get a shot from below. Otherwise, hope for snow or wet going and prowl the oaks, moving in the pathway openings among clumps. Be alert and ready. Three hunters or more can make very successful drives in the oaks, keeping one or two men low in a draw and at least one high up on either side.

Open Country and Desert

Much mule-deer range in parts of the mountain states, such as eastern Wyoming, is in wholly open country. Many hunters bypass such areas, thinking no deer live there. Don't be fooled! Some old busters hide out in such terrain. In general the land is rolling to hilly and nearly treeless. But there are areas of low brush along dry and running creek courses. More important are the shale buttes and hills atop which the deer bed down, and the numerous deep gullies, some of them running for miles. All these features hold deer. One hunter following the bottom of a deep wash, another walking up top along the rim makes a mop-up combination for this unusual terrain. Ranchers often have alfalfa patches in this region. Watching one early and late also pays off.

The desert mule deer is a subspecies that lives in the authentic desert flats and mountains of western Texas and in parts of southern New Mexico and Arizona. To a hunter accustomed to Rocky Mountain mule deer, it seems incredible that animals could be here on the wide-open, seemingly barren slopes where sotol, yucca, ocotillo, Spanish bayonet, lechuguilla, and various cacti are the chief cover. I have glassed a completely treeless slope in the Big Bend country of Texas and picked up as many as a dozen 10-point bucks on it.

What finds these deer? A routine of cruising passable vehicle trails with pauses for glassing, or walking and glassing, or sitting long to study a whole mountainside. You may spot deer at a watering spot just after dawn. Shortly after then they move up the slopes to bed down. Late in the day, after 4 P.M., foraging deer can be picked up on the slopes. But it's hard to tie them to any one food.

Desert mule deer have odd bedding habits that can undo them. Many of these deer go up to the rimrocks and rocky points that jut over a valley. (So do Rocky Mountain mule deer.) For either variety of mule deer, the rims and points offer excellent short-shot "jump shooting" for a climbing hunter during the middle of the day. But very commonly these desert mule deer move up a slope and lie down in the meager shade of a single small bush, sotol clump, or bayonet. Here again, infinite patience in glassing is what finds them.

If you make a stalk on a deer that you've found on its feet, watch for it to hide if it spots you. Often the desert mule deer will trot away, go around behind a single yucca or bayonet, and lie down, head stretched out flat. Or it will trot up a slope, circle behind a tiny motte of brush, whirl into it, and stand immobile. The best protection this deer has is that visitors to its bailiwick just won't believe a wide-open hillside covered with grass and a few scattered bushes could possibly be alive with deer.

As a final tip about cover, let me simply remind you: all deer of whatever variety must make do with the specialized elements each particular domain offers. Among those elements will be some too widespread and scattered for you to use as a focus in finding deer. But among them also will be one, for sure (whether *food, water, comfort,* or *safety*) that will be either least abundant or most concentrated. *Vegetation, moisture,* and *topography* are the three keys to a deer kingdom. Astute judgment of which one is most pertinent to any given cover situation is what will consistently put a haunch in the oven!

How About the Old Stalk-or-Stand?

Ever since I began deer hunting, I've heard hunters argue over which is better: 1) to take a stand and wait patiently for a deer to come into view, or 2) to get off your duff and wander the woods, carrying your campaign actively to the quarry. Anybody can win the argument, regardless of which side he takes. Or both can just as easily lose.

Let's suppose that a hunter elects to take a stand. He selects it ineptly, and maybe he sits for 30 days straight and never sees a deer. The other hunter rams around the woods, scoffing at the stand-sitter, and spooks every living creature in the whole forest. He also fails to see a deer. What it amounts to is that both haranguers are partly right. A hunter who is the patient, relaxed type, and who knows how to choose a sitting place to his best advantage, can—as most of the astute and stoic stand-sitters claim—collect a deer every season. The hunter who scoffs at sitting, but who is an expert prowler, can also kill a deer every season.

Neither result, however, proves much. Each man wastes time that could be better spent doing just the opposite. If each is happy, that's fine. There is, however, a better way—an approach by which success can be enhanced and a conclusion arrived at in less time. It is simply a matter of doing what the deer do—splitting the day into periods of activity and rest—but giving the proceedings a reverse twist.

In its most basic form, the routine of a deer's day begins by the animal's winding up its feeding and getting a drink if need be along about or before 9 A.M. Then it moves to a favorite resting area and lies down or stands placidly. It may get up and move around every hour or so, but it may not move more than a few yards, then bed down again. Along about 3:30 or a little later in the afternoon—and, of course, I'm talking now about fall and the hunting season—the deer gets up, moves off to a favorite feeding ground, and feeds and fiddles along until, for the hunter, shooting light has disappeared.

So, again at its most basic, the deer has three general areas where it spends daylight hours: 1) on feeding areas early and late, 2) on travel routes from feed to bed and from bed to feed, and 3) in bedding areas that offer both safety and comfort. It would seem obvious, therefore, that the hunter should be doing just the opposite of whatever the deer is doing. When deer are feeding or traveling, a hunter—if he knows how to pick his spots—will sit and let the deer come to him. When the deer are bedded and resting, the hunter would be foolish to sit in the same spot, because he won't see anything. He should be quietly prowling, seeking bedded deer or deer that are standing in cover.

That's the fundamental philosophy. But since deer are deer and hunters are hunters, the details may not always work out quite that pat. Some hunters just cannot sit still more than a half-hour or so at a time. I'm one of them. I don't *want* to sit. I'm bored, it's dull, and besides (in my view) there isn't much craft to it. I love to fool a buck, get to him when he doesn't suspect I'm anywhere near, and take him on my feet, whether he's feeding, traveling, or resting. Conversely, expert stand men will tell you that they find walking unproductive and that they know how to pick a spot where a deer—in due time—will almost certainly present a shot.

One old hand has told me many times: "I can sit from dawn to dark. And mark my word—sometime during that long period, a deer will show." It's tough to argue with this gentleman, because invariably, and eventually, he does bring in venison. Nonetheless, both he and I would undoubtedly arrive at the gutting process more quickly and surely if we each did some standing and some stalking.

What makes the fundamentals iffy are the endless influences—discussed in some detail elsewhere in this book—that are brought to bear upon deer. There is the effect of weather on a given day, maybe what the moon is doing at night, how abundant watering places are, how much food is on hand, whether food and cover are together or separated, and whether or not the rut is in progress. All such influences can upset the equation. Should you stalk, or should you take a stand? Every day, as one friend puts it, is another day and another decision.

One fall I hunted with a farmer friend who had some winter oats coming on, and deer were going after the green sprouts in great shape. In the area where I live, it's rather common to plant small fields of winter oats purposely to help deer along through the winter. My farmer friend told me he'd seen several nice bucks feeding at dawn and dusk in the short greenery, and he invited me to come out and see if I could get one. Well, it was an appealing offer. His place is tough hunting, as tough as my own, all up and down rocky canyons, physically wearing and besides, in our region with no snow, horribly noisy. Sneaking around on dry days alerts deer two gun ranges distant.

It was a few days before I could get out there. Meanwhile we had a sharp frost. I went out and sat watching the oats. Not a deer showed. I just couldn't believe it. So I stopped in to see my farmer friend and get his opinion. He grinned.

"I meant to call you," he said. "The cold snap started acorns dropping by the bushel. Never was a deer born that wouldn't leave green stuff to munch acorns. They get fat quickly on them, and a good crop always tides them through the winter."

I know a good bit about deer and acorns. I watch deer in my front yard each fall when we have a crop on our live oaks. They practically live on acorns and hardly move out of the way when we drive out the driveway. But hunting isn't quite that simple. During a year of heavy crop, when every tree is dropping forage, the deer don't have to move around much. Only in the years of spotty production do they go beeline to the trees with the heavy mast crops. That, incidentally, is a hot tip. Find the full-bearing trees during a scattered crop and you can even kill a deer moving bed to tree, if indeed not under it, they go that straight and regular.

The fall in question, however, all the trees were full. On the canyon sides and the ridgetops were tons of food. This influence knocked galleywest the nice pat theory about sitting when the deer move and moving when the deer bed down. Most of the deer were feeding and bedding in the same places, so movement was at a minimum.

What was a sitter to do? Darned little. Certainly a single deer might show, somewhere. But the deer sure weren't moving much. And anybody who'd go into the oaks and sit down would run out whatever was in there. Obviously prowling was indicated, the stalk. I suppose that technically "stalk" means to make a sneak on a quarry already seen. But I use stalk here more loosely, to mean movement of the hunter in search of deer.

I can't truthfully say that my own craft was the control factor that brought me the good buck I soon bagged. What happened was that we had a front move in and a pleasant, all-day drizzle. With the woods wet, I eased around, now able to operate silently. A heavy overcast gave low light in which to work, and I collected a deer that never knew about that next acorn,

Everyone knows how a switch in the weather can spark or turn off the all-out rut. On a number of occasions, and in several states, I have experienced a sudden extra-warm day in midrut that shut off deer activity like turning off the TV. To be sure, either prowling or sitting

126

It's a waste of your time to sit and wait elsewhere when the deer in the area are doing what these two are: feeding back in the oaks during a time of acorn abundance.

is a reasonable tactic during the rut. Bucks are less likely to be spooky, and often a hunter can make a successful sneak. And, when bucks in the rut are running, a stand overlooking a valley with scattered cover or a hillside is perfect. Though the main activity will probably be early and late, it may go on all day.

But when that emphatic weather switch occurs from crisp to hot, the bucks will invariably give it up. A seasoned deer hunter will sense what's happening, will give up sitting, and will go after the bucks just as if the rut hadn't even started. If the next day comes on with a cool breeze whistling, he'll go back to his stand again.

There's a possible variation. I recall when a series of hot days held back the bucks that had started the rut. But each dusk a good breeze sprang up, with cooling effect. Bear in mind now, the stage had already been set. The sharp-witted stand-sitters prowled the thickets during the day, then took a stand just before dusk—when the bucks were aroused by the brief temperature change and couldn't resist traveling.

At times I get the impression, especially from reading scads of gimmicky magazine stories about deer hunting, that writers too often confuse their readers about just how many deer-hunting methods there are. Certainly there are many variations on the basics. But whitetail hunting really has only two fundamental approaches—moving or sitting. For example, driving deer is avidly practiced in some parts of whitetail range. Driving is simply a variation of the generally used term "stalk."

I have never been comfortable among deer drivers. On occasion I have prevailed upon the drivers to lay aside their weapons. This move eliminates part of the danger. But in whitetail cover from which deer are to be moved by walking men, the blockers (shooters toward which the drive is headed) can't always stay in line either. Drivers notoriously get ahead of each other and wander into each other's line of drive. Thus, I'm always wary of the method. And I don't much like the idea on principle besides. I realize that a well-coordinated drive requires craft by the planners, and that drives at times work very well indeed. Maybe I'm just not much for group sports. The arrangement of one hunter and one deer suits me.

One type of drive can be made safely by two or three hunters. Generally this tactic is effective only when deer are bedded—the time during which hunters should be moving. Let's say that a small open area, just nice rifle-range across, lies in a valley. On either side, a steep slope runs up to heavy cover that's known to be used by resting deer.

The shooter goes well around the area and takes up a position along the edge of the opening. When he's had time to get into position, two hunting companions spread apart and drive the thick resting cover atop one of the bordering ridgetops. It is understood that the shooter down in the valley will accept only shots on his own level. That is, he won't shoot up toward the slope. He must wait for a target to appear running or moving around the perimeter of the field or opening he is watching.

On our ranch we have just such a place, and very occasionally we drive it. The drivers don't even carry guns. Nor do they whoop it up noisily, as some deer drivers claim should be done. Our idea is not to wildly spook deer off the top but to let them hear us walking slowly, become alerted, and simply drift off well ahead. If deer are badly frightened by noise, some will double back or pour off the sides. But by our casual walk-through, we have put several deer out of beds and down to the waiting shooter a number of times. When the drivers

128

come to the edge of the steep slope, they call out from cover to the shooter down below, who, of course, has already done his shooting if any opportunities materialized.

So, this might be classed as one variation of the "stalk." The more common ones, however, are simply prowling around until a deer is spotted within range, or until one is spotted distantly and a true and final stalk is made. And then there's the matter of pausing to glass and then going after a deer. For our purposes here, I don't class glassing as "stand hunting." Glassing is a temporary occupation. When I'm moving around, my own practice is to move a few steps, use my binocular, and then repeat the sequence over and over. I simply couldn't hunt deer without a good glass. I use it both in and out of dense cover. It's surprising how often a glass will pick out an antler or an ear of a deer in its bed, one quite close, that the naked eye passes over. Then, just before the hunter breaks out of heavy cover, the glass scans everything over as much distance as possible—and with infinite care—to make certain a deer in sight is not spooked. Often it is from the edge of dense cover, as the prowler comes out, that a true stalk is just about to begin.

Becoming a good prowler and stalker is not easy. In fact, it requires more patience and discipline than sitting endlessly on a stand. Most deer hunters never realize that. They walk along making more noise trying to be quiet than any listening deer will tolerate. They go much too fast. Any move-around whitetail hunter should make a first rule to time himself. If he covers two miles in an hour, he's going about four times too fast. Consider the fact that when you jump one deer or a group, and they run, they may alert others along their course. Certainly a prowler will see deer he doesn't wish to shoot, and he will probably alert them. But he may also see what he wants in the first deer that never knows he's there.

Watching where your feet are going, every step, is one of the secrets of learning to sneak. If a tree is in your path that has dropped many dry leaves, and you can get around its carpet on grass or rocks, make the detour. Every step is important. Take one or two steps, pause, then look. Always keep covered (i.e. keep yourself invisible from the quarry), always try to keep as open a shooting path as possible, and stay ready. It should be obvious that stalking and prowling must be done into the wind, or at least quartering into it.

Although these are the fundamentals of the stalk, only long experience can tell you under which circumstances this is the way to hunt. In Michigan one season, a friend and I went out into the Pigeon River State Forest when it might have seemed foolish even to be out. A vicious snow storm was in progress, with wind whistling. Under such conditions, deer in that region and elsewhere across the North commonly move into the greenswamps, those dense accumulations of varied conifers, often cedars and balsams. The deer lie up in this cozy cover until the storm passes.

Under storm conditions, we were going to the deer. It would have been ridiculous to sit somewhere waiting for a deer to move into view. The noise of the blow covered any sound we might make, and of course, the snow muffled everything. As it happened, that day we saw only does and fawns. But the previous season my partner had taken an excellent buck under similar conditions in the same greenswamp.

Elsewhere in these chapters I have discussed the influence of bright moonlight on the movements of deer. To avoid much repetition, just let me say that when the moon is bright, deer commonly move more by night and rest more by day. It is logical that taking a stand has less chance of producing action at these times than moving into the bedding grounds of the quarry.

The cover and terrain type in which you hunt also has an important bearing on whether to stalk or stand. I went on a deer-photographing expedition several years ago in a piece of Deep South deer cover, part swamp and all of it exceedingly dense. In that region, dogs are legal for hunting deer. Hunters who know the terrain take stands where, from past experience, they know they may have a chance at deer ahead of dogs. But to just take a stand in such a place without experience would be silly. You might hear a deer move within range, but probably you wouldn't see it. By doing the moving yourself, however, very slowly and ever alert, it is possible to get shots—as I proved with my camera.

Your situation is quite different in semiopen whitetail country. We have a lot of quite open scrub woods on ranches near where I live. Deer utilize these places, but if you prowl around there you won't get many chances. Under these circumstances sitting is usually a much more productive scheme. But obviously, you should plan to be in your waiting spot when the deer are most likely to be moving.

I can recall several farm-woodlot hunts I've made in the Midwest. Sitting beats fiddling around the woods here, because the deer are very uneasy about any disturbance in their scanty blocks of cover. Of course, you'd want to concentrate your efforts early and late in the day here. Not often do deer in such situations go gallivanting around during the middle of the day.

The most common stand-hunting approach is to select a spot not necessarily along trails, but at least where you know that deer forage

When you find evidence like this that deer are repeatedly using the same route to travel from feed to bedding grounds, you might well get your deer by taking a stand nearby.

or where they move from bed to food and back. I like natural runways such as a dip in a ridge, a ledge system that cuts slanting across a rough, rocky ridgeside with cover, a crossing on a creek where bluffs seem to guide the deer to a particular place and draws that lead from ridges to valleys. These are classic examples of logical stand sites.

But, as I've noted in another place in this book, a setup near a buck scrape during the rut is all but a guarantee of action. Your rattling of antlers also is done on a stand, and so is using a call. Both these are dealt with at some length elsewhere in this book. I remind you of them here because they are variations of stand hunting.

It should be obvious that a stand looking toward the sun in the morning, and ditto in late afternoon, is just about worthless. You can't see, and the deer can. Switch it around and you put the deer at a disadvantage. The same applies when stalking. Sometimes, though, the breeze doesn't cooperate. In that event, sit where you can watch across the breeze, or move so that it's blowing toward one shoulder. You'll disrupt things on your downwind side, but you have no choice.

One other important bit of lore to remember is that when light first comes up in the morning, and deer first come out into fading light late in the afternoon, they're inclined to be at their wariest. First light strips them of the cloak of darkness. Last light brings them into areas they haven't checked out for some hours, so they're extrasensitive for possible danger.

Regardless of whether you stalk or stand to try for your whitetail, remember that whitetails never move across a totally open place if there's any possible way to go around along the edge. (And there always is a way.) Feeding deer will invariably be along the fringes of openings, not out in the middle of them. Whitetails will cross small openings, of course. But if such an opening has scattered bushes or trees, or even a single bush, you can bet the deer will move to keep the wisps of cover between it and what it may deem a dangerous direction. And if it pauses to look around, it will pause behind or beside a bush, not out in the open.

I recall a hunter from Pennsylvania who told me that he judged whether to move or sit by what he heard around him. "If I'm on a stand and don't see a deer for an hour, and hear no distant shooting from other hunters, I know this is like a survey—a lot of other hunters aren't seeing deer either, so it's time to start moving." In uncrowded woods this listening for shooting isn't valid, but it is a fairly reliable clue where many hunters are operating.

Where many hunters are concentrated, most of the sharp ones elect to sit. It's a sure bet that among today's great mass of deer hunters a husky percentage are inept. They in effect become bumbling drivers who keep the deer moving. Deer under such circumstances are always spooky. A stand such as I've described will show you running animals, because the deer are accustomed to traveling certain routes and whitetails usually run back along the same routes they traveled in getting to where they were frightened. By contrast, a stand contrived in an out-of-the-way spot where few hunters would bother to look may show you a big buck sneaking off at a slow, alert walk, headed for a secret hideway.

The decision on any occasion whether to move or sit is finally based on your analysis of deer needs. They must eat and drink, and they must rest in secure areas that they deem safe for relaxation. Whether the deer are active or resting, they will use their three sentinel senses—sight, hearing, and scent—to monitor their surroundings. Hearing and sight are not difficult to thwart if you take a stand. And if you select your stand with good sense, you also thwart the most important of the whitetail's senses—scent.

An astute stalker can also neutralize all three senses: by moving with infinite slowness and always screened from the quarry, by making no fast motion and watching where he places his feet, and by facing the breeze.

Should you stalk or stand? There's no cut-and-dried answer. All the influences I've touched upon affect which method will be best for that place, for that day, and for various times of that day. The adamant sitter and the never-sit prowler are each a kind of halfway deer hunter. The best tack to take in any situation, one experienced friend of mine says, is simply to do what the deer aren't doing!

CAN YOU RATTLE UP A BUCK?

It has long been most surprising to me that the sport of "rattling up" whitetail deer has not caught on over wide areas of the United States. This is a very old method of bringing a buck to you—a technique that originated many years ago in south Texas, in the cactus and thornbrush of the Mexican-border country. It's without question the most dramatic and thrilling method of deer hunting ever invented.

Hundreds of big bucks have been collected by hunters using this unique approach. Many of these big, wise old bucks never would have been killed or even seen if it hadn't been for the antler-rattling technique. And yet, odd as it seems, thousands of U.S. deer hunters don't even know about rattling up a buck. Thousands more who have heard of it simply refuse to believe it, or else they believe it will work only in the relatively small area of south Texas where it began.

If you do it properly, and at the proper time, rattling will work anywhere. Be assured of that. Twenty years ago people in the Texas hill country, which is roughly 200 miles north of the border, were saying the technique wouldn't work, even that short a distance from its point of origin. But a number of interested persons swiftly overcame that doubt. At the YO Ranch, nationally famous for its guided package hunts for whitetails and exotic game, scores of big whitetail bucks are rattled up each fall. Bob Ramsey, a noted hill-country rancher, has for years been rattling up bucks as a hobby. One fall I rattled up 14 in one day and made only 9 stands of 15 minutes each to do it. Over a 10-day period, I brought in 57 bucks. Some were 10-pointers that came in as close to me as 25 feet!

You sit rattling and watch a big fellow with his hackles up and eyes wild come running as fast as he can right at the spot where you're hunkered down in the brush. You watch him slide to a halt only a few steps away. Then he sticks his tail out stiff and straight behind him, lowers his head, and starts on in, closing the distance until you think for sure he's going to get right in there with you. About that time, you begin to wish it didn't work quite so well!

On a bright, crisp mid-November morning one season, shortly after dawn, I drove out through the live oaks and parked my pickup. Not a breath of air was stirring. Cold and still, a perfect kind of morning for rattling. The man with me had never seen this done, and I knew he was skeptical. He had the idea that I was really trying to pull his leg a bit.

We eased out of the vehicle. I motioned to him not to slam the door and to move quietly, with no talking. He had his rifle, I my set of "rattling horns." We walked quickly a hundred yards away from the pickup, over the lip of a small draw where the pickup would be invisible from the position of any buck in the draw or on the opposite ridge. I selected a small thicket of low shin oak with one live oak about six inches in diameter thrusting out of it and with several old dead snags out front. We got down into the shin oak so that we were well hidden but could still see out. I then clashed the antlers together, rattled them loudly, scraped the bark of the tree, whacked the brush, clawed the ground, thumped the ground with the curved back of one antler, then rattled again.

This sequence took possibly 45 seconds. It was a wild burst of sound rolling out over the still landscape. What that sound was saying to any listening deer was that two bucks had got into a fight. This being breeding season—the rut—this buck battle would be over territorial rights, dominance. Any buck within hearing and not already with a doe would instantly have one of two schemes turning in his love-addled head: 1) he'd come on the double to mix in this fight, perhaps even because this was *his* territory being invaded; or 2) he'd sneak in, curious, maybe take on the winner, or find an also curious doe watching nearby.

You can believe it or not, but before I had even completed that 45-second sequence, I saw a buck coming. He was a big fellow, and he came down off the opposite ridge running. He came right across the open bottom of the draw and up toward us. I didn't alert my companion. He hadn't yet seen the buck, and I wanted him to be surprised. I got more than I bargained for.

All of a sudden my friend heard the big brute throwing gravel. By then the deer was within 50 yards and still coming. My rifleman, instead of raising his gun, blurted, "Great gods, look there!" and he stood up and pointed.

The buck put on the brakes, slid to a stop, and stood staring. I whispered, "Don't move a muscle." I tickled the antlers very gently together. I knew the buck was going to go, now that he'd run head-on into a human at close range, but at least maybe I could get my hunter to shoot.

The deer whirled, ran off a short way, stopped, turned to stare again.

"Shoot him!" I said. "He's a dandy!" But my hunter just stood there dumbfounded, frozen, until the buck finally took off.

My friend turned to me then, his mouth open, and said, "Did you see *that*?" It was one of the most comical hunter remarks I have ever heard.

Don't for a minute think, however, that bringing bucks in this way won't shake up even the hardest-nerved old veteran. Yet the ridiculous thing is, you don't need to be a veteran to bring off this exciting business. You can be a first-time whitetail hunter and rattle up a buck just like a veteran if you'll learn the fundamentals, be willing to stick with it, and have faith that it really does work.

The entire technique is based on the fact that bucks during the rut are pugnacious, jealous of their status, and jealous of their staked-out home territory. Rattling won't work just any old time. Bucks must be in rut, some does in heat. To be sure, this requirement limits your rattling opportunities. But the breeding season for whitetails is longer than most hunters realize, and in numerous climates—latitudes—it can be off again, on again, because of variations in the weather, and does available intermittently over a period of weeks in breeding condition.

Pretty obviously, the breeding season varies from South to North. On the Mexican border, the peak of the rut may occur—often will, in fact—the last week in December and first week in January. In hill-country Texas (where I live, and where whitetails are abundant) bucks commonly are in full rut when the deer season opens in mid-November. Texas has in most counties a six-week season—to the end of the year. This means that no season there goes by without a chance to rattle up bucks. This long season may, in fact, be one of the reasons why Texas and antler rattling have so long been associated.

However, although bucks come most quickly and most eagerly to rattled antlers during the peak of the rut, the "peak" simply means the period during which the greatest *number* of deer are breeding. The fact is that whitetail deer breed over a period that usually extends at least 40 days and may stretch out for some stragglers over as much as 5 months. I have authenticated that bucks can be rattled up in my area (just for fun; no open season) as early as September, and I have personally seen several different bucks running does in January.

136

The rut is triggered by influences of weather, and diminishing hours of daylight. Does come into brief estrus periods—monthly until conception is achieved. Bucks are ready as soon as velvet is rubbed. An unseasonably warm spell may dampen activity. But let the first cool night come, and at dawn you'll find bucks running does again. In the warmer climates, this weather change may be slight, a drop of only 10 or 15 degrees. It is probable that in the colder climates the rut, all told, is a little shorter and cuts off more precisely. When I lived in northern Michigan, I observed bucks in rut commonly in late October and early November, and often during the two-week late-November season they were really going all out.

If your deer season falls at a time when the rut is at its peak—that is, with most does ready to be bred—your chances are the very best. The odds are far greater at that stage that a buck will come to the rattle of antlers. The competition for does is greater. But your season can actually fall outside what is generally considered the rut peak and still permit you rattling sport. You'll have to stay with it harder and longer, and make more "sets," but after a while some buck, still at least mildly interested, will show up.

However, if you were to hunt a season up North, let's say in late December in a lot of snow, or somewhere out West during a very early season, like September, I'd say your chances of rattling success would be slim indeed and probably nil. One thing that has held back this endeavor is that some persons have overrated it, or claimed it will work any old time. It won't. Nor will you call up does by this method, except in extremely rare instances. On two occasions I have had does come walking up to look, and I'm reasonably sure they came out of curiosity. Most of the time you can rattle your brains loose while a doe stands off some distance feeding and pays you no attention. This method is for bucks that are in rut.

Don't be too hasty about shooting the first buck that shows, if it happens to be a spike or forkhorn. These young bucks sometimes act positively silly. They'll run in to rattled antlers, stand around, jump and hop, and twitch their tails. I have even spoken to them out of curiosity and made all sorts of movements and noises without driving one off. Watch such a deer, however, if he hangs around. If you see him looking over his shoulder or cocking his ears in a certain direction, you can be pretty certain a bigger buck is out there somewhere.

So that you will understand what may happen, let me describe how mature bucks come to rattled antlers. One may crash right through brush, barreling in as if ready to tear everything apart. If you hear

137

such a ruckus, just give a brief, low rattle, and get your gun ready. It's better to have one man shooting and one rattling. This wild-eyed buck won't need any further urging. He's coming—period.

Another may come sneaking in with absolute silence. I've had bucks come up behind me almost within touching distance, scaring the daylights out of me when they spooked.

Still another you may spot moving 200 yards off, on a ridge. This often happens in midday rattling. The buck has heard and got out of his bed to have a look. He'll come slowly. You keep coaxing, gently, with a loud burst every now and then. He takes a few steps, stops, takes a few more, stops to look and listen. One time I rattled one for a friend, and it came at least 200 yards. Then it stopped in the open about 75 yards away. I knew it wasn't going to come closer, and my partner shot it.

An annoying habit of big bucks is to come silently and stand in a dense copse at some distance, or sometimes quite close, remaining immobile and watching and listening. Such a buck takes careful handling. He may leave without giving you a shot. Or if you stay with it, rattling very gently and briefly with quiet spells in between and keeping the antlers close to the ground to make them sound more distant, this cautious devil may suddenly step right out into the open.

A still, crisp day is best. Cloudy, cool weather may be good all day long. On bright days, the most action occurs from dawn until about midmorning or from midafternoon until dark. Dusk is a fine time on any day. It's cool, and it's when the big boys get started.

High wind is bad. It makes hearing difficult, makes deer nervous, and whips scent around on odd air currents. A small breeze is all right. If there is any breeze at all, pick your rattling spot where you can see down wind and watch the whole 180-degree arc. Any buck will circle around to come in from downwind. Use one of the popular disguising scents on such days. At least it will help mask human odor.

In selecting a spot, look first for buck rubs—the places where a deer has polished its antlers and, earlier in the season, rubbed them free of velvet. These rubs, invariably on small saplings, will tell you a buck calls this general area "home." Then look closely for "scrapes." This is a pawed-out spot usually in dry ground, and above it there will almost always be branches within reach of the buck's head. He scrapes the ground with his front hoofs, pawing out a small area, but it is quite distinct. He urinates in the scrape and on his own hocks. The tarsal gland, the one on the inside of each hind leg, is wet with musk at this time, and many a buck becomes smelly indeed with the combination of musk and urine.

At the corner of each of the buck's eyes, near his nose, are the preorbital glands, sometimes called lachrymal glands. These ooze a substance that the buck uses as a territorial marker at the scrape site. The buck will reach its head up to the branch overhanging the scrape, often nibble tentatively at a twig, touch it with an antler, and then rub one or the other of the eye glands against a leaf or twig. Hunters have occasionally witnessed this maneuver without having any idea of its meaning.

Scrapes are the marks a buck leaves to stake out its territory and to announce to other bucks, and does, that it is at stud and available. There may be several scrapes scattered around a buck's domain, and they're made only during breeding season. And does in heat also come to scrapes—which they find easily by scent— and often urinate in them as an announcement to a buck that they are ready to be bred. A buck patols his bailiwick looking for does in heat, and also to drive other bucks from it. He will, however, also make forays into the territories of other bucks, fight if necessary at times, and attempt to run off ready does. It is rather common to see a buck with its nose to the ground following a doe track. When she's in heat, a doe leaves a distinct body scent. All deer also have an interdigital gland, between the toes of the hoofs, which produces a gummy substance used as a track marker.

Locating a scrape, or several, tells you all you need to know about the buck that has the territory marked out. (Rubs are also a good indication of a buck in the area, but a buck doesn't usually return to the same rubbing tree.) However, a buck is tied to his scrapes. If you make a set near a well-used scrape, you're in one of the best rattling locations possible to find. For one thing, the buck that made the scrape is certain to return from time to time. Besides, the sound of a fight near his marker is infuriating to him.

You want a spot where you'll be well hidden but from where you can see out. A small clearing in the forest is excellent if your position is in the edge of the timber. In more open country, the side of a draw will be a good vantage point. Camouflage is a good idea. But color as such—like red—doesn't disturb deer unless you move.

Now let's see about what constitutes a good set of "rattling antlers." They should be fairly heavy and have either 8 or 10 points. The antlers should be brown, not white. The dark antlers have more resonance. Saw each antler from the skull just above the burr. Saw off the brow tines. If the antlers have any crooked points or small odd points here or there, saw these off also. Now with a rasp (coarser than a file) smooth down all the edges of the cuts you've made and smooth off any

Dalrymple, with completely prepared set of rattling antlers, shows how to grip them to begin. The resulting "music" sometimes produces amazing results.

burrs on the antler butts. The butts will be your handles, and you want them easy and comfortable to grip.

Most rattling enthusiasts drill a hole through each butt near the end and run a thong through so that the pair can be carried easily over a shoulder. Some practitioners leave the burr on each antler and tie the thong above it.

There are different ideas about how to hold antlers for rattling. Some switch hands—that is, use the deer's left antler in the right hand, and vice versa. Some hunters hold the antlers just as they came off the deer. I have seen some pairs of rattling antlers that were made from two lefts or two rights and were rattled with the curves cupped together. I don't care for this variation myself, but, of course, it works just as well. Your finished set should be symmetrical and mesh nicely as you bring the two together. If the antler points are extremely sharp, saw the tips off and then round them a bit with a rasp. On public hunting lands, it's a good safety precaution to paint the antlers flourescent orange. I don't because all my rattling is done where no other hunters are present.

There are all sorts of rules and taboos among expert rattlers, but most of them are just whimsy. Some hunters say a pair of rattling antlers must be exactly thus-and-so, or that mule-deer antlers won't work on whitetails. A great number of whitetail bucks I've rattled up were brought in with a small pair of antlers sawed from a mule deer. Bucks with all sizes and styles of antlers fight now and then. So bucks know well that different antlers make different sounds. Don't worry about it. A buck in full rut could be rattled up with two sticks whacked together. It's been done.

Rattling procedures vary a good bit. My sequences go about as follows: When I get all set comfortably, I bring the two antlers together with a resounding whack, then intermesh the tines and rattle them hard. Then I draw them apart, whack them again, and again make them rattle. By now I can be absolutely certain that any buck within hearing has my spot precisely pinpointed.

I try always to select a spot with a rough-barked tree in front of me and some brush within reach. I now rake the antler tips hard against the bark, clawing it. Then I instantly switch to whacking and beating and clawing the brush. Now a quick clash and rattle. Then, placing the tips of one antler on gravel or dry leaves or rocks, I rake it around as if a buck were slipping and clawing with his feet. Then back to rattling, but not so loud now.

If I'm anywhere near a buck, he has probably already arrived and been shot by now. If not, at this juncture I stop momentarily. Then I seize the right-hand antler and pound the butt or the back of the antler smartly on the ground. This sounds much like a deer stamping his foot and it can be heard a long way off. I have brought in bucks that had come partway and stopped by simply whacking the ground like this at intervals. At each whack, such a buck will take a few steps closer. Then, when I have his full attention, I barely tickle the antler tips together, and usually he can't resist.

The exact sequence of the rattling and other sounds is not especially important. Only experience can teach you when to make noise and when to keep still. Some bucks will be very much intrigued by constant rattling and clawing and raking, and some will spook off instantly.

If a buck comes in and stands behind a screen of brush, I usually try the coaxing technique: very gentle tickling of antler tips, very light ground raking, and so on. A hesitant buck like this shouldn't be allowed to see you move.

On the other hand, a buck that comes wild-eyed often is expecting to see movement. I've experimented by purposely moving the brush and wallowing around. On occasion, such movement seems to be an attraction. Yet I'd be cautious about movement. The old rule is never to let a buck see you or see you move. Make him hunt for those "hidden" fighters. Much depends on how badly you want to kill a buck. If you're rattling one up for the rifle, then you should exercise every care. If you've killed your buck and you're just practicing, then try different approaches and techniques.

Pick your stands carefully. If you have seen a buck in a certain area, he probably lives not far off. If he's undisturbed, he'll come to your racket. Ordinarily, in regions where deer are abundant, 15 minutes on a stand is enough. But bucks have been rattled up after an hour or more. When you change stands, however, move at least half a mile. It's better to be clear out of the bailiwick of a buck you may just have been trying.

The spots you select to make your stands become more important, of course, if deer are scarce. In our territory, where whitetails are extremely plentiful, location won't make so much difference as in an area where deer are scarce. In the regions of scarcity, scout your territory thoroughly before you begin. Find a spot where you are fairly certain a buck actually is in residence. Then, if breeding season is on, your chances will be excellent.

Don't be ready to give up if you get no results. Be fully assured that rattling *does* work. Don't get up in a tree to rattle as some hunters do. Stay close to the ground. Sound will carry best and most naturally there. If you happen to hit the time of a full moon, you're at somewhat of a disadvantage. Bucks will do much of their running at night. In such an event, place your emphasis on rattling late in the afternoon and right up until shooting light fades.

If you go through an entire rattling sequence without result, yet you feel your stand should be a good one, remain quiet for 15 minutes and start over. A buck traveling around looking for a doe may have moved into hearing during that time.

The most important rule of all, however, is to *check out carefully the time of the rut in your hunting area.* It will differ from year to year as weather dictates. But its general timing should remain reasonably constant.

Let me emphasize what I said earlier: the chief reason that few hunters outside of southern Texas rattle bucks into range is that they aren't convinced it will work, and so they don't try. Or else they try with little confidence or perseverance and fail.

Some time ago a New York City writer did a magazine article that

142

This unique idea in providing a rattling stand (folding chairs on a plywood panel atop vehicle) allows hunters to see over nearby brush. This "stand" can stop anywhere so that hunters may rattle antlers. Check state laws before you decide whether to try this approach in areas you hunt.

scoffed at rattling. His references in the story were rather obviously to me and to several things I have written about this method. He stated that he had tried rattling on two occasions in the Adirondacks with no result. I gathered that he might have spent in total a couple of hours. His conclusions were ridiculous, a classic example of a little knowledge being dangerous so far as conclusions are concerned. He may have discouraged his readers from trying—and even bagging a few trophy bucks.

I have no doubt that the abundance of whitetails in parts of Texas is a big help. But whitetail bucks fight during breeding season in Maine, Michigan, Mississippi, Florida, New York—everywhere they

143

live. Numerous readers who have read material of mine about rattling have written me testimonials to their own success with it. Letters have come from practically all parts of whitetail range—the Ozarks, New England, the Great Lakes region, Pennsylvania.

On my own ranch I've gone out on a certain day when I knew the rut was in progress and rattled my head off with no success. That result doesn't discourage me. Once you've experienced the astonishing thrill of having a big buck come right to you—well, if I thought it would happen once in a hundred tries, I'd certainly stay with it. One sidelight to keep in mind is this: a whitetail doe is in heat only briefly, possibly a day and a half. Nonetheless, studies show that on almost all whitetail ranges, an extremely high percentage of does are bred annually. Few are missed. The hunt by bucks for does—and indeed much of the time vice versa—therefore is intense. The fewer the does, the more willing a mature buck is to battle for their favors in his domain. Obviously, as I've said, you must do your rattling where a buck in rut hears you.

It's strange, but not very much is known about the reactions of mule deer to rattled antlers. I have tried it, but so far without success. There may have been logical reasons. In each instance my rattling opportunity was either too early or too late in the season—or so I believed. Further, mule deer are far more gregarious animals than whitetails. And though some sensational battles between big mule-deer bucks do occur, most of the time they're not as aggressive as whitetails. It's not uncommon to see several mule-deer bucks with a group of does when it is obvious they are "rutty," yet aside from a bit of pushing and short charges, serious fighting seldom occurs.

In my opinion the reason so few hunters have tried rattling mule deer is that the mule deer lives in habitat where it is far more visible. A hunter seldom finds the need to draw one out of dense cover. The slopes of mule-deer ranges offer endless vantage points for observation over open or partially open country.

The whitetail situation, particularly where big bucks are concerned, is drastically different. Big whitetail bucks are awesomely shy, masters at keeping their lives secretive. Using antlers to rattle one out of its dense habitat during breeding season is a most intriguing and dramatic endeavor. Even if it improves your chances only a single percentage point, it's worth a persistent try, regardless of where you hunt.

ODDS-BOOSTING WHITETAIL TIPS

On the fifth day one whitetail-deer season, I sat watching for a shootable buck—just as I'd done each previous afternoon of the season. Up to that time I'd passed up five legal bucks, not because I was seeking a record pair of antlers but because I wanted a rolling-in-fat meat animal. On this fifth afternoon, at about 5 P.M., I shot precisely the deer I wanted. But without question I would have muffed my chance, except for close observation of the movements of another deer.

Out in front of me at the time were four does and one goofy little spike that was hardly dry behind his nubbins. The does were feeding and jittering around, occasionally scaring themselves by rattling a stick or catching some minor whiff of scent that disturbed them. But presently one doe looked up, not at me but off to my right.

As she did this, I was just getting ready to shoo them all off in disgust and leave. I'd sat for two hours—more than I can usually endure—and I was sick of it. But now as the doe swung up her head and looked toward her left—she was facing me—a very exact movement she made forced me to stay put.

If you've ever taken time—which you should—to observe deer with close care, you'll know that a deer that looks at a man or some other danger real or imagined, holds its ears not completely forward, but slightly forward of a right angle to the plane of the head. But you will also have noted that a deer, when looking toward another deer, and sometimes just when looking toward some other common animal of its domain such as a rabbit, will cock its ears as far forward and cup them in as far as possible.

Going further, there is an extremely fine distinction, one not always possible to observe, between the way a deer looks toward an approaching doe and toward an approaching mature buck. Of course, I'm talking about deer season, which generally pretty much coincides with rut or prerut.

This doe threw her head high and then stood perfectly still. Her ears were fully forward and cupped close in. I knew instantly that she was looking at another deer. I also knew that this deer was *approaching*. I have often watched a whitetail stare like this, then look away or go back to feeding, saying perfectly plainly, "My neighbor there just crossed over the hill." But when a whitetail looks in this manner and keeps on looking, sometimes (but not always) moving the head a bit or shifting the feet, then you can be almost certain the deer it's watching is coming in to join it.

I got my gun into position. I will admit there was a margin of error possible. The doe could have been staring at a jack rabbit, rock squirrel, skunk, or wild turkey. But because of her level of vision, because she kept on keenly staring, and because she made no movement of her tail (which might indicate fear or annoyance), I was willing to bet she was seeing another deer not yet in my range of vision. I also was willing to bet it was a buck. Rut was close, but not yet in full swing. Both bucks and does, as I had observed in past days, were interested. There was that hard-to-define intentness about this deer that just yelled "boy friend."

Presently, I could hear the rustle of movement. I saw her raise her nose a little and sway ever so slightly. She liked what she saw. Mature does very often vie with each other or get into scraps. A doe during prerut looks like this and acts like this only if her own fawn of the year is moving in or a virile he-deer is approaching. In a moment he showed, swaggering—an eight-pointer round as a butterball. I put the cross hair on his neck and took him to the locker.

Except for learning the few obvious indications deer give of their intent by physical movements, most hunters have mined this field of deer-hunting lore very little. Every deer movement has meaning. And this body language of deer indicates mental reactions. Upon those mental reactions depend, more often than not, hunter success.

In using the term "movements" I mean to include all physical reactions—sounds as well as the flick of an ear or switch of a tail. One great advantage of seeking hunting knowledge from the deer themselves is that your study—with few exceptions—needn't be done during hunting season. This study opportunity gives a deer hunter wonderful excuses for getting into the woods anytime he can.

Among my deer-hunting friends are two ranchers who are in the woods and brush practically every day. For years they've made a hobby of observing deer. They spend little time getting their deer when the season opens. Part of this record can be credited to their knowledge of the hangouts of the deer on their land. But in their hard-hunted area, the deer are extremely shy. Most of the consistent success of these hunters comes from the fact that they know deer, period. They can tell practically by the flick of its eyelash what any deer is going to do, and why, and when.

For example, when you hear a deer snort or blow, a deer you don't see, what does it mean to you? Suppose you're sitting on a stand and all of a sudden you hear this snort. Do you get up and cuss a little and walk off, certain the deer has winded you and left in high gear, spooking everything else in the vicinity? If so, you're making a grave mistake.

Not long ago I sat until I was bored stiff, hoping a shootable whitetail buck would cross my range of vision. None did. Presently, however, a deer snorted—possibly 70 yards in front of me. What's difficult about deciphering this sound is that usually it comes as a surprise. This keeps you from listening as intently as you should. Was this single snort a "test?" Or was it a "goodbye?"

Usually the doe will do more snorting than the buck. I'm not saying bucks never snort. A deer suddenly startled by sight, sound, or scent of danger at close range will let off a single rousing snort and be long gone. You can actually tell by the abrupt, slam-bang sound of it that this is a badly frightened animal. But a deer that's only mildly startled will emit a pretty good one, followed by several shorter ones as it runs away. It may not run far.

A deer that's unsure may get a minor scent wafted to it and give a *whew* of modest volume that neither begins nor ends with a solid punch of breath through the nose. This is a tough one. You can't tell whether the deer has just demonstrated mild alarm, a little bit of uncertainty and curiosity, or not. You must gamble. It's very possible the deer making this sound is a buck—not an old wise brute but a middle-size buck with middle-size not-quite-sure experience.

That was the sound I heard on this day in question. I checked the breeze and decided it was possible that the deer hadn't been aware of me at all and had whistled because of some lesser disturbance. Because the sound came only once, I was more than ever suspicious that a buck was nearby. I decided to wait.

Here was my reasoning: On many occasions I had watched a doe that had actually got a whiff of my scent, or had seen some movement of mine, that—while not enough to put her to flight—had aroused her highest suspicions. She had on such occasions stared, uncertain and alerted but not yet positive enough to run. I could almost see the wheels turning in her head. Maybe a snort would unsettle whatever it was she had seen or heard or scented, force it to give itself away.

There is no doubt that deer use this sound now and then to "spook" whatever they're suspicious of. Their reasoning—if it can be called that—seems to be that if it's a harmless rabbit, fox, or bird, it will either pop out for a look or else flee. If it's real danger, that too will show itself at the sound—and the deer will flee. It isn't very safe reasoning, but deer don't know that.

Such a deer, having snorted once, seldom stops there. She will whistle again. Sometimes she will repeat a number of times. Then, deciding she's being a silly old fool about it, she'll put her head down and begin feeding again. On the other hand, if she's positive she has caught a scent at fairly long range, she'll usually walk—along a ridge-side perhaps, on a level with a hunter—and she'll make part of a circle around him, snorting every few steps.

Naturally the hunter doesn't always get to see what's happening, so he may not realize what's going on. But he can make very certain of one thing: this kind of performance is to force some suspected danger into giving itself away, and no mature buck during the fall of the year (when he is an awesomely wary cuss to begin with) is going to fool around with such nonsense. He'll be long gone.

If he and some does are around when one doe starts such a scene, the buck will disappear quicker than scat, leaving the does to their silly ways. Nor will he join the busybodies in a departing snort. He won't say a word, and he may not make even so much as a sound in going. In the same manner, when you're walking and break out at close range upon a doe that is unaware, she may let out a beaut of a snort and plunge away. Nine times out of ten, a buck that's come upon in the same way will plunge away without any vocal sound.

And so now I sat, adding up all these items I had previously put into my mental card file over the years. The answer I got was that there was a good chance a buck had made the low snort, and that he was not really spooked at all. I had him figured for a buck of modest size, maybe two or three years old.

I listened with full concentration for some small sound of a deer distantly running away through the heavy brush. I heard nothing. I kept my gun ready. I had sat for possibly half an hour, watching and listening, knowing full well that my assumptions might all be very silly, but knowing, still, that there was a chance they were not. It only takes that small chance on the hunter's side, plus a split second, to put a buck on the turf.

Suddenly there he was. Right in front of me at not a step over 30 paces. His nose was in the air and he was snuffing away, gently, trying to locate whatever was bothering him, which now at least was undoubtedly me. He hadn't made a sound in coming. I lowered the boom

148

on him without his ever knowing anything more about it. Exactly as I had doped it from adding up past observations, the animal was an eight-pointer and by his teeth about 2½ years old.

I'm not claiming you can make such deductions work every time. You can't. But what if they turn out only occasionally? Counting up the knowledge that goes with them from previous precise observation of sounds and movements of deer, such deductions still give you a little bit better chance than ordinary. And sometimes just a little bit is enough, the difference between venison and none.

Deer are not very vocal creatures. A fawn, even one well grown, will occasionally blatt if it has lost its mother or she has been shot. Such a young deer will sometimes emit this rather loud and disturbed blatt over and over, trotting along as it does so. This sound is not especially useful to the hunter, unless he is an any-deer hunter prepared to shoot a small, young deer.

But a low, pleading bleat, softly and most sparingly given, is a different matter. Even this one you seldom hear. When you do, you can be certain it's from a mature doe and that she's telling a buck she doesn't mind a bit if he courts her. On such an occasion, he will be nearby, perhaps right at the doe's side. He will also be as addlepated as a buck ever gets. It is not at all impossible to steal up within a short distance and collect him. His mind is on other matters.

A buck, too, makes a sound rather often when running a doe. It is a low, guttural grunting, repeated several times in quick succession. Not loud. You must listen closely if you expect to hear it. When you do, however, you can kill the buck with ease if you use good judgment. He is not readily disturbed. Just be careful that he doesn't scent or sight you as you get up into position to bring him down.

The sound of bucks fighting is very occasionally heard. It's not common enough, however, to let you plan on killing a deer that's in a battle. But it's a real racket of crashing brush, quite different from the sound made by a running animal. And you can also hear antlers strike together. This sound, of course, emanates steadily from one place. Now and then a buck is taken by surprise while in a fight.

A most interesting sight to witness is a buck rubbing his antlers on—or sparring with—a bush or small tree. Practically every deer hunter knows a rubbing tree when he sees one, with its bark scuffed and small branches broken. Once I stole up to within a few yards of a buck that was busy at this business. His own racket and his intentness covered my stalk. The sound is one worth listening for. It's not likely to be heard often, but it should be recognized when it is.

In shale country or rocky areas, especially where large chips of rock overlay larger patches of rock, the clink of stone on stone as a deer walks and inadvertently turns over a piece of shale here and there is a dead giveaway. Many times in the Southwest I've been alerted to the approach of a deer by this sound. You can read into it, too, the fact that the deer itself is not alerted. Otherwise it would travel with extreme care, trying its best to avoid making such sounds. The popping of twigs as a deer moves unconcernedly through its domain is one more instance of how sounds that deer make can have meaning important to the hunter.

Now let us sift a little more of the evidence of deer intent that can be drawn from their observed movements. The tail of a deer, particularly of the whitetail, is an all-important barometer. Let's say you're watching a doe and don't want to frighten her away. Her presence may reassure a passing buck that everything here is serene. But some mismove of yours alerts the deer. She's not spooked into flight, but she does throw up her head and stares straight at you. If you remain absolutely immobile, she may not run unless she gets your scent.

She stares intently for a long time. Then she gives a little switch-switch of her tail. She does not raise it but simply switches it from side to side. Do you know what this means? It is an okay signal. She has made up her mind that for the present, although she's still nervous about things, she will stay. Invariably that tail switch indicates the breakoff of her attention to you. She puts her head back down to feed, or she looks away. She may go through this routine a number of times. Don't crowd her too far now, for it won't take much to send her away.

If it's a buck out there, and you are trying to get into shooting position or waiting for a shot you want, don't bet so heavily on the switch of his tail. Occasionally—especially with young bucks—a tail switch may be read exactly as you'd read the same gesture with the doe. But a mature buck may switch his tail with a quick whip—and bound into flight.

After a while you get so you can tell by the way a buck switches his tail whether he's staying or going. This knowledge is important, with both buck and doe, because it allows you to plan your next move in accordance with the intent of the deer.

Several years ago I concentrated all season on watching to see just how deer used their tails as signals of flight. If a deer of either sex stares at you (or at anything else) and begins to raise its tail, be prepared to see it flee. But watch closely how the tail is raised. If it is flopped upright—I'm speaking, of course, of whitetail deer—with a *whoosh,* that deer is undoubtedly already beginning to bolt. If you intend to shoot, you had better be quick.

150

If the tail is raised slowly and held not quite at half mast, you have an extremely suspicious deer on your hands that just may take time to walk away but will most certainly bolt at your slightest mismove. On the other hand, suppose you sight a deer that hasn't been spooked or alerted. You cannot see its head, but you do see it walking stiffly with tail half raised. Chances are it's a buck and that he's either following a doe or has his temper up over another buck.

I have long felt that a hunter who watches the does closely improves his chances of killing a good buck. During my last season of deer hunting in the Great Lakes country, I had a doe dart out of the woods right behind me. In fact, I had barely passed the spot. I heard her and turned slowly. I was in plain sight, but she seemed not to be aware of me at all.

She trotted a few steps and swung her head around erratically. Her ears flopped as she did so. Down to the ground went her nose, and right up again. She trotted another few steps ahead, impulsively. Then once more her ears flopped as she swung her head to look behind. Any old hand at deer hunting would know immediately that a buck was behind her and that the breeding season was in full swing. If I had glanced back, noted that the deer was a doe, and gone on, I would have missed her message. As it happened—ungallant as it may seem in cold print—I waylaid her pursuer.

The other side of this picture is the buck that's following a doe. For years I had wanted to collect a real old buster of a whitetail from the brush country along the Texas-Mexico border. This is the Texas area from which a number of record-book heads have come. There are many enormous-antlered deer there. But they're possibly the most difficult of all whitetails to kill, because of their habitat. But one season—because I got excited and didn't heed my own advice—I muffed a marvelous opportunity at a tremendous trophy.

I saw a deer move on a ridgeside. Then I saw the massive antlers. He had his nose to the ground, and he was trotting. He threw up his head and glanced my way, then disappeared into the brush.

The late Paul Young, Sr., of Laredo was with me. "Don't shoot now," he said. "Get him where you want him. He won't leave."

It was sound counsel. That buck was very obviously following a doe. He was glassy-eyed with romance. When he looked our way, he didn't even see us. A doe pursued by a buck, and willing to accept him, will almost never run off in a straight line. She'll trot a little way, turn and circle, or zigzag. Sometimes this ceremony will go on for half an hour or more with very little distance covered.

Sure enough, in a moment a doe came out of the brush and passed, in the opposite direction, the place the buck had just entered. He came along soon. And I, like a fool, shot at him when too much brush was in the way. All I had to do, in this terrain particularly, was wait until I got him broadside in an opening. I missed. Even then the two deer were in no hurry to leave, but they did fade from sight too deeply into the brush for another shot to be worthwhile. The lesson is that under such conditions a hunter should, whenever the terrain permits, wait out a shot until a good one is presented. The deer won't leave unless he's forced to.

There are innumerable small bits of lore you can learn. And, of course, much said here of whitetails also applies to mule deer. There is the stamping foot, a gesture ordinarily indicating that a deer is uncertain. It is both a warning to other deer nearby and an attempt to urge the "unknown" into action so that the suspicious but unsure deer can better appraise it. On occasion a buck can be lured into showing himself by a hunter who hits the ground with a stick or stamps his foot to make a sound like a deer stamping its foot. I wouldn't bet on this as a surefire method, but it's worth researching from time to time as you hunt and especially as you have an opportunity to observe deer when they use the gesture.

A deer that lifts each foot deliberately and sets each one down solidly as it walks, meanwhile throwing its head backward and forward with an exaggerated motion, will have its ears cocked and every muscle alert. It will almost always be a doe, one that is extremely suspicious. She may prance like this clear around a hunter who stays immobile. And if a buck is watching nearby, usually he fades away. He can take a hint. But if it's a doe you're after, you'll usually have plenty of time for a shot when one acts this way. You can take a chance on letting her get into a good position for you.

Stances certainly are not "movements," but they do belong in this discussion of deer body langauge. How many times have you heard a hunter say, "I didn't know it was a buck." This is an anguished postmortem that is always blurted out after the deer runs away. Actually, a close observer can tell with fair certainty at long distance, which deer is a buck and which a doe, just by the stance.

A whitetail facing you that looks extremely narrow in the chest and stands with its front feet splayed, that is, with decidedly less distance between the shoulders than the feet, is unquestionably a doe. The same whitetail seen broadside will look a little bit like a long triangle. The neck and head will be the point, and the body of the deer will form the two long sides. But a buck will look broad-chested when seen head-on, and from broadside he'll be much more of an oblong—like a steer.

The neck of a doe always looks puny and slender and too long when seen from the side. The neck of a buck, not necessarily swelled in rut either, looks short and thick and bull-like. It is carried more arched, as if the weight of antlers forced this stance. You can observe and learn scores of small details that will instantly tell you which sex you're seeing.

One time I watched a deer come out of low overhead cover. It was a doe. Next came a deer that clung along the edge. I couldn't see antlers. But the deer moved with its head and neck low, and the neck was on a plane with the center of the body. The head was then carried as a kind of extension of the neck, straight out with nose thrust forward. Immediately I knew this was a buck. He was mildly interested in the doe. This is a common buck stance at such a time.

On dozens of occasions I have seen bucks, both mule deer and whitetails, stand in cover such as dense cedars, with head low and nose thrust forward, watching a passing hunter. How could I know they were bucks? Well, I've shot a few of them. The others I'm just as certain of. Their antlers get in the way in close overhead cover. They habitually duck and thrust the nose forward so they may see out. This is such a typical buck pose that the hunter who knows about it seldom can be mistaken.

On one occasion I was riding in a jeep with another hunter who was new to the terrain where we were. I was well acquainted with it and knew about where I should be looking. We weren't hunting but were enroute to the place where we planned to hunt. On a narrow, rocky trail bordered by dense cedar, I happened to catch the outline of a deer back under the dark, twisted trees. The instant I saw it, although I saw no antlers, I knew this was a buck.

It was a big deer. The broadside stance, plus the low thrusting out of the neck and head as it watched us from beneath the cedar branches, were dead giveaways.

I whispered, "Buck." The driver jammed on the brakes and rolled out with his rifle. He started to aim, then turned and said impatiently to me, "I can't see any antlers even through the scope."

About then the deer burst from cover, crossed a tiny opening, and disappeared into the next thicket. It had very substantial antlers. I realize that a hunter in a bucks-only area should not shoot without being absolutely certain. But if you know the tell-tale signs, at least you're forewarned. I would have been prepared to shoot instantly at sight of antlers because the various stances of deer was a pet subject of mine. He was not prepared, and the deer got away.

And so indeed, every movement of deer, every sound they make, every pose they strike has meaning that should be carefully studied and interpreted by the hunter. Habitually successful hunters know these things without even thinking about them. Less-experienced hunters can double or triple their own chances of success if they're willing to learn.

Special Mule-Deer Savvy

It was midmorning, and the east side of the steep canyon was deep in shadow. The Montana weather was crisp. A man hunting along the bottom of the canyon was bound to feel the night's chill that hadn't yet been banished from there by a bright sun. It seemed logical that any mule-deer buck that had spent the night here would certainly be on the west slope, soaking up the warmth that streamed through scattered pine, juniper, and sage.

I paused and carefully glassed the sunny slope. Obviously the sunshine, if sidelighting a good set of antlers there, would make them shine as if they were ivory. I knew, too, that the sleek side of a big muley will just seem to glisten when slanted sunshine strikes it this way. But as I suspected might happen, I found nothing. Finally, I turned the glass to the much darker side of the canyon.

It took a few moments for my eyes to adjust to the drastic decrease in light. Then I saw him. The binocular seemed a bit ridiculous. The buck was so close he filled the circle. He was standing on a crumbled ledge among stunted vegetation, wholly in sight. He was broadside, head lifted and turned as he stared at me.

It may be that he felt secure, hidden by the deep shadow as it contrasted to the sun across the canyon from him. It may be that he sensed immobility was his best protection. But I don't think so. I think he was just being a mule deer. This wonderful game animal is to me possibly the most intriguing antlered creature we have in the United States because it is such an enigma.

I lifted my rifle and began as usual to breathe hard and shake a little. The deer continued to stand. Through the scope every detail of him showed. I could detect no alarm. Some people might say I took unethical advantage of the situation. I don't think so. He was the very deer I had come for. I eased off the safety and collected him then and there.

The reason I tell the incident to begin this chapter about hunting

This hunter, sitting on rocks in a valley and glassing, is doing what is probably the most important part of mule-deer hunting. He scans nearby ridges, looking for an antler or some slight curve that says "deer."

mule deer over their vast U.S. range is that the experience makes the muley seem—as many observers have claimed he is—plain stupid. I'm quite sure no whitetail buck, or at least only a very rare whitetail buck, would have stood that way to stare, within mere feet of a moving hunter. The whitetail would have panicked long before and would have turned himself wrongside out getting the heck far gone from there. But just as the whitetail is a definite personality, so is the mule deer—though a far, far different one. Understanding the personality of the animal (and how it differs from that of other antlered game) is what will make you a successful mule-deer hunter.

As everyone knows, the densest U.S. human population is in the East and across into the Midwest. Here live the most hunters, and several million of them hunt whitetail deer each season. Meanwhile, year after year, more and more hunters from whitetail country excitedly plan trips westward into the mule deer's extremely varied domain. As the figures on nonresident-license sales and hunter success from Western states show, there's a tremendous interest in the abundant and prolific mule deer among hunters not native to mule-deer range. And hunters who live in one kind of mule-deer range have a great interest in how to collect a good trophy in another kind of range.

Over a number of years, I've had a rather unusual and most fortunate opportunity to pile up experience in hunting mule deer from border to border: from the mountains in Montana to the bald sage plains of Wyoming; from the canyons of Utah to the rough, treeless country of west Texas, the saguaro-studded deserts of Arizona, the high shin-oak mesas of Colorado, and the divide country of New Mexico. Previous to that I had chased whitetails from Maine to Michigan, Mississippi, Florida, and Texas. There was ample opportunity to compare and evaluate, and I believe the sum of that experience can be helpful to hunters whose hearts thump mightily at thoughts of the big-eared, big-necked, big-horned, string-tailed buck of the West.

If you're a whitetail hunter going after mule deer for the first time, the first advice *not* to listen to from friends is that the muley is dumb. I've seen a big mule-deer buck, in Utah, move slyly from a position in the open to stand beneath a low-spreading piñon, there taking a position with antlers thrust up among the branches and head low, watching. If he had run, he'd have been spotted instantly. Because I knew that mule-deer bucks work this same trick rather often, I happened to spot him. I was looking for just such a ruse. Of course, a whitetail buck in a like situation undoubtedly would have raced away, and probably would have escaped. This difference in behavior doesn't make the muley stupid. It simply illustrated that he is totally unlike his relative in his reactions.

The best way to put it is this: the mule deer is a much calmer, much less skittish, and much less nervous creature than the whitetail, and probably less wary. Mule deer are almost invariably fatter than whitetails. Sit sometime and watch a group of muleys feeding along. They don't jitter, jump at shadows, or snort and bob their heads, as whitetails do. They seem to be stoics, the workhorse type, not the racehorse kind. That's why they wax fat and lazy. Some of this personality, I've always thought, may have come from the immense solitudes in which the species has lived for centuries. In the coulee-cut sage, the high mountains with their open parks and stands of timber, the aspen glades and the open meadows atop the mountain mesas, mule deer can see farther, as a rule, and hear better, than can the whitetail in its more confined habitat. The mule deer has very few enemies, except for the mountain lion, and the press and pressure of man's civilization has, until recently, been slow in coming.

I've seen what might almost literally be called "herds" of muleys in high-country Colorado that didn't seem to have more than a vague idea of what danger was all about. Obviously not, for there was seldom any intrusion. But this, mind you, is the sort of experience that can lead you into a common pitfall, into the belief that bagging a big mule deer is always a snap.

Sometimes it is. Often it is not. And so the hunter can never settle on what might be called a hunting pace, as he can in whitetail hunting. The mule-deer hunter is always off balance, simply because his quarry is such a puzzle: sometimes utterly naive, sometimes fantastically crafty, always quirky.

A few seasons ago I was hunting in Wyoming, and I spotted a big buck lying in the cool eroded recess at the head of a deep coulee. This is a very common place, incidentally, to find mule deer in the more open country. The deer had spotted me before I spotted him. What he did struck me as little short of amazing. He laid his head flat out on the ground, his neck stretched and his lower jaw hugging the turf. Obviously this was to keep from showing any more outline than necessary. There were some small bushes among which his antlers were thrust. It was almost, I thought, like the trick of a rooster pheasant caught at close range. It was a crafty reaction. But what happened next is the sort of thing that makes mule-deer hunting interesting, the kind of thing that throws newcomers off balance and loses them a trophy.

A smaller side coulee ran at right angles, directly across from where the deer lay. He had only to burst from his bed and dash into it and I'd be foiled. The way in which he was lying was, from my approach point, not good at all for a shot. I couldn't see enough vital area, none in fact that was acceptable. A natural hunter reaction would have been for me to make a running climb out of the coulee and across where I could see down into the side draw, thus putting me in position above where the buck was sure to go. But I'd had experience with mule deer in coulees, and I would have bet he wasn't going to do what would seem most logical. After acting very smart and lying flat, he'd wind up doing something that mule deer in such situations do almost without fail. And in the next instant he did it. He reared up in a swirl of dust and action and ran straight up the steep side of the draw. Here he was in plain sight all the way, moving upward sharply, which, of course, somewhat slowed his speed. I was all ready for this sequence because I had witnessed it several times before. I concluded my hunt then and there.

To be sure, the great variety of habitats in which mule deer reside will affect what individual deer do. But you can just about bet across the board that when a mule deer has a choice, he'll go up. Knowledge of this fact has assisted hunters in collecting more mule deer than perhaps any other bit of lore. I recall one big deer about which I wrote in *Outdoor Life* magazine some years ago that succinctly illustrates the point.

This was in the open sage country of Wyoming. I was walking on flat ground, with a deep coulee near at hand. The big buck below—which I didn't know was there—had only to run along the winding coulee bottom, unseen, and he would have gone free. I'd never even have been aware of him. But when he heard me and became nervous at my close approach above along the rim, he ran straight up the other side, into plain sight, and streaked across a flat where not a single bush grew. He was heading for a distant rocky hill, but he never made it.

This upward movement of mule deer occurs in all sorts of country. Let's say you're hunting in timbered mountain country where likely draws, wide at the bottom and narrowing at the top, cut the sides of the slopes. Assume further that you know some hunters are working the sides of the slopes. All you have to do to kill a deer—and this is just about guaranteed in the case when deer are resident there—is to take a stand atop the mountain near the head of a good draw. Deer moved by the hunters on the slope won't run downward to the brushy bottoms. Almost without fail, they'll move into the draws and proceed upward.

A striking illustration of this behavior occurred several years ago in southern Utah. Two of our hunters had elected to go up into the aspens on top of a big mountain. Several of us were to work the slopes with horses. Now I realize that horses are indispensable for getting you around in mountain country. But I happen to believe from a number of observations about horses and mule-deer hunting that continuous riding is just about the worst possible way to get yourself a deer. More about that later.

At any rate, several of us floundered along the slopes on horseback, going as quietly as was possible in the timber and rocks. This is to say that we undoubtedly moved every deer on the mountain, probably some of them from half a mile distant. I kept feeling certain there wasn't a chance of jumping a deer and killing it. The deer wouldn't necessarily be badly spooked. They'd just drift away from the commotion. And so they did. And *where* they drifted was precisely where mule deer by their very nature were sure to go: up. The two hunters up on top were at least a mile from us. But they killed two good bucks as the deer came walking up the draws above us and into the aspens.

There's another very interesting angle on this upward movement of disturbed mule deer. Sometimes when you know you've jumped a good buck and that it's "going up," you may do well, if you don't have a clear shot, to hold your fire as he runs away. If the place where he'll top out is open, there's at least an even chance that you'll get your best shot, from below, right there. For mule deer have one curious habit reminiscent of antelope. They'll very often run up a mountainside almost to skyline, then stop and look back.

A good illustration of how strong is this desire to have a last look, is an incident that happened to me one recent season in west Texas. We were driving in a pickup and I saw a buck that seemed to be all antlers. Just as I spotted him he disappeared over a small ridge. Ahead of the deer was a big semimountain of jumbled rock. I hurriedly made my stalk, fearing he'd get so far away I'd not be able to take him. But as I came over the ridge, puffing and blowing from altitude and fast climbing, he was at about 150 yards, with a group of does and smaller bucks.

With so many eyes watching, naturally one deer and then another saw me. They all ran—uphill, of course. As much as it pains me to tell it, I shot five times at that big buck as he dodged around rocks on his way up, and I failed to crease a single hair. You'd think he'd have streaked over the mountain full out. But what he did instead was to stop briefly, short of the top-out. Looking bigger than ever, he stood broadside spang atop a rocky spine. The distance was about 350 yards I presume, by no means an impossible shot with such a perfect target for the .264M I was carrying. But my gun was empty, and so were my pockets. Had I held my fire on the zigzagging animal, I'd have had a wide-open standing target. That kind of shot presents itself many times with mule deer.

By far the major share of mule-deer range is in mountainous country. But not all. The southern deserts of Arizona, where mule deer live, are often flat to rolling. The plains of eastern Montana and Wyoming and the western Dakotas are likewise. In the plains areas where no mountains at all occur, the coulees, eroded gullies, and stream bottoms take the place of high rimrocks and other lying-up spots for the deer. I've often felt that not enough attention is paid by hunters to these open mule-deer ranges. They offer beautiful opportunities for really getting at the deer. But many hunters don't realize the deer live in these less-scenic areas. Most such hunters have had experience only with whitetails.

On the whole, the mule deer is much more an open-range animal than the whitetail is. In west Texas, thousands of big mule deer of the desert subspecies live in country that has no trees whatever. It's rough, mountainous, with Spanish bayonet and some brush. Right in the same region are high-up, small oases of timber on a few large mountains. Here piñon, oaks, and madronas grow. These isolated bits of country have the small Carmen Mountain whitetails, a diminutive whitetail subspecies. They seem unable to spread from these tiny timbered "islands," but the mule deer are happy anywhere.

In western Nebraska today, some extremely big mule deer are killed in range that is cut with eroded draws and that has only scattered brush and short timber. The western Dakotas and eastern Montana have excellent mule-deer hunting in some similar territory. All down across the eastern edges of the mountain states that lie along the Continental Divide are hordes of mule deer in treeless range. This is some of the most interesting hunting available, and no deluge of hunters utilize it. They go instead into the timber, where it's much more difficult to kill a big buck.

In all of this open-country hunting, there are a few rules that, if well rehearsed, will bring you success. Along stream bottoms, with their usual cottonwoods, the deer will drift down into these during the night. But seldom will you find any good bucks down there during the day, even though small bucks, does, and fawns are there and it may seem to you, as you look at the barren-appearing country, the only place worth hunting. The good bucks will be in one of two places, depending on the character of the country. If the area has high hills with at least a few rocky or shale outcrops, the bucks will most likely be up there. You will, unless you're experienced, look at such bald places with naked eye or even glass and discard them as totally unlikely. They just look like "nothing." If the area has no such hills, then there are sure to be eroded draws and coulees, and that's where your trophy will be.

There's one exception. Country of these types often has high smooth hills with scattered juniper growing on them. Mule deer love to bed down in the black shade of these small trees. But the thing that's puzzling to most newcomers to mule-deer hunting is that the deer get into such hiding places so early. If you want to catch one actually moving up—or down into a coulee—to its daytime bed, you must be out before the sun is up. The big bucks almost without fail will make the move either before sunup or just as light is growing. And they seldom will show again until late afternoon.

Of course, if the time of the rut has begun, that's a different story. But in normal routine during normal seasons, after about 8:30 A.M. at the latest and until 4 P.M. at the earliest, you've got to drive out the big boys if you expect to get one. That's not easy.

The reason behind all of this goes back to an interesting sidelight on the incident with which this chapter opened. Recall that I found and shot this deer on the cold, shady side of the canyon. A man thinks a deer ought to enjoy lying in the sun. Mule deer will feed out in bright sunshine, particularly in late afternoon when much of the heat has gone. But muleys are fat, lazy deer. They dislike even mild heat.

There are exceptions, obviously, but you can just about bet that a good big fat buck will spend more time in the shade than in the sun. I've seen them many times, early in the morning, not out where the sun is warm but right along the chilly, dark sides of the mountains. When they move up to the rimrocks or down into the deep draws shortly after daylight, they select the shady places. The sunny side of the mountain top or rocky outcrop is mainly a waste of time for the hunter, unless it has deep recesses that are cool and shady. The dark side is the one on which to hunt all day. And in flat country, the shady coulee heads are the places.

I can recall my own attitude when I first started hunting the treeless regions for mule deer. I couldn't imagine deer even living there. You look out across the sage and there seem to be no hiding places whatever. But start walking or driving this undulating range and you'll constantly come to deep cuts with high sage and some brush. This is where the deer live all day. This, and the shale hills previously mentioned.

Whether you're hunting on such ranges as these in southern Arizona, eastern Wyoming, or elsewhere, you should know some curious side angles to help bring success. As an example, one time in Arizona I sat and glassed for a long while a bald old rocky knoll without a tree on it. Numerous big deer tracks were all over the lower country, and I was sure this high knob would be the bedding place of the deer. Finally I spotted what I wanted: a set of antlers in the dark recess of a ledge. So up I went from the opposite side.

At last, working around, I saw the deer leave its bed and quietly circle the top of the rocky knoll. My partner, left down below, kept waving signals to me. The deer didn't run, nor did it ever leave that high place. Exactly like a squirrel going round and round a tree, that

162

buck kept sneaking out and around, staying on the opposite side. After a time both my partner and I lost him. Where he went I'll never know, but I have seen good bucks do this squirrel act on several other occasions.

Another interesting bit when you're trying to move mule deer from such bedding places is this: you can't spook them out as easily as you can a whitetail. A mule-deer buck resting in the shade of high rocks, or down in that coulee cave, will lie nine times out of ten as tight as a covey of quail locked up by a brace of good dogs. You've got to all but step on him to move him. This trait has been the downfall of many trophy heads. But it has also been the frustration of many inexperienced hunters.

One method that sometimes works quite well to move mule deer from beds on rocky slopes, or on slopes with jumbles of rock interspersed with timber or gnarled juniper, is to roll rocks. Sometimes you have to be persistent. When mule deer, especially bucks, don't want to move and give themselves away, they're stubborn. During a recent December, I hunted in awesomely rugged, scenic mountain country north of Alpine, Texas, with Jim Barbee guiding me. Jim is a native of west Texas and has long hunting and guiding experience.

During the bulk of the day, we'd stay far up atop the mesas, driving up there in his four-wheel-drive rig and then walking to the overlook points, always on the shady drop-offs. Some of these would make a hunter dizzy just looking down to the valley far below. This is a region of unbelievably huge, dark boulders interspersed with jumbles of smaller rock and shale. There are scattered piñon, juniper, oak, and madrona, and thousands of spots where a big buck can bed down.

First Jim and I would sit and glass down onto the massive expanse. Now and then we'd locate a bedded deer. But in the shade this was not especially productive. Finally Jim would start pitching rocks down. A size that will bound and roll seemed best. It was interesting to me in this instance—and I've observed the same reaction in several mule-deer states in similar situations—that most of the does would move out to have a look immediately. They wouldn't necessarily run. They'd stand and stare around. If we continued the racket, they'd move at last along the mountainside. But it took sometimes half an hour of rock rolling to move bucks from their beds.

On one occasion we sat and visited on the rim for nearly 45 minutes, periodically rolling or hurling rocks down below. Our voices easily carried far below, I'm sure. At long last we heard a distant clatter of hoofs. We picked up the movement and put the glass on a big buck racing down the rough slope, bounding among rocks. When others heard that one, they left their beds. We put five bucks off that slope, all too far to shoot at. If I had tried, I'd have been scared I'd kill one. What a chore it would have been to get it!

I must interject here that rock hurling works even better with whitetails in comparable country. John Finegan, owner of Dolan Creek Ranch on Devils River in Val Verde County, Texas, is a master at driving them out this way, with his own unique approach. This big ranch is renowned for its package hunts for whitetails. Some 200 hunter-clients usually fill their tags here each season. Finegan showed me some years ago how he uses a sling—not a slingshot, but a leather sling about like the one David used against Goliath—to send rocks clattering far off into a canyon to put brush-bedded whitetails to flight.

The terrain in this region is remarkably similar to much desert-mountain habitat for mule-deer. It's exceedingly rough and rugged, steep, rocky, and sliced by sharp and narrow canyons. During the day, whitetails move into these lie-ups. If a guide walked a hunter into and out of a few of these canyons, they'd both be exhausted for a week. Further, a chance for a shot would be a long gamble in the heavy cover at the canyon bottoms. So John drives in a four-wheel-drive rig on rough trails along the ridges. Then he gets his hunters out and walks them to a canyon rim.

His leather sling has long thongs and a pouch that will hold a rock of baseball size. Finegan is a masterful "slinger." He loads the sling, winds up, and puts all his power into the throw. When he makes the release, you can hear the buzz of the flying rock. It soars far out and drops into the canyon. With whitetails, it requires sometimes only a single throw, and certainly not more than two or three, to put every deer to flight. To get out of these sharp canyons they usually go somewhere up a side or up the header and out. I've never hunted mule deer this way, but I'm sure that if a hunter made himself a good leather sling and practiced with it, he'd be onto a worthwhile scheme for those times when mule deer are on slopes such as those I've described but aren't anxious to leave their beds. The rough-country whitetail hunter should note this method for reference, too.

Sometimes mule deer at close range try to sneak away. One time I spent a whole morning carefully working out a high jumble of rock above flats where I knew some big bucks had been feeding. It was exhausting work. One area I combed several times. I never saw any sign of a deer. Then I sat on a rock and rested for 10 minutes. Amazing as it seems, within a mere 30 yards of me a good buck suddenly appeared as if from nowhere. He was sneaking, head down. He looked as if he were on his knees. Only bits of him showed. Not until he had a big pile of rock between himself and me did he run. Then, with a great clatter, he was off and away. My only chance for an open shot was when I saw him, still running, several hundred yards distant down on the flat, heading for another mountain. Had I not paused to rest and thus made him nervous, he would have let me go on past.

I also vividly recall several southern-Arizona bucks a few years ago that scared me half to death and went free because of it. They were lying up under bushes near a high waterhole and let me pass before they broke from cover. I don't believe they would have flushed then had I not stopped. The moral is: when you hunt the bedding places in rimrocks and draws, hunt very slowly, quietly, and thoroughly, and stop often. If you do get a shot by this kind of hunting, it will be a close one, probably a running shot, which I personally dislike. But if you're a good enough "sneaker," you may get a chance at a buck in its bed. It's an interesting and excellent midday hunting method.

Mention of the waterhole bucks brings up another point. Certainly the streams and the watering places have a value as hunting sites. But I have never been much of a believer in using them as traps to catch big mule-deer bucks. Sometimes, just at sunup, I've seen good bucks pausing to drink at a stock tank in the sagebrush country. But keep in mind that a deer knows its range far better than do you, the infrequent visitor to it. When the deer's country is disturbed by intrusion, it generally doesn't have to use the obvious watering places. Hundreds of small puddles and rock depressions hold a bit of rain water. Canyon bottoms may trickle flows year-round.

Nonetheless, if you are in a sparsely hunted region, watching the obvious or inobvious watering places at dawn and dusk may get you a good deer, especially in the more arid regions. Stock tanks in the Southwest will invariably have deer nearby.

A stream crossing is something quite different. Like all big-game animals, mule deer will select certain spots where they commonly cross a stream. There seem to be no sure rules for spotting such crossings. You just have to search out the sign. Such crossings may not be watering places, except incidentally. They are places where deer move back and forth from feed to bed grounds or vice versa. These provide excellent possibilities for stands. Because of the rough character of most mule-deer range, you can usually find a vantage point that will overlook a stream crossing.

Mule deer are far more gregarious and sociable than whitetail deer. This difference has a bearing on your hunting. Many times I've watched groups of whitetail does and fawns together, and always there seems to be much bickering among the does. Further, as a rule you frequently see nubbin or spike bucks with the groups of does, but not so commonly the larger bucks. And when you do see a whitetail buck or two in a group of deer, that's usually about the limit.

By contrast, it's very common to see, in heavily populated mule-deer country, a group composed of as many as three or four bucks and an assortment of does and fawns, all consorting with reasonable congeniality. It is even extremely common to see a number of mule-deer bucks hanging around together.

One fall on a high mesa in Colorado, three of us jumped a group of mule-deer bucks that contained eight individuals, all with fair to excellent antlers. They were all fat as cattle, and like a bunch of schoolboys on vacation. One season, in an especially good mule-deer area of west Texas, I kept count of groups of bucks. There were many groups of four running together, seen in fact several times together. I killed a big fellow from a group of three. We saw several five-buck groups and one of six.

My reason for going over such details can best be explained by an experience I had. In New Mexico one fall, I talked to a very downcast nonresident from Indiana who had long wanted to make a trip after big mule deer. As he told me his story, it was obvious that he'd made about every mistake possible. He was trying to hunt his trophy just about the way he'd go after a whitetail in the Great Lakes area. Things just weren't the same. At last, however, he got his chance, but only at a small six-pointer (total count). It came walking out of a stand of conifers into an open mountain park.

Because his hunting time was nearly finished, the man shot it. As the deer went down, he told me, the edge of the strip of forest seemed to be alive with deer. He counted six more, all of them bucks. Apparently they couldn't tell where the shot had come from, and they scattered in every direction, right out in the open. Several he guessed at 10 points or better and one, he said, was the biggest deer he'd ever seen.

The moral when you hunt mule deer is, of course, to wait it out. You might shoot the first whitetail buck you see, for he probably will be alone. But right behind any modest buck mule deer, a huge old devil may be coming. So don't be hasty, be certain.

Mule deer are not only more inclined toward open country than whitetails are but also the general character of a mule-deer range is one of far more large openings. In addition to the deserts, rolling plains, and treeless or near-treeless areas, there are the high mountains, with their continual broken character, a stand of timber, a large meadow, over and over. Hunters who have traveled to any of our national parks, such as Yellowstone and the Teton country, will have seen ranges that are typical. This is not to say, of course, that mule deer avoid timber. But the most densely timbered regions of the West are undoubtedly the poorest mule-deer range. Oddly, some of the best elk and moose country of the Western mountains has the fewest mule deer. These are not infallible rules, but it pays to remember them. Besides, it is far easier to get a trophy in the more open ranges than in the dense ones.

There is something else here also. I spoke just before of being skeptical about hunting mule deer from horseback. I've done quite a lot of it. You will hear some persons say—never the really good hunters—that on a horse you can ride right up on a big buck. For every time this approach works you'll spook 20. I made a hunt in northern Arizona a few seasons back during which a not-very-expert guide and I rode constantly, he always a bit ahead of me, as if this caste system established our relationship. I would have bet money we'd never kill a deer if the hunt lasted a decade. We didn't. Horses are noisy. Riding, a hunter must be quick to get down, to get his gun out of the scabbard, and fire at close-in deer. Horses make much more racket than a man. The noise will drift the deer right on ahead of you or around you.

If you don't believe me, go riding sometime out of curiosity, as I did before one deer season in rocky but treeless mountain country. This experiment was done in a region where the deer are hunted very little and are about as gentle as mule deer ever get. Three of us rode along, not talking, and as quietly as possible. We could actually hear groups of deer running a quarter-mile or more away, hear their hoofs striking rocks, just as they had long since heard the hoofs of horses. On another occasion I rode for several days (hard riding, too) in timber and rocks, in Utah. I failed to see a single deer, even in country where they were thick. The reason was that we *rode too much.*

Even many guides have a total misconception about how to utilize horses in mountain mule-deer hunting. The use for the horse is to get you where you want to hunt and then to help you pack the deer out. Aside from these before and after uses, the horse is more often than not a detriment. Keith Stilson, for years a widely known and very expert big-game guide in Wyoming, told me once that he spends more time letting his horse graze with its reins down, while he lies on a mountainside glassing a vast region, than he does riding.

I was with Keith one season and saw a classic example of the way

167

I think the horseback hunter should operate. We rode for about two hours, climbing up, up, up. Finally we got into a position where we could graze the horses in a timbered opening while Keith and I lay on a slope commanding miles of surrounding territory. We now spent two hours without moving from the spot. We constantly swept the whole region with glasses. I should add that this was a photo-taking expedition, but it's exactly the same way Keith Stilson hunts. During the two hours, we saw numerous elk, two moose, two black bears, and plenty of mule deer.

This horseback hunting method in mountains gives a hunter a tremendous advantage. When you spot your trophy, it's wholly unaware of you. You can then decide how to make your stalk on foot, or you may decide you can ride partway and then begin your stalk.

Of course, you must become adept at selecting places where the glassing can best be done. If nothing shows in due course, you can move. But indiscriminate, incessant, all-day riding in timber country is simply a good way to drive every deer ahead of you. This advice does not apply, obviously, if you stake out part of the hunters and then use horses to drive out bucks from rimrocks or coulee bottoms. That's all right, and a very good method.

Of all the slants and angles on mule-deer hunting, probably temperature is one of the most important (and most neglected) to the greatest number of hunters from border to border. As noted earlier, mule deer don't like heat. This aversion to heat is relative. In their southern ranges, muleys can't avoid it some of the time, but they'll always gravitate toward the cooler places. Since most of their immense and highly varied domain is mountainous (or at least has slopes and variety of elevations) the general rule is: search them high up when it's hot, lower down when it's cold.

Mule deer spend the summers up on the high cool mesas and slopes. They stay right there, if food is good, clear on into hunting season, unless there's an extremely severe weather change. Shin oak, mountain mahogany, juniper berries, and piñon grow in profusion up high. As long as the food lasts and snow doesn't cover it, the deer will stay put. I have seen many persons from the East and Midwest in the Rockies at, let's say, 6,000 feet, in places where deer food was extremely abundant. Yet, no deer were there. The animals were higher.

Whitetail hunters have difficulty understanding this behavior because mule deer, unlike whitetails, go "south" for the winter. "South" to them is a drop to lower altitudes, where they can find food and protection from the violent winter storms and heavy snows of timber-

168

line. You may hunt an almost deerless area over which high slopes and mesas loom, when by moving up only a thousand feet you'd be into herds of mule deer. In mountains, you can never make a mistake by hunting as high up toward timberline as you can get when the weather is mild in fall, or even when a modest amount of snow is on the ground. It takes quite a lot to drive the muleys downward.

But when they do start, then comes some of the best and easiest hunting of the year. There are places—the vicinity of Meeker and Rifle, Colorado, was long a classic example—famous for their mass migrations of mule deer from high elevations down to winter range, places where the great majority of deer follow the same general route downward. When such a late-fall trek to winter range is under way, hunters who are in the know can easily get a deer.

The best time of all, however, is the late-season hunt. Several states periodically have such hunts. Personally, I prefer to hunt in pleasant weather. But it can't be denied that the so-called post seasons or trophy seasons in late November and December that occur occasionally are the real bets for fast shooting and big deer. What happens then is that winter has really settled in. Snows have driven all the animals down from the high country. Bucks from places totally inaccessible to hunters, bucks who've never seen a human in their high-elevation solitude, now are forced into winter ranges that are more confined.

Here deer by the hundreds may be concentrated. Once in Colorado two friends of mine made a post-season hunt of three days, during which they glassed 56 shootable bucks from their jeep. Of these they selected eight, because the license that season allowed four deer to each hunter. This is how the biologists crop deer herds from high altitudes that never get hunted otherwise. Of the 8 deer they shot, not one had antlers that measured under 28 inches in spread, and all weighed over 200 pounds. Those times may be gone forever, as human population crowds the deer. But if you don't mind cold and snow, check periodically with game departments about a possible post- or late season (usually restricted to specific areas). Such a hunt will almost certainly result in a real trophy for you.

Of course, not all mule deer make a vertical migration. In numerous areas where elevations don't reach much above 6,000 or 7,000 feet, the deer live on the same range all year. Check on the migration or lack of it where you intend to hunt.

All of these things I have learned about mule deer during a good many seasons of hunting, seasons that have taken in ranges all the way from the Canadian border to the Mexican border. If you become fully familiar with the whimsical personality of this most interesting quarry, and come to understand how it lives in its amazingly varied wilderness domain, with just a pinch of luck thrown in you can nail one down on every hunt.

How to Find Spooked Deer

For well over a decade, many deer hunters have been overlooking the single most important factor in success over a vast portion of deer range. Fundamentally it is a negative factor—the influence hunters themselves, as a group, have during hunting season upon the deer population in all heavily pressured states.

Time was, long ago, when a hunter quietly slipped into a selected domain of whitetail or mule deer on opening day of the season, and with little or no disturbance went about the business of collecting trophy and venison. In those bygone days it was unlikely that anyone had been bothering the animals to any appreciable extent since the previous season. A hunter might meet one or two other hunters. But with only a nominal number of hunters operating in any given area, many a deer lived to old age without ever being more than mildly startled a few times by a human. So certain accepted deer-hunting techniques worked well.

We all know how drastically all that has changed. Burgeoning human population, the spread of industry, and the whittling away at habitat by highways and other developments has forced deer in numerous places to learn literally to live on the fringes of civilization. Those animals, therefore, have had to become more secretive in their habits. Meanwhile, hunters have increased dramatically in numbers. Some of the better deer states now sell over half a million hunting licenses each year. The preponderance of the territory hunted by most hunters often has by far more hunters crisscrossing it than there are deer. In some of the most heavily hunted areas, anywhere from 20 to 100 hunters may comb a single square mile of deer range during a single week.

Obviously such an invasion has a profound effect upon the quarry. It totally spooks them. Not only does this spooking occur during season, but also it begins in many places long before season. Hunters meticulously scout their intended hunting ground well before season.

Most of these scouts, intending to sharpen their craft, succeed only in sharpening the wariness of their targets. Millions of words have been written over late years instructing hunters how to stalk deer, where to take stands, how to make drives, even how to get on a buck track and follow it to the end and success.

This information is useful. It is based, of course, chiefly on the known habits of deer that follow a normal routine. However, the very practice of much deer-hunting advice by the vast modern-day horde of hunters and preseason scouters in crowded habitat is self-defeating. The habits of the deer there are totally changed by all that human activity. In those areas much of the conventional wisdom is worthless. In all of the hardest-hunted deer range, it is estimated that in practice not more than two out of five deer at most are killed by craft. The other 60 percent are bagged because they run into one hunter while running away from another!

So the most fundamental and important knowledge needed by many a modern deer hunter is not how to hunt deer that are leading a normal existence. What these hunters need to know is how to find thoroughly spooked deer.

What does a deer do when exposed to undue disturbance? Where does it go? How are its feeding, drinking, and resting habits changed? The hunter who sees plainly the importance of these questions is the one in today's crowded hunting world who will most consistently hang a deer on the camp meatpole.

The place to begin is to put out of mind all those nature-faker ideas too commonly kicked around. Deer are not unerring, supremely intelligent, unbelievably canny creatures. They do not have telescopic eyesight. They cannot hear the grass grow. They do not pick up your scent a mile away.

Deer are certainly intelligent. But they're creatures of instinct, not of involved thought processes. Their eyesight is excellent for detecting movement, but overall it's probably not any better than yours, if you train yourself to observe. The hearing of deer is keen, but not magical. Their sense of smell, granted, is extremely sensitive, but any hunter can defeat it by watching wind direction. Further, deer are not infallible. They make scads of mistakes. Otherwise every deer would live to a ripe old age.

The instinctive reaction of a disturbed deer is purely and simply: *to get away from what disturbed it and to find a place where it will not be disturbed.* The job of the hunter seeking spooked deer is, in its simplest form, to figure out what places are most likely to furnish quiet inviolate hideaways, that are difficult to approach. Because whitetails

172

and mule deer are quite different both in personality and in preferred habitats, and also in their reactions to disturbance, consider them separately.

Finding Spooked Whitetails

Whitetails live mainly in or near dense cover, are chary of crossing openings, and are far more wary and more easily spooked than are mule deer. Most hunters underestimate how easily whitetails become disturbed. Let me illustrate.

On our ranch is a high ridge covered by a heavy cedar brake. The trees are large and have limbs that arc low. Grass and browse grow underneath, and a few interspersed oaks drop acorns in years of good yield. This ridge is a favorite midday bedding spot for whitetails.

No one lives on this ranch. From season to season, no one even walks through the cedars along this ridge. So, on opening day we often make a drive here during the middle of the day. As we move east along it, deer jumped from beds run ahead, go off the end of the ridge and down into or along the edge of a small clearing that leads to a brushy creek bottom. The shooter is placed to oversee this clearing. Almost without fail, this brief and quite safe drive presents a shot or two for a waiting hunter. Sometimes as many as a dozen deer, several of them bucks, pour off the ridge. From that first drive onward (our season lasts six weeks), we can seldom again raise a buck there for at least a month.

The reason is simple. That cedar brake on the ridge is an inviolate place where for nearly an entire year the animals have rested without fear. Once their hideaway is invaded, they desert it. They sense that it's no longer a trustworthy haven, and each day we hunt they hear a vehicle or a hunter, see one of us, or pick up a scent. They won't readily return to such an obvious place. Does and fawns may try it again within a week. But not a buck, except if he happens to cross it. A hunter must get it straight in his mind that whitetail bucks and does are like two different species. You may see a doe and fawns three days in a row in the same general area. But if you run a buck out just once and then continue hunting the same place, 90 percent of the time you're wasting your effort.

This state of affairs is a main reason that many buck hunters fail with spooked deer. They may see does and fawns, and they're sure a buck or two must be nearby. However, except for the brief rut period when bucks do become addled and incautious, you might as well forget about antlerless deer if you want to locate spooked whitetail bucks. That's the first rule. If you learn how to locate spooked bucks, you can far more easily find jittery does, and you'll do so in the process. The bucks are the ones you must concentrate on.

Study the terrain and try to dope out just where a supersecretive buck *could* be. This invariably will be a place, maybe a very small place, where hunters aren't. To be sure, a spike or a giddy forkhorn may not have learned the intricacies of total secretiveness. So always think in terms of mature bucks. That's how to become a crafty hunter.

It may not make sense at first, but the fact is that the harder the hunting pressure, the easier in some respects is the job of deducing where the bucks will be. The more hunters an area has, the fewer are the undisturbed places where a buck *can* be. In northern Michigan one year, two friends and I started out hunting an area of excellent cover along a swampy stream. We quickly discovered we were far from alone. Hunters were everywhere. The stream was tributary to a larger forest-bordered river. We went far around by vehicle, following an old lumber trail across a hip-deep swamp to try the far edge of the main stream. Conditions there were the same.

That evening we made our scheme. We spent the second day going to town and renting a canoe. Both streams, you see, were too deep for hunters to wade except possibly with armpit-high waders, which we guessed none had. The two streams made a long semi-island that ran back from their confluence, and the swamp at the far broad end of it cut off ready access there. Whitetail deer, we knew, live individually on rather small home ranges. Some hunters believe the bucks "run right out of the country" when disturbed. Don't you believe it! Where would they run, except into more disturbance? They're simply experts at seeking privacy in seemingly least-likely places.

Where was the best chance for privacy? On that swampy island, which turned out to have high ground in its interior, with excellent cover and ample food. We crossed to the island in the canoe and hunted in hip boots to get through the wet stuff. There was no sign of other hunters. In a flurry of action during a half-mile prowl down the high ground, both my partners killed bucks, and I unfortunately missed one. Meanwhile we jumped several other deer we didn't see, maybe does, maybe bucks. The animals had simply retired, when the invasion of hunters began, to this place of peace and quiet.

To make your hunting easier, bear in mind that a whitetail buck won't stand around thinking, "Let's see now, where can I hide?" The deer doesn't know what a gun is or what "hunting" is. It simply has an ancestral fear of unnatural sights, sounds, and scents. What the deer *does* know, in infinite detail, is its own bailiwick. It knows the location of every stump, rock, tree, copse, gully, ledge, meadow, swamp, trickle of water—everything. If it is mildly harassed, it may have a lot of places in which to seek solitude. But if it's harassed from every angle, the hiding places diminish. The hunter needs to think sharp, and not necessarily in an orthodox manner, to find his buck.

A friend of mine in Arkansas had seen a real trophy buck several times during late summer. He knew where it lived and mentally had his tag on it long before season. Here was the terrain picture: a broad river-bottom stand of dense hardwoods along the lower White River, interspersed here and there along the outer edge of soybean fields with more wooded country on the far side of those fields. During the first several days of deer season, the hunter was exasperated because the woods swarmed with other hunters. They hunted the entire wooded region. Obviously nobody hunted the open soybeans, and no whitetail would cross these fields, at least in daylight.

Very few deer were killed, and the big buck, it seemed, had vanished. There was no report of it. On the third day, as my friend related it to me, he was coming in disgusted near dusk. He paused on the edge of the outer fringe of woods and for no logical reason ran his glass over the far edge of a soybean field. In it, perhaps 75 yards from the bottomland woods on that side, was a small motte of trees and underbrush out in the soybean field, left for some unknown reason when the land was cleared.

He could hardly believe his eyes when he saw in the dim light an enormous buck step tentatively out to the edge of the small patch. The hunter took a solid rest and with a good scope was able to drop the trophy. It would be easy to say that the buck thought up this ruse. However, because the woods on both sides of the fields were swarming with hunters, the buck had few choices. No one ever walked in the open field, and so undoubtedly the buck simply moved into the only logical spot left for it. The lesson here is never to overlook the offbeat. Think about where you'd go if you were a wary old buck wanting to be left alone.

In hilly country, hunted whitetail bucks seldom hide out in the low places. They move up where they can hear and see and gather scent best. They have a great liking here, especially in dry areas or when leaves are down and no snow covers them, for the headers of small draws. Such draws gather many dry leaves. Typical ones may be 50 yards wide at the bottom of a hill, but up at the top, the hiding pocket will be 10 to 30 or so paces below the ridgetop. It may be only six feet wide. Midday thermals bring scent uphill. Dry leaves make approach from behind or below impossible without alerting the deer. Cover in the header is invariably heavy—brush with large trees overhanging.

You cannot successfully stalk such spots. Anyway, the deer won't move during daylight. That's another part of hunting spooked deer. When pressured, they all but cease feeding in daylight. As most hunters know, deer are active during moonlit nights. But don't believe for one minute that they must have moonlight in order to see to forage. The eyes of a deer have tens of thousands more rod (light-gathering) cells than the human eye. That's why the eyes of a deer shine in bright light and those of a human do not. To bag a buck that is using a hide in a draw header, you must waylay it. When it arises, it will almost without fail come out the way it went in—that is, it will move carefully downhill, down the draw.

On our own ranch we've had some classic experiences with this kind of hunting. We check the small draws running up from the creek and the side canyons. One season we discovered tracks of a large deer going both ways in soft black earth spread by runoff across a rock ledge near the bottom of such a draw. The late afternoon was utterly still. My son, Mike, prowled with infinite patience up to the rock ledge. An hour before dusk, he sat against a low-growing juniper, facing up the wooded draw.

When shooting light was all but gone, he heard the deer. It was coming down the draw—a few steps, pause, and repeat—obviously listening, looking, scenting. The caution of the deer, relayed by the sounds of the dry leaves, indicated a big old buck. Mike got the gun up and ready. He had a fairly open sighting path for about 50 yards. He correctly deduced that after he'd been sitting for an hour his scent might have oozed out over a circle of quite a few yards. Thus he decided to fire the moment he established the target. That was a sharp decision. The buck suddenly came into sight, hauled up, instantly very tense but puzzled. It was a good one, and the hunt was instantly concluded.

Indicated in this experience is the fact that when whitetails are under hard hunting pressure, the early-and-late hunting rule is all the more important. Be on your stand or hunting ground well before daylight and settle in to take advantage of the first shooting light. Stay late into the afternoon until the last shooting light fades. In these circumstances, a good scope for low-light hunting means the difference between success and failure.

It should also be obvious that any astute low-light hunter will plan his approach so he faces quartering or fully away from the light at both dawn and dusk. Breeze direction will dictate the exact angle. One other low-light rule of which many hunters are unaware is this: whitetails, especially, are slightly less wary when moving to hideaways at dawn, after having been up and moving during the night, than they are at dusk when, after having been long in hiding, they venture forth into an unknown situation. One other rule is that standard deer sign, such as a well-used trail, for example, is not as valid after deer have been choused around. They are forced to change routines.

Sometimes you have to "go in after whitetails," hunting in places you'd not normally traverse. In years when food is abundant, whitetails—and particularly mature bucks—may find places in heavy cover where they can simply stay around the clock, bedding, feeding, getting enough water, and never coming out. To invade such places, you need full camouflage, even to face paint and camo gloves. You need wet or moist footing for quiet, and you need to learn the patience to move one step at a time and only 50 to 100 yards in a full half-hour. This is the most difficult of all whitetail hunting, but it is challenging and often gets the big spooked buck.

Mule Deer

Mule deer are far more placid animals than whitetails, more gregarious by far, and by no means as jittery and wary. Curiously, however, they seem unable to tolerate much intimacy with human settlement and have been unable to adapt as have whitetails. In addition, mule deer are animals of far more open and, in general, wilder country. Sportsmen who have hunted in the areas of the heavily forested Rockies often wrongly envision mule deer as deep-forest animals. They aren't. The mountain meadows, the timberline summering areas of low willows and open terrain, the foothills of sage, scattered juniper, and the fairly open aspen stands of higher country all are their prime bailiwicks. Mule deer also are perfectly at home in numerous arid areas of desert terrain that are virtually treeless.

In addition, mule deer are animals of the slopes. I don't mean they're never found in flat country. They do gather in valleys and flats between ranges of hills or mountains. But the plains themselves have always been a barrier to the enlargement of mule-deer ranges. Basically the muleys seem unable to live without slopes and high places nearby.

What all of this means is that shots at mule deer are generally more open and often are presented at longer range than are shots at whitetails. Spooked or disturbed mule deer have an altogether different hiding problem. Their favored terrain presents opportunities that are mainly quite different from those available to the dense-cover white-tail. This is a fundamental the hunter must absorb.

Also, it has been said often that a fleeing whitetail looking for a safe place will take the easiest route to safety. This is probably an exaggeration. Anyhow, easy and difficult are all the same to the mule deer. Muleys are born to steep country and can bound up a mountainside with speed, grace, and ease, and usually they do. Seldom does a mule deer—I'm speaking chiefly of mature bucks, the real prizes—move downhill when disturbed. *Up* to a mule deer is for some reason equated with safety. Over the ridge is where safety lies. In fact, it often does.

Perhaps the plainest view of mule-deer reaction to disturbance is to say that as a rule the deer do not flee in wild terror. They are simply true wilderness creatures. When they're disturbed, they move not only up but also farther back. Ordinarily individual ranges are not extremely large, but distance means something quite different to a mule deer than to a whitetail.

For example, one of the most beautiful sights I've ever seen was a group of six big buck mule deer all feeding on the same slope before season opened. As I watched and glassed them from possibly 500 yards, they slowly but uneasily moved over the ridge and disappeared. The next day they were there again. And again they moved away, not in panic, but not liking the intrusion. On the third morning the season opened. The deer were not there, and they didn't show again.

The region was a series of quite open rocky ridges with a few scattered junipers. It was not until a week later that we found those bucks. They weren't really hiding. They were four ridges back— maybe two miles from where they had first been seen—hanging out in a snug, peaceful little valley between two steep ridges, a place hard to get into without alerting them, and one easy for them to quickly get out of. The bucks hadn't gone to any devious lengths to hide. They had simply drifted back away from disturbance.

Most hunters don't walk over four ridges. A great many hunters in mule-deer country cruise the vehicle trails, look over the obvious meadows and close-in slopes, and wonder why they see few deer. After a single day of much harassment, mule deer simply drift away. And the larger and older the bucks, the quicker they react and the farther they go.

There's an old saying among trophy hunters after mule deer: "If you want a record-book deer, go back in several miles past the last hunter you've seen." Absolutely correct. The whitetail may lie up, as did the one I described, in a tiny clump of trees and brush in an open field, listening to hunters all around. Not the big buck mule deer! Not that it is especially skittish. It is simply a denizen of big, wild country, and it cannot tolerate the incursion of mankind.

Yet oddly, mule deer select what to the uninitiated hunter are some most unusual places to find solitude. I once found an enormous buck in Wyoming, out in a treeless area near Arvada, lying on a ledge atop a barren shale hill out in the middle of nowhere, while hunters combed the region. My crafty stalk ended in failure. The deer simply arose and went around the hill, slipped into a wash on the hillside, and trotted down to enter a winding gully that cut across the open. I finally saw it down there, far out of range and trotting along.

One of the greatest traps to set for a big mule-deer buck is in a deep wash that meanders across an open valley. I recall such an experience. There were two steep mountains with slopes stippled by meager brush clumps, scattered juniper, and large rocks. Between them lay a grassy valley. The distance from mountain to mountain was probably two miles. There was not a tree in the valley. But there was a deep wash that started in a draw at the foot of one mountain and wound in tortuous loops and oxbows partly across and then down the valley.

Meeting this big wash were several tributaries, some coming from the opposite mountain. A few leafless shrubs and small trees sparsely bordered the cut edges of these eroded lanes. Two friends of mine were hunting one of the mountains. From far out in the valley I saw with my glass a big buck come off that mountain and disappear. It hit me that this deer had entered the wash, and I would have staked anything it was heading for the opposite mountain.

I went as fast as I could toward the main wash, hoping to get in ahead of it. The buck had other ideas. Somehow it sensed the trap. I arose afer a long wait and climbed out. The buck had turned into a side tributary wash barely deep enough to cover it. It emerged as I did, too far for a shot, and at the foot of the other mountain. We left it alone that day. But the next day we ran it off the new mountain and waylaid it far over toward the other a half-hour later, in the big draw where it had no choice. This action is so typical of big buck mule deer—crossing open places by traveling washes—that it is a hunting method of illimitable value when you're after disturbed mule deer in places that have such terrain.

Of course, the hideouts of mule deer basically bear some resemblance to those of whitetails, in that muleys select spots where disturbance is less likely. It's simply that in mule-deer terrain many such spots aren't always quite as obvious. However, mule deer almost without fail—mature bucks that have been spooked—select a spot where they can't easily be trapped. Glass from below the side of a steep mountain and look at rocky points, even very small ones, thrusting out above a valley. Here a deer will lie, scenting midday thermals, watching everything below. But examine the place from up there and you'll note the deer can reach the lie-up peak from either side. This means it can go out either side.

Never overlook rimrocks. Almost all mule-deer country has them. Many places also have jumbles of rock with twisted old junipers or other growth at the bases of vertical cliffs. At a distance, even through a binocular, both types of hides look as if you ought to be able to see an animal here. Get close, however, and you'll see that each is an intricate labyrinth that could hide scores of deer in an infinite number of tiny pockets. Disturbed mule deer love to retreat to such places. Such hides require you to hunt slowly, arduously. Many a big buck will let you all but walk over it and will stay put. Many another will slip out behind after you've passed, or practically crawl on its knees out of a rock crevice around a corner before you get to it. It won't show itself until it is streaking off far out on the flat below.

Probably the best mule-deer advice possible is to try to get as far away from other hunters as possible. If you can get away, then scout the country and hunt all the places where you don't think a big deer is likely to be. Never underestimate the brass of a big mule-deer buck either. I've seen one lie with head flat out, under a single scrawny bush on a totally barren desert-mountain hillside the entire day, while vehicle after vehicle cruised along a valley trail below. I can never decide whether such a deer is dumb or uncannily clever. Surely such a spot is one *least likely to be scrutinized.* That characteristic in fact is the basis on which to establish your approach to hunting spooked deer of either species.

WHERE TO FIND A TROPHY BUCK

For a good many years I've been claiming I'm not a trophy hunter. I had just repeated the claim on a recent hunt when I saw an especially good buck while I was being driven along a mountain trail by a companion to whom I'd made the statement. Suddenly I was flailing my arms and yelling for him to stop, knocking my hat off trying to reach my cased rifle in the back, and in general creating a commotion. The driver told me I reminded him of a Southern small-town lawyer friend of his.

He'd just lost a case in local court during which his prize witness had been accused of outright lying. The judge asked straight out if the lawyer thought his witness would lie. He replied, "I've never known him to, Your Honor, although I confess he does have a reputation for just mildly messin' around with the truth."

Probably every deer hunter is to some extent a trophy hunter. He may not be a purist record-book addict, but he wouldn't let a record run off if he had a chance at it. He may not go out with mind closed to anything but an exceptional head, but that big one had better not stick its head out of the brush. A deer hunter may not wind up with a mounting monster, but if he's honest he'll admit he feels a little tinge of envy when his buddy brings one in.

Yes, practically every deer hunter dreams of the massive rack he'll collect. In the long run, much of this dreaming runs into compromises. Dreams often are relative to what is available. Where I presently live, in the hill country of south central Texas, we have scads of deer. But one dollar gets you ten that no hunter is going to come up with a record-breaker from this region. Yet every year quite a few very good heads come out of this piece of country, compared to the average head there. So when I'm hunting there, which I do every season, I would shoot a buck and call it "big" even though down in the brush country 200 miles south of me it wouldn't even remotely qualify for that term.

Deer hunters take "trophies" all over the nation—trophies judged

This whitetail buck certainly wouldn't qualify as a candidate for the record book, but it's beautifully symmetrical and a true trophy. I collected it by hunting the general area from which almost all Texas whitetails have been taken.

within narrow regional confines. But on a national scale, it becomes a different matter. What's considered a trophy in one state, or one part of one state, may not be worth bragging about in another. When it comes to close focus on trophy hunting, you have to first decide what "trophy" means.

At that point I believe we must forget the regional meanings of "exceptional" and look at the subject on a continental basis. Further, you must differentiate between "trophy" and "record." A small number of hunters do indeed go out strictly to try for a record-book deer. An even smaller number are determined to crack the all-time top record. Some of these hunters will go year after year without firing a shot, seeking precisely what they want. It is an admirable attitude, but obviously this style is not for everybody. On the opposite side of that highly selective stance is the gent who will settle for any deer. That's all right, too. In many states this hunter is wildlife management's best friend.

The any-deer hunter is not at all a specialist. The trophy hunter is pursuing such a highly specialized endeavor that his sport comes not so much from the hunt as from the determination to be best. He has passed the point where he even gets much of a kick out of just a "great big buck."

182

Between these two extremes we find what can be called the average trophy hunter. He doesn't really want to settle for just any small buck or for a doe, although he may take such a deer rather than go home without tying on a tag. Conversely, although he'd eagerly take a crack at a record-beater, he isn't primarily hoping for that. He simply holds out as long as possible, sometimes—like the record-book addict—until too late. He can identify a set of antlers that would be classed as outstanding not just in one area but nationally, and that's what he has his heart set on. He'll admit he isn't too keen about how close it comes to a record-book score, and he may not have any special spread or inside measurement in mind. He simply wants one to be darned well proud of—a deer worth mounting regardless of local standards.

It may seem curious, but the record-book specialist and the somewhat less discriminating trophy hunter have quite a lot in common. Both wish to give themselves the best chances possible, and so both, sensibly, try to set up a hunt where the odds seem most in favor of a chance of a good head. A study of the record book, which shows where the record deer came from, is an invaluable aid.

Look at it this way—antlers basically are products of two influences: 1) the soil and 2) genetics. A trained deer biologist can tell you, for example, where in his state the big racks come from most consistently. It may be that an exceptional one occasionally turns up where least expected. But over the long haul the same counties, or sectors, or stream courses, or stretch of hills will produce the best bucks year after year, unless some drastic habitat change occurs. Certain soils contain the elements required to grow the best and most abundant deer forage. And certain soils contain the specific minerals, passed along by plant growth, that influence outstanding antler growth.

So a number of excellent deer continue to live on these optimum ranges as long as man doesn't make sweeping changes that deny them the superb habitat. Strains of quality animals beget more of the same. Somewhere along here the genetic influence appears. The combination of proper genes and ample protein produces an unusual number of excellent heads.

What a study of the record book does is point you at some of those quality spots. A good many states never have had a head in the book. Others have one or two. This absence doesn't mean some of these same states never produce bucks with mounting-size racks. Some certainly do appear. Some other states have a lot of records, sometimes scattered all over the state. A state like that has just got to have exceptional amounts of what it takes to produce those animals, both in forage quality and in gene pool. Some other states and provinces have just a few counties in which all or most of the records originate.

A classic example is my adopted state of Texas. In the Boone and Crockett record-book edition current as this is written, Texas has 57 whitetail heads. Forty-nine of those came out of a cluster of a few counties in what is called the brush country, between San Antonio and the border. This fact should tell a Texas trophy hunter that there's no question about where to try for an outstanding deer in this state. The other five records, if they had come from one county, would also have told him something specific. But they didn't. They're scattered here and there. Of course, that also is a statement—that these extra-fine heads just "happened" to turn up where they did, perhaps old bucks that avoided detection and were able to grow.

Now the next step. Again, we're interested in the records only to the extent that they say something, when concentrated, about an area that produces (or fails to produce) extra-large antlers. If a few counties in southern Texas had enough big ones to put the major share of the records into the book, we can logically infer that this same region must have produced a lot of other bucks that weren't quite book measurements but were still stunning trophies.

Indeed, it is true. I know the region well, have hunted it for the past 20 years, and have seen some eye-poppers season after season. In fact, for some years I did a week of strictly trophy hunting down there. In that time I collected three tremendous heads, not records by any means, but exceedingly respectable. I also missed several more, turned down some big ones just because I wanted something bigger, and didn't get a shot at numerous trophy animals that I got at least a look at.

So if you really want to find a trophy buck, the best scheme is to set up a hunt in an area that has produced a substantial number of records and trophies. A great many deer hunters nowadays are convinced the trophies and the records are pretty much all killed off. Don't you believe it! All you have to do is again study the book and see when the entries were made. Obviously a head that went into the book 40 years ago might not mean much. But if some others, a respectable percentage of the total, have gone into the records steadily over more recent seasons from the same area, then this is a valid place to try. Again using Texas as an example, about 20 percent of the whitetail records from those same brush-country counties were collected and made the book within the past 15 years.

Now, of course, *exactly* where to hunt a trophy deer, and *how* to hunt one, are other areas of the craft. Elsewhere in this book are numerous pertinent discussions of those matters. What we're concerned with here is where in general the trophy bucks are most likely to live in fair enough numbers. Such deer, of course, are never abundant or easy to take. But if you know the big-deer (antler) areas of the continent, you're started on the first leg of the stalk.

The easiest varieties to pin down are the little Coues (Arizona whitetail) and the Columbian blacktail. Both of these—compared to mule deer and other whitetails—have quite restricted ranges. The Coues, of course, is not only the smallest of the whitetails taken by trophy hunters but also has the smallest range. Within the United States it lives in extreme southwestern New Mexico and in southeastern Arizona. I won't say that you couldn't take a very handsome Coues head in New Mexico, but a look at the book shows that of the 100-plus heads only 3 are from there. The rest, excepting a few from Mexico, are from Arizona. Some of the tilt toward Arizona came about because the Coues range is near two large cities—Phoenix and Tucson—and because a lot of Arizona hunters have been interested in this little deer for years. In New Mexico the area is rather remote from large centers and not as easy to get into. The small individual mountain ranges of southeast Arizona and southwest New Mexico are the places to make a try for a good Coues trophy.

The blacktail (properly, for our purposes, the Columbian blacktail) lives along the west slope of the Pacific coastal mountain ranges. (The Sitka deer of southeastern Alaska and northern coastal British Columbia is also a variety of blacktail but is obscure so far as records are concerned.)

The southern end of the Columbian blacktail's habitat has always produced the most records and trophies, and these big heads grow progressively scarcer, even though deer are abundant, the farther north you go.

For example, counties of northwestern California have produced approximately 56 percent of book heads, a number of scattered west-slope counties in Oregon have put less than half that many into the book, Washington (also with rather scattered records) has registered a few less, and southern British Columbia (chiefly Vancouver) has produced the least of all. It is logical to conclude that the best opportunities are directly related to the records. But even though California has the most record heads, remember the chances are still good in Oregon and Washington.

Mule deer come next in complications in tracing trophy regions. Be aware that all mule-deer records are of the Rocky Mountain mule deer, the so-called type species. It's not that subspecies such as the desert mule deer (which ranges in western Texas and spottily across southern New Mexico and Arizona) wouldn't be welcome. This mule-deer subspecies sometimes grows exemplary antlers, but their biggest never are as large as the big ones of the Rocky Mountain variety.

This brings up another point. Let's suppose you wish to hunt desert mule deer. I consider this among the finest of deer hunting sports, and I've killed a number of desert muleys. You simply must realize that even though you may come upon an excellent desert mule-deer specimen (one in fact so good that if you were hunting in Rocky Mountain mule-deer range you'd also take it) it could be close to maximum size for the desert subspecies but would simply be the size of a respectable head in the Rocky Mountain variety.

It's difficult to state flatly what should be considered a trophy desert mule deer. I don't think any variety should be pinned down to an exact size that will or will not be shot—except by the strictly record-book hunters. However, I'd say that a desert mule deer with heavy antlers and a spread of 24 to 26 inches would certainly be amply acceptable. Like the Coues and the blacktail, this deer has well-defined areas: the Big Bend region of western Texas, the southwestern counties in New Mexico and a few places across the southern fringe of that state, and the foothills of southern Arizona. This is all prime range for the desert mule deer. No heads are listed in the records, so there's not much evidence to help you pinpoint the best spots. Fact is, a good head can turn up just about anywhere in the range. They do, every year.

The Rocky Mountain mule-deer range in Canada, from parts of British Columbia across to Manitoba, has never been much for trophy specimens. Some big ones, yes, but not very many spectacular heads. Nor does the eastern fringe of the range over in the western Dakotas and Nebraska and Kansas show much. The trophy mule deer come almost entirely from the region that gave this type species its name—the states down the backbone of the Rocky Mountains.

At the end of this chapter you'll find a listing of the states and provinces, showing the total numbers of records for the several deer, indicating which states have none, and also listing the general regions of each state and province where the preponderance of the records have originated. These locations are where the big-headed bucks live. In these locations, you'll know you're hunting where large numbers of book heads have been collected, and where also scads of racks worthy of the taxidermist have been produced and are produced and killed year after year.

I want to emphasize again that these locations that show the heavy accent in the record book—and this applies to the Coues and the blacktail (and the whitetail when we get to that) just as much as to the mule deer—are almost without exception as valid today as they were 20 or 30 years ago. In fact, the consistency with which certain regions produce good racks is a fascinating aspect of the deer-hunting lore. Looking at blacktails, for example, I see that in the past 15 years the Pacific Coast states and British Columbia remain in precisely the same positions they've always had: California first, Oregon next, Washington third, British Columbia last. These statistics make a very important statement about where the big heads still remain to be collected.

The same pattern is true of mule deer. Over those recent years, the states with the high numbers of records have stayed in just about the same sequence. But you have to read mule-deer statistics carefully to make sure you have the correct answers, because these deer have had their difficulties over some seasons now. They are by far more vulnerable to hunting pressure than whitetails, but they are also far less adaptable to the changes man makes in their environment. Game managers readily admit that mule deer often are more and more perplexing in our modern day. Nonetheless, year after year some terrific heads show up right where they're supposed to.

The tricky part is looking at records for a state like Arizona. Most of its total of 42 in the book edition used here came from the North Kaibab. But if you check closely you discover that big heads no longer come from there. A number of influences upon the Kaibab deer forced management of that once-sensational herd into a different kind of hunt. The lion's share of the Arizona mule-deer kill still originates there, but few exceptional heads are included. The shift, a study will show, has been to the west, to the more remote strip country north of the Colorado and bordering on Nevada and Utah.

Colorado still has its astonishing way-out-front pace, even though its mule deer saw some hard times during the late 1960s and early 1970s. This state has produced more record-book and trophy deer than any other mule-deer state. And it still does. It has put slightly more than a third of them on the list during the past 15 years. Percentagewise, Idaho has done even better. Almost two-thirds of Idaho's record heads made the list in the same stretch. So the trophy bucks are still there, and in just about the same places.

In New Mexico, one of those classic illustrations occurs. Rio Arriba County, up in the northwest part of the state, has turned in almost all of the state's 49 records. Note well that over half of this total are recent. How come? Because the Jicarilla-Apache Indian Reservation there made such a splash with its opening some years ago to hunters.

187

An astonishing number of large deer have come from there.

I have saved whitetails until last because the record-book and trophy whitetail situation is one that most hunters may find difficulty in believing. If you were sitting in on a pow-wow among a group in a deer camp and someone came up with the statement that for the best chance at a trophy whitetail you should hunt the West, either in the United States or southern Canada, you'd probably make a mental note not to listen to him any longer. But you should be listening because it's true.

Beginning in southeastern Manitoba on your map, draw a line from north to south, on down the eastern border of the Dakotas, and wind up along eastern Texas. That divides the continent's deer range just about in half. A check of the Boone and Crockett Club's lists will show the rather astonishing fact that a whopping *two-thirds* of all whitetail records since they've been kept have come from *west* of that line!

In one way, that figure may be a little unfair. It's based on the total number of record whitetail heads from the United States, southern Canada and northern Mexico. That takes in the range of Coues deer, which is in a record class by itself because of the smaller size of both its body and its antlers. OK: deduct all Coues records from the whitetail total. You still come up with the startling statistic that approximately three-fifths of all records for the large varieties of whitetails are from the western half of the continent.

It's also an eye opener to note which states and provinces the majority of these records have come from. The largest number of both typical and nontypical record heads has come from Saskatchewan, an aggregate total of 95. Consider that figure against 5 record heads for the great whitetail state of Maine. Or, skipping representatively around the eastern half of the United States, 16 for New York, 10 for Georgia, 10 for Michigan, 14 for Pennsylvania, and 3 for Louisiana.

Texas is second in the West, as previously noted, with a 57 total to 42 for third-place Nebraska, another state most hunters wouldn't guess. Then comes Montana, followed by South Dakota, then Alberta and Manitoba. I find it intriguing that Washington (which most hunters don't even realize has any whitetails) is next with 21 heads in the book. That Washington figure is remarkable and a hot clue for trophy hunters. Compare it for example to an Eastern-half state like Wisconsin, always a high-score location. Wisconsin shows a husky 61 heads in the book, about 3 times what Washington has. But Wisconsin has a whitetail herd averaging from 10 to 14 times as large as Washington's!

With the exception of Texas, which has the largest whitetail herd in the nation (estimated at 3 1/2 million) and the highest annual kill (275,000 to 350,000) there are, of course, far more whitetail deer east of our line than west of it. Some western states have none. In most western states that have whitetails, the range is quite restricted. In addition, herds there compared to mule-deer herds are small. But in numerous locations the deer are busters, and the top-rank showings they've made over many years in the record book, as I've said, well illustrates, just by the few figures given, that there's a high percentage of excellent heads among the modest numbers of deer.

There are—or were—17 different races of whitetails within U. S., Canadian, and north-Mexican ranges. The so-called "type" species was the Virginia whitetail. Odd as it may seem, this big deer, the first seen by the colonists on the Eastern seaboard and, therefore, the one from which all others were named as subspecies, is today practically extinct as an authentic race. It came close to extinction years ago. It's been so diluted with introduced blood that it probably no longer exists as a true type.

The same situation exists in the West with the burly Kansas whitetail, another big subspecies now phased out by dilution. The Texas whitetail, another subspecies, is (as I've said earlier) at its regal best in southern Texas. The Dakota whitetail is the big and rugged deer of the stream valleys, the northern plains, and the badlands of most of the Prairie Province ranges of Canada; and on down into parts of the Dakotas, Nebraska, northeastern Colorado, and even parts of Montana and Wyoming. While pheasant hunting in Dakota corn fields, I've seen them so fat they could barely waddle. This is the deer subspecies that is the basis of the famed Saskatchewan trophy herd.

In its prime range (such as northeastern Washington), the Northwest whitetail of southeastern British Columbia, western Alberta, parts of eastern Washington, northern Idaho, and western Montana and Wyoming is one of the best trophies of all. This deer not only is generally of large body size but also commonly has very wide-spreading antlers. Three counties in Washington produce the preponderance of that state's kill. All the heads in the record book came from this area of northeastern Washington, which encompasses Stevens, Pend Oreille, and the northern part of Spokane counties. The northern counties of Idaho and the northwestern counties of Montana—Flathead, Lincoln, Sanders, Powell, and Mineral—have this same big deer.

Those are brief examples of what the West has to offer in trophy whitetail hunting. Of course, the majority of whitetail enthusiasts will still stay at home, which means in the Eastern half of the United

States, and they'll certainly have their chances at deer with racks to brag about. But there are problems nowadays throughout the traditional whitetail range that slim down the chances. While putting together this book, I got in touch with management experts in all of the states and provinces where deer range, seeking information about modern deer difficulties.

Practically everywhere, the loss and degradation of habitat are severe. But where these problems are most emphatic is east of the Mississippi, within the classic whitetail states. Human populations are dense there. Cities sprawl, and highways constantly encroach deeper into deer range than is true west of the river. Granted, the same difficulties are evident throughout most of the West, but in lesser degree. In Wyoming, for example, whitetails have been increasing their range, and the state is not anxious for this spread to continue. The whitetails need to be contained, for otherwise they'll encroach on mule-deer range. Mule deer just aren't as flexible as whitetails are in adjusting to human progress.

Loss of habitat east of the Mississippi has not yet drastically cut down the numbers of whitetails. That, in fact, is a most perplexing slant for management. Whitetails have learned how to cope with civilization so well and are so prolific that deer overpopulation is evident in numerous states. Crowding results in disease, a decline in average weight of animals, and a decrease in antler quality. Overpopulation—more deer than the available range has the capacity for—forces managers to constantly try to get the herd cut to size by hunters. Several states now have limits of one deer a day or four to six deer a season. All these states must use antlerless permits or any-deer hunts to keep the animals in check.

The antlerless hunts sometimes compound the problem. Most hunters nowadays have been convincced that does and fawns must be cropped. But some influential people haven't. Many land owners still fight the idea. Worse yet, here and there a state government refuses to let its game department have full control and refuses to allow any or enough antlerless cropping. Because of ignorance and politics, the quality of the deer herd is degraded. In Vermont, for example, whitetails have been starving in winter for years because of overpopulation and lack of department authority to allow the shooting of does.

Where deer must be constantly and severely cropped and any-deer regulations are in effect, it's obvious that few bucks become old enough to reach trophy proportions. Under conditions of a thin population and little hunting, certainly some bucks would live to be four, five, six, and even seven years old and would show excellent antlers.

190

On optimum habitat, as studies have shown, bucks of three years may have authentic trophy-size antlers. But where hunters are counted in the hundreds of thousands—Pennsylvania is a good example—and 100,000 to 150,000 deer are killed annually (again Pennsylvania is an example, with an added road kill of another 25,000-plus) what happens is that deer managers simply try to keep the animals in check, to keep them from ruining their ever-shrinking available habitat. That's all that can be done, but it is not a situation conducive to raising many record or trophy bucks.

So in much of the eastern half of whitetail country, trophy hunters may have to scale down their hopes, and perhaps redefine what a trophy is. The following table shows you where the records originated and gives you clues to where your chances are certain to be highest for taking a record, or at least of scoring on a memorable trophy.

Record-Book Deer—Where The Most Came From

NOTE: The listings here are totals taken from Boone and Crockett records, current at the time of this writing. A later edition will contain a few more listings.

Record totals listed here are aggregates of both typical and nontypical antlers. Key: "Wt."=whitetail; "M."=mule deer.

Where records are few and scattered, it is evident that the state or province offers a slim chance but that a trophy may possibly turn up almost anywhere. Where records are numerous but also scattered, it is obvious that trophy chances should be fair throughout deer range in that state or province.

To clinch the fact that trophy, and record, heads are still available, note the percentages of the all-time total records that have been added within the past 15 years: blacktails, approximately 25%; mule deer, roughly 30%; whitetails, approximately 25%. States and provinces with five or more entries in the past 15 years: blacktails, California, Oregon, Washington; mule deer, Colorado, Idaho, New Mexico, Utah, Wyoming, Arizona; whitetails, Saskatchewan, Nebraska, Wisconsin, Missouri, Texas, Minnesota, Washington, Montana, Alberta, Kansas, Idaho, Manitoba, South Dakota.

State or Province	Total in B & C Record Book	Trophy Areas
Northeast		
Maine	Wt. 5	North
New Hampshire	Wt. none	
Vermont	Wt. none	
Massachusetts	Wt. none	
Rhode Island	Wt. none	
Connecticut	Wt. none	
New Jersey	Wt. none	
New York	Wt. 16	West
Central Atlantic		
Maryland	Wt. 2	no pattern
Delaware	Wt. none	
Virginia	Wt. 7	West
North Carolina	Wt. none	
South Carolina	Wt. 1	no pattern
Appalachian		
Kentucky	Wt. 4	No pattern
Tennessee	Wt. 3	No pattern
West Virginia	Wt. 1	No pattern
Pennsylvania	Wt. 14	South central and southwest
South		
Louisiana	Wt. 3	No pattern
Mississippi	Wt. 3	No pattern
Alabama	Wt. none	
Georgia	Wt. 10	Scattered, National Forests, river courses
Florida	Wt. none	
Great Lakes		
Minnesota	Wt. 48	Scattered, north, south, east
Wisconsin	Wt. 61	North, west-central, southwest
Michigan	Wt. 10	Upper Peninsula and scattered
Illinois	Wt. 17	Scattered
Indiana	Wt. 2	
Ohio	Wt. 27	Northeast, south, southeast
Midcontinent		
North Dakota	Wt. 15 M. none	Stream courses
South Dakota	Wt. 26 M. 2	Eastern farm region
Nebraska	Wt. 42 M. 2	Eastern half, scattered (Wt.)
Kansas	Wt. 16 M. 1	Scattered
Iowa	Wt. 24	Big rivers, south, southwest
Missouri	Wt. 24	Northern farm country

192

State or Province	Total in B & C Record Book	Trophy Areas
Arkansas	Wt. 16	South, southeast
Oklahoma	Wt. 4	No pattern
Texas	Wt. 57 M. none	South
Intermountain		
Montana	Wt. 32 M. 24	Wt. northwest, eastern river courses
		M. northwest; scattered, south, southeast
Wyoming	Wt. 10 M. 34	Wt. northeast;
		M. central west, southeast, north central
Idaho	Wt. 6 M. 68	Wt. panhandle;
		M. southeast, Salmon River
Nevada	M. 11	Elko County
Utah	M. 47	Exceedingly scattered
Colorado	Wt. 1 M. 181	Western half
Arizona	Wt. (Coues) 102	Southeast
	M. 42	North Kaibab (no longer valid)
New Mexico	Wt. (Coues) 3	Southwest
	M. 49	Northwest
Pacific Coast		
Washington	Wt. 21	Northeast
	M. 14	Southeast, northeast
	Blacktail 68	Pierce, King, Lewis Counties, scattered other
Oregon	M. 17	Scattered east of Cascades
	Blacktail 85	Scattered, west slope Cascades
California	M. 3	Modoc County
	Blacktail 125	Northwest
Alaska	Sitka blacktail-none	
Canada		
British Columbia	Wt. 4 M. 9	Both southeast
	Blacktail 11	Vancouver
Alberta	Wt. 24	Southeast
	M. 6	Southwest
Saskatchewan	Wt. 95 M. 13	South and southeast
Manitoba	Wt. 23	Southwest, southeast, interlake
Ontario	Wt. 1	No pattern
Quebec	Wt. none	
New Brunswick	Wt. 5	Scattered
Nova Scotia	Wt. 3	Scattered

Hunting Desert
Whitetails and Mule Deer

The mental picture that practically all enthusiasts have of deer hunting is a dramatic experience played against a backdrop of snow, mixed evergreens and hardwoods in New England or the Great Lakes region, or of wooded blue ridges and moss-draped stream bottoms of the South, or of high-country aspen and spruce of the Rockies. Even calendars and Christmas cards invariably show deer—mule deer and whitetail usually interchangeable!—against forest backgrounds.

Perhaps this view is logical. Where else would deer be? Who, for example, would envision deer standing among prickly-pear cactus clumps and thorny desert chaparral? Well, for one, I would.

Unquestionably those of us who are enthusiasts of desert deer hunting are few compared to the hordes of others. Many hunters, especially east of the Mississippi and across the North, don't even realize how successfully both whitetail and mule deer eons ago colonized portions of the Southwestern deserts. Most people, indeed, think of "desert" as meaning an expanse inhospitable to all but meager wildlife, a barren wasteland. The fact is that our deserts teem with wild creatures, far outranking in species numbers any forests of the continent. Curious as it may seem, deer are often more abundant there than in their better-known locales. Hunting desert deer is a quality experience.

For example, in my estimation the most difficult, challenging, and rewarding whitetail hunting on the continent is in the virtually tree-less, endlessly rolling expanses of desert scrub thornbrush in southern Texas. The bucks, at maturity, are busters, a substantial number of which have found their way into the record book. Granted, the mule deer that range across western Texas, southern New Mexico, parts of southern Arizona, and, of course, across the border into the deserts of northern Mexico haven't so far made it into the records. This is because they're the desert mule-deer subspecies, which is slightly smaller both in body and in maximum antler size than the Rocky Mountain mule deer. Nonetheless, heavy antlers with gratifying

194

For the newcomer to desert deer hunting, it is difficult to get accustomed to the idea of seeing deer right out in the open. Mule deer in particular are habitual feeders on the flats and bare slopes.

spreads of 24 to 26 inches are fairly routine there, and spreads of 30-plus turn up on occasion.

Regardless of trophy considerations, something is superbly provocative and intriguing about hunting deer in the somehow "unreal"—to a newcomer—desert terrain, where it just doesn't seem that deer belong. I wasn't born to the desert. Perhaps that's one reason I'm so captivated by hunting it. Two introductory experiences come to mind.

About 25 years ago I traveled from my home in the North one winter to make a javelina hunt—my first—in southern Arizona. Levi Packard, originally a Wisconsinite but for many years now with the Arizona Game and Fish Department, was a warden at Tucson then. He squired me around. We were prowling the desert one afternoon looking for pigs, and I don't recall that the idea of deer being in such country had even crossed my mind. Suddenly a big blocky desert mule-deer buck with a rack that seemed to me enormous burst from its bed in a clump of brush, practically from underfoot. I was so startled and excited I was breathless. I vowed someday to come back to that desert for just such a deer. In due time, I did.

The other experience happened the first winter we lived in Texas. I received an invitation to hunt deer near Laredo. When I arrived, I simply couldn't believe there could be whitetail deer of any consequence in the vast sweep of cactus and thorns of this so-called brush country. To my mind, it just wasn't whitetail habitat.

My host was driving me along a *sendero* in his old hunting car when I saw movement on a distant ridge. He stopped, and I glassed the spot. I was looking at a deer that wasn't possible. Its body was enormous. To this day I'm convinced the head was of record proportions. I literally fell out of the vehicle, wrestled my rifle around, and loaded it. I missed the deer five times, and I was shaking so hard as it went over the hill that I had to sit down to recoup. You can bet I've been back many times since and have even been fortunate enough to collect a few of those trophies.

These big whitetails are of the subspecies *texanus.* This deer ranges throughout most of Texas, but it reaches such large size only in the southern brush-country counties, a seemingly sparse habitat where a casual observer would think they'd be at their smallest. It may surprise many whitetail hunters to learn that although on a continent basis Saskatchewan has the most whitetails in the record book, and Wisconsin is second, Texas is a solid third with 57 total, aggregate of typical and nontypical heads. And the clincher is that of the 57 from Texas, all but a few are from the relatively small area of the brush-country or south Texas desert counties.

The Texas whitetail sweeps on across southern Texas even to the far west, across the Pecos River. Some among a modest population in the Big Bend region are very substantial trophies. There are two other whitetail subspecies within the desert range we're talking about, but technically neither is an authentic desert dweller. One is the Coues (Arizona whitetail) of southeastern Arizona. But this small though handsome deer is almost always found up in the oak, juniper, and grass at around 6,000 feet, not out on the desert floor. The other is a similar case, the diminutive Carmen Mountains whitetail, scattered in small numbers in the oak, piñon, and madrona at an altitude of 5,000 to 6,000 feet in the Big Bend country of western Texas and across into its namesake mountains in Mexico. Although both offer some highly interesting hunting, neither strictly fits the desert environment I'm discussing here. Yet both occasionally are present on its fringes.

Several facets of south Texas cactus-patch whitetail hunting espe-

196

Can you spot the trophy whitetail whose fine rack barely shows above cactus and thornbrush? This home area of his seems wholly improbable to many a hunter of woodland deer.

cially frustrate newcomers—and often old hands just as much. A deer can be anywhere. Everything looks the same, and the terrain is seemingly endless. There are few breaks in the cover. On some ranches, dozers have cut swaths through the brush, or root-plowed patches, and then sowed hardy grasses for cattle grazing. Very early and very late in the day, deer may move into these. But the deer are also fond of plentiful native foods, such as the feathery leaves of *huajilla* bushes, and thus can stay in dense cover for days at a time. You just can't bet on a spot as you'd select an edge along a northern forest opening or on a well-worn eastern trail along a stream.

For stand hunting in the desert, two locations produce best. One is a tank (a pond bulldozed out in a low spot that fills when it rains and serves cattle and wildlife). Most tanks will have numerous deer tracks, so a hide nearby may eventually pay off. The other good place for a stand is along one of the many crisscross *senderos*—trails. Some are used as ranch roads, and some are gridded by seismograph crews looking for possible oil-drilling sites.

197

On the desert, deer forage is totally different from what is in other areas. Included in the desert deer's diet are such odd items as the fruit of the prickly-pear cactus, shown here. A buck mule deer might even munch the spiny cactus pads. Your hunting success depends heavily on your learning the desert plants that the deer like best.

Deer on some days may follow the low ridgetops. On others they'll move lower down in the so-called "creek bottoms." These aren't creeks except briefly after a hard rain. At other times they're dry washes. But the most dense brush grows along them, and the white-tails recognize this brush as their best protection. I usually make a stake-out beside a *sendero* at the crest of a ridge it crosses. From there I can scan washes in brief valleys that run parallel on either side. If the valleys are abrupt enough, you're also within range of other long-shot ridges.

Any deer moving even briefly cross-country in its bailiwick must cross the open *sendero.* But such a trail is narrow, just about pickup-truck width. A doe may dawdle there, but a buck usually stands just inside the brush, has a look each way, and then—*zip*—is across before you can raise a rifle. This is a horrible exasperation. However, your close scrutiny now and then catches the buck as it surveys the trail crossing. Mostly you get a neck shot or nothing. No great quantity of bucks are bagged this way, or any way in the brush country. It's a tough kind of hunting. During one seven-year period, I killed two while strictly trophy hunting, passing up so-so specimens. But the thrill is illimitably grand.

Another exasperation is not being able to judge precisely whether a deer will show up above the low cover. Much of it is so thick you can't possibly see into it. And though it looks low, even a big whitetail is not as tall as the average hunter imagines. The deer moves easily, accustomed as it is to the spiny environment. But the buck won't be visible unless it's a monster or else the brush is especially short. I get exasperated just thinking about the time I watched a set of superb antlers move casually, their tips—nothing else—above the tangle. I watched, and I crept along pursuing that buck for a quarter-mile. Never once was a remotely possible shot presented. Finally the deer simply faded away.

Although this brush country is best described as "rolling," some of the ridges are high enough to overlook a large area. A position atop such a ridge, always just below the crest so you're not sky-lighted, allows you a good view down into the gray-green sea of prickly pear, scrub mesquite, blackbrush, and retama. Deer blend perfectly into such stuff, especially on overcast days. On bright days and particularly with low-slanted sun, sometimes a glint of a well-polished, mahogany-hued antler gives away a prize. Such a stand is for meticulous glassing. This terrain is, in fact, the only whitetail country I know where steady glassing even for several hours is likely to put a great rack on the wall.

One of the largest whitetails I've ever brought down was found just this way. You see, distantly the cover looks as if a hunter should be able to see everything. But when you're *in* it, it's something else. I had swept a 180-degree arc over and over, hoping to find a buck moving along a ridge or down into the broad and broken valley. Possibly an hour after I'd taken the stand, I picked up a spot that I had seen and been momentarily excited about when I first came. I'd thought there was a glimpse of a deer—but no, close scrutiny proved it to be a tangle of thorny branches across a dead pear clump.

But now as I happened to hit the spot again, there was the deer! Plain as could be. In all that time, it had moved only a few feet. The shot was long, the brush dense. If I moved, the deer would instantly spot me. My only hope was to wait it out and try to control my

This desert mule deer is moving up to rimrock to bed down early in the morning. Desert mule deer aren't quite as large at maximum as are the Rocky Mountain deer, but they can be excellent trophies.

excitement. The antlers surely had 10 points and extended way, way outside the ears. During the next 45 minutes, the buck fiddled about, nibbling here and there.

Once it turned back and disappeared, and the wind went out of me. But as every patient hunter knows, it requires only seconds when things jell to conclude a hunt. The buck was suddenly there, standing in a small wide-open patch of *saladillo,* a plant that grows close to the ground. Later I was to reflect that it was a good thing the deer had disappeared momentarily. My excitement, and shakes, had been snuffed out. Seeing it suddenly, I was calm. I took a rest across one knee, and when the shot laced across the brush, the deer was down.

Hunting desert mule deer is in many ways parallel to desert whitetail hunting. When you move west from the area I've been describing, once you cross the Pecos River in Texas, you're in desert mule-deer country. A line drawn very roughly north from Langtry to Sheffield, west to Fort Stockton and along U.S. 285, from there to the southern border of New Mexico, will enclose, to the west of it, all of the Texas herd of desert mule deer. Of this area, unquestionably the Big Bend country and its fringes have the greatest concentration.

In New Mexico this deer is restricted to the extreme southern portions, and in altitude to the Upper (3,500 to 7,000 feet) and Lower (500 to 4,000 feet) Sonoran Zones. Beginning in the east in Eddy County and stretching across westward through the southern tier of counties, a fair number are found. The best regions are in the foothill country of the individual desert mountain ranges of the southwestern counties: Hidalgo, Luna, and Dona Ana. In Arizona, the range is restricted to the southeast, taking in the counties of Pima, Cochise, and Santa Cruz, and parts of Graham County.

The bulk of desert mule-deer range actually lies south of the United States–Mexico border, sweeping far down into the deserts of central Mexico, where occasionally some exceptional specimens are taken. In all of this range, as soon as you move too high up and into timber, this deer disappears and is replaced by various subspecies of the whitetail.

In both Arizona and New Mexico, the ranges of the desert mule deer and the Rocky Mountain mule deer overlap slightly. This "in-between" zone of central and eastern Arizona and central New Mexico commonly has intergrades, or crosses, between the two subspecies. These deer are extremely difficult to identify. If you're after a typical desert specimen, you should stick to the central or southern part of the range. Texas offers little or no opportunity for contact with the mountain deer, and so the desert strain is quite pure. Some hybrid desert–Rocky Mountain mule deer range in parts of the Panhandle.

The desert mule deer is the subspecies *crooki*. It has some close relatives. North America has at least 10 subspecies of mule deer, plus the type species, which is the Rocky Mountain mule deer. It's the Rocky Mountain mule deer that has the widest range of any of our big-game animals. Along the coast of southern California is the southern mule deer, an extremely dark race that is probably somewhat distantly related to the desert deer. Eastward, the burro deer, *eremicus*, another subspecies, is found along the Colorado River, usually below the altitude of 1,500 feet. In Arizona's Pima and Yuma Counties, some of these deer are present, and they range on down into Mexico. The river-bottom mesquites and willows are the chief habitat of these deer, although they push on out somewhat into the true desert.

A fairly close desert-country relative, the Peninsula mule deer, inhabits lower California. This is a light-colored race. And on Tiburon Island, where presumably a race isolated from others evolved, is another subspecies. Possibly there are other races. Scientists are inclined to either lump all mildly similar forms together or split hairs over setting them apart. At any rate, these mule deer of desert and semidesert terrains are probably closely allied to the true desert mule deer.

The west Texas mule-deer terrain, where I have hunted successfully for many seasons, is composed of desert mountains. In between are valleys with sweeping flats covered by creosote brush, scattered prickly-pear and cholla cactus, Spanish bayonet, and sotol. Much of it is not as dense as the south Texas whitetail country, but it does have awesomely rough rocks and steep, severe washes. An endless skein of brushy draws lead up into the towering, barren-sloped mountains.

At the base of the mountains, scattered juniper begins. There are also dry creek beds (commonly 40 feet deep and lined with scrub trees) that meander for miles across the flats. If you go high enough, you eventually get into low oaks, piñon, and more juniper. Mule deer will be on the flats, along the winding bottoms, in the brushy draws, up in the bare rimrocks—that is, practically anywhere. And right at the edges of the vertical zone changes, where cover switches from low and sparse to more timbered, in a few places the big *texanus* whitetails are found. This evidence proves quite well that whitetails and mule deer are capable, under certain circumstances, of living on almost the same range. In fact the muleys do commonly overlap hereabouts into the favored whitetail hangouts.

The country is much the same in New Mexico. In Arizona, it is somewhat changed, more like an exaggeration of the south Texas whitetail range, because much of the desert here is densely covered. There are literal "forests" of thriving cholla higher than a man, huge, gaunt saguaro cactus stalking the slopes, and a welter of shrub varieties cluttering the landscape.

In all of it, a mule deer can be anywhere. I was hunting one year in the brushy draws along the mountain bases west and south of Marathon, Texas, figuring this was just the spot to knock over a really good buck. I jumped several forkhorns. Going back some 10 miles to ranch headquarters in my vehicle, I had to cross a creosote flat. This shrub seldom grows more than three or four feet high. Nothing eats it. It never holds big deer. Or should I say that?

I saw a buck to make any hunter catch his breath. It came trotting across the flat, head high, going straight away from the mountains. I could see where it had to cross open yellow grass, beyond which the line of a winding wash showed distantly. Odd as it may seem, a variety of stunted walnut commonly grows along such washes. It is a scrub tree, not tall like northern walnut. But it serves as cover, and I knew mule-deer bucks—usually big ones—love to follow these bottoms.

I put the glass on the deer and watched the angle at which he finally disappeared into the gully. Then I went like hell in my four-wheel-drive, drawing a dust plume behind me along a ranch trail. When I was at least half a mile past where the buck had disappeared, I raced cross-country, left the vehicle, and ran a hundred yards or so to the dry creek. The wind was perfect. Both sides of the creek were open grass. Ample walnut and varied brush covered the sides and bottom. I hunkered down, waiting, trying to get my breath. Within 20 minutes the deer appeared, walking.

Believe me, staying put was difficult. But I knew better than to rise and try a shot even of 100 yards. Too many branches. And a wise old brute like this would simply wheel and bound off, back the way he'd come. So I trembled and gasped and let him come. He was within 20 paces when he sensed something and hauled up, ears spread, all senses revved up. He never knew what had disturbed him. His very heavy antlers had 10 points and a 24-inch spread. From his dressed weight, we estimated him at around 240 pounds on the hoof. For a desert mule deer, that's a big one.

Just as with desert whitetail hunting in south Texas, long glassing is what brings most success with desert mule deer across all of their ranges. The only difference is that the mule-deer range is much more rugged, steep, and vast. You move more. Cruising ranch or other trails, pausing to study the slopes of the mountains, the rimrocks, the flats with your binocular is what locates the deer because you cover a lot of ground. To be sure, does, fawns, and forkhorns are often in evidence on open slopes or flats, standing to watch. They're far more naive than whitetails. But the big bucks, though more placid in personality than their flagtailed relatives, nonetheless are crafty, wary animals.

If you're patient, you might find it very effective to take a stand below a ridgetop, as in whitetail country, especially where you can oversee several brushy draws and washes and an opposite slope within range. Walking can also be effective. In fact, putting the breeze in your face and walking the dry creeks for south Texas whitetails, where the cover is most dense, is possibly the sportiest method of all. Quite similar is the walking of brushy, winding washes on the desert floor in New Mexico or Arizona for muleys.

In either case, when you get action, it's like being hit over the head, a bright explosion of action and drama. But you had better be fast with a rifle, have your scope turned low for a short shot, and be able to pick up a going-all-out deer in a hurry. If you aren't adept at running shots, don't do it, regardless of the excitement involved. It's too easy to wound a deer, and odds are it'll be a big one.

I have hunted most of the country I've described—southeast Arizona, southwest New Mexico, west and south Texas. On several occasions I've taken a desert whitetail and a desert mule deer the same season, and by identical methods. Glassing, in my opinion, is the best method. You get to study a deer carefully, and it's usually unaware of you. If you've never spent hours plucking cactus spines and varied thorns out of your hide after a session of desert deer hunting, you should have the experience. Painful? Sure. But the memory of how they got there will sustain you throughout your agony!

Secret Weapon: The Silent Float

The whitetail buck was a good one, and he was feeding placidly on acorns in a flat beside the stream when we eased the boat around the base of the rocky cliff on the bend. Mike, my older son, who was 13 then, was to do the shooting. He motioned me frantically to shore. He had the .243 ready, and he wanted to get out and get a solid rest.

"Take your time," I whispered. "He doesn't know we're here."

I tried to dip the oars quietly. But so intent was I upon this operation that I didn't realize the front end was swinging around close to where the rock ended and the grassy flat began. There was a sudden reverberating *"boing"* as the prow banged the jutting rock. The aluminum skiff was like an echo chamber. The buck threw up its head, then its tail. In a clatter of flying shale, it trotted to hit the foot of the ridge and then faded instantly into the cedars.

Mike looked at me. "Some show!" he said reproachfully. "Maybe you ought to let Terry take the oars, Dad, and you just direct!"

Terry is younger than Mike. He was then 10. From behind me he giggled. "Yeah, maybe Mike's right."

"Oh, it was just a deer." I replied.

"That's what we're here for," Mike needled me, grinning and sure enjoying it when the old man messed something up.

I swung the boat back away from the rock, and we eased along toward camp. We were having one of those "different" deer hunts, an idea we had hatched with some excitement when the boys and I, weeks before season, had seen a good buck run over a steep, rocky ridge and down into a flat beside this section of stream that we couldn't get to without a stiff climb.

We were on a big ranch in the scenic hill country of south central Texas. A stream ran across it and for some distance was obviously floatable by a small boat. But in places there were rock bluffs going literally straight up. Then, past these, there'd be a lovely flat, a brief

The only success I had in shooting this deer was through the telephoto lens of my camera. As we came ashore, I banged the prow of the boat against a rock, immediately spooking the buck.

little valley with tall oaks and with whitepatched sycamores closely guarding the stream.

Mike had said, "Boy! How'd you like to bust that one?!" when we saw the good one rollick over the ridge and head for the cutoff flat.

"Not down there," I'd told him. "How would you get him out? That's steep."

"Easy," Mike replied, with the quick ingenuity kids so often show. "Use a boat."

Right there the idea had been sparked and we had started planning the hunt. It seemed that each time we roamed this place to which we had access we always saw deer by the stream. This was logical. This was a rather dry piece of country. But that's not all of it. Good feeding conditions are usually found, anywhere in deer country, along the stream bottoms. Water is handy, and good hiding places are many. On numerous deer hunts from Maine to Michigan to Montana, I reflected, I had hunted stream courses. They're naturals. And they lead through country in which they're often the only "trails."

So the idea grew. In the Texas hill country we don't have very large deer. These Edwards Plateau deer are a race of whitetails of only modest size. It takes a good one to weigh 100 pounds dressed. But we sure have scads of them—far too many on lots of the ranches. However, regardless of how numerous deer may be, bucks still act like bucks. They're shy. And, one problem in hunting them is that our terrain, like many other places, is awfully noisy country for walking.

And so, as season opening neared, we made our preparations. We wouldn't walk much, because of rattling dry leaves and clinking rocks. We'd set up a camp and hunt by boat. The most important angle of this was that by boat we could get to places we'd never be able to hunt otherwise. And we'd have a good chance at deer that were lying up on the steep, rocky bluffs where they felt safe and relaxed. Besides all this, it would be a unique experience.

With a pickup, we pulled a small camp trailer down to our hunting ground the day before. We jockeyed the trailer in among cedars on the stream bank and then gathered wood for a fire. Mike pointedly threw a rope over a limb out in front.

"Who'll be first?" he said.

As it happened, he was slated to be. For as we eased the boat back toward camp on that opening morning, after I'd spooked the buck in the flat, we saw a secluded bluff that looked perfect. Without a sound, we tied up to a leaning Spanish oak. While Terry and I stayed put silently, Mike clambered out and sneaked along a ledge. Quite often, we had observed, deer would come off the ridgetops and lie up on these ledges among blackjacks just under the rims. Here they could see for long distances, and quite obviously—to them—nothing could bother them from below. We had stayed close to the bluff, well hidden by overhanging timber, as we drifted along.

Suddenly we heard Mike clink a small rock. I turned to Terry and grinned. *I'll bet Mike is mad at himself,* I thought. But at that instant another sound came from above. We craned our necks to peer up, and we saw among the trees a small buck doing the same, craning its neck to look toward where Mike must be. Obviously the deer had been lying down and had got up to investigate the sound. That was his error. For at that point the little .243 let go its bark of authority. The deer hit the rocks instantly, kicked, and slid a short distance, and lay still.

In a moment Mike appeared, his face split in a grin. "He's not very big, a six I think. But he'll sure look good hanging in camp."

He and I went up and brought the deer down. It was certainly easier to get it down than it would have been to take it up! About the only way would have been to labor to the top and then put it on a horse, or else make a long, difficult carry. And so already our float idea had worked well. I doubt we'd ever have got to Mike's deer, or found it, otherwise.

Back in camp we hung the buck and took some pictures. It was a satisfying scene: cozy trailer beside the water, venison cooling in the breeze. I reflected that it would be a mighty good thing if all fathers could, or would, spend this kind of vacation hunt with their kids. I'm sure a father establishes a rapport that is more solid and genuine than can be done in almost any other way. But besides the deeper significance, what we had done here by use of the trailer and boat was to turn a rather familiar place into a place of new adventure. It was as good as being a hundred miles from the nearest civilization.

This kind of approach is possible just about all over the United States. I think everyone should be cautioned, however, that state laws must be checked thoroughly to establish precise legality of boat use in deer hunting. In Texas, for example, it would be illegal to shoot from a boat except where you own the land along both banks. In other words, you could *not* float a public stream and shoot onto somebody else's property. Nor could you use a motor to pursue or actually *hunt* a deer.

This is true almost everywhere. And many states also have boat-hunting laws on public property. I recall when I lived in northern Michigan floating a stream in a small boat to get to a deer-hunting area in which I wanted to operate. Nothing illegal about that. But to shoot a deer from the boat as you drifted along would have been most questionable there. To shoot a deer *in* a stream was at that time at least patently illegal. In other words, many states may specifically forbid *hunting* deer from a boat—that is, shooting them from a boat. But no law that I know of prohibits hunters from using a boat or canoe to get to the place they'll hunt or to bring out a deer that's been shot.

Floating opens up all sorts of hunting grounds to you. Think of the hundreds of thousands of acres of public lands that lie along large impoundments or other large lakes all over the United States. Deer in many of these regions are underharvested simply because so few hunters get to their territory. Think of the millions of acres of public lands, much of it roadless, through which floatable streams run. Along many of these streams in roadless areas, only horseback hunters ever penetrate.

It seems curious to me that deer hunting reached by way of the water never has grown into a generally popular method. It also seems odd that shooting a deer from a boat or canoe is generally illegal but that moose hunting has been done this way legally since early days of settlement. Of course, the moose is definitely a water-oriented animal

Thousands of big lakes offer the opportunity for making a boat trip to reach an area far from other hunters. You may decide to camp and hunt one area or to move on after a short time.

in parts of its range, for example in eastern Canada. I've hunted moose in Ontario from a canoe, and also by using the canoe to get to a place where I wanted to do some walking. "Stalking" moose from a canoe is in my opinion a most exciting and challenging method.

In a few places, to be sure, the canoe has long been a means of travel to deer-hunting grounds and of bringing out the kill. The classic use of this method is in northern Maine. I have native friends in upper New England who for years have been getting into otherwise hunter-less country by canoe and bringing their bucks out the same way. Here and there in the West, astute hunters have used various craft to get to a remote deer-hunting area.

I remember visiting with a man from Montana who, with a group of friends, made an annual hunt by traveling on a big raft down a large river in order to reach a sizable island that was swarming with white-tails. Many Montana hunters dislike going after whitetails, which are present in parts of the state, because they are so much more difficult to hunt than are mule deer. But these hunters had found out about the island deer, so the scheme to put together the unique hunt just grew. They built the big raft, transported all their gear, made a camp, and usually were quite successful and certainly without competition. After the hunt, they floated on downstream and were met by prear-rangement.

One summer on a fishing trip in Montana, I talked with a native in the eastern part of the state who hunted along the huge Fort Peck Reservoir. The area has many miles of roadless country. He and a friend used a boat just as other hunters would use horses, only with far greater ease. Friends of mine in New Mexico have in past years made combination hunt-fish trips in fall on the Navajo Reservoir. This also is a spot where few roads or trails cut into the region. By careful timing, these fortunate sportsmen were able to hunt ducks and deer and to catch trout, bass, and kokanee.

On large lakes, and also on streams, boating to a campsite and setting up on shore avoids undue disturbance of surrounding country. In addition, it's quick and easy to change locations several times if the first doesn't seem suitable.

If you carefully check your state laws and the public lands border-ing various available waters, you will undoubtedly discover many new places you can hunt in this novel fashion. If a stream is easy enough to float down but too tough to come back up, you simply arrange to be picked up somewhere downstream. Make your hunt by floating into the country, then hunting afoot here and there in new territory, and eventually loading your kill aboard for the trip out.

Usually, however, the slow, easy streams are the most pleasant. A certain unique and delightful thrill comes from drifting or paddling silently along, or dipping a pair of oars gently, all the time looking for game. Even if you've fished the same stream, you get a different feeling from searching the banks and bluffs for game. And I can promise you it's the easiest way to get a deer out of a back-in spot.

That afternoon, my two sons and I started off again. We quickly saw a small spike and tried to get Terry a chance. Any deer was legal in

210

our area. But it was no go. Of course, we didn't have a really long stretch of water to hunt. But the stream did pass through several hundred acres, a whole lot more than we'd hunt on foot.

It pays to be especially careful with guns in a boat. We did *not* carry ours loaded, and we took only two. It was agreed there'd be no shooting from the boat, unless I did it, and only then if I had a really good chance. I had checked thoroughly beforehand with our warden supervisor. As long as I shot onto the property where we were and didn't use any means of sail or power for the skiff, we were within the law. Regulations from state to state are highly varied, so check those that apply to where you'll hunt.

A good thing I'd checked the law. For suddenly I saw a buck away up on an oak-and-cedar-covered bluff above us. The bluff thrust almost straight up from the water line. I loaded the .243 and told Mike to try to keep the skiff steady and broadside. Believe me, it's tricky shooting. The deer started to run. I held fire. Stones clattered, and then almost at the top, he paused to look back. More by luck than good management, I presume, I let him cleanly down.

But now what? It looked as if we really had our work cut out. The deer would be straight above us if we nosed in to the bluff, and we had no chance there to climb. We looked for another way. I rowed back a bit. We got out. Finally we found a place where we could climb up to the deer. While Terry stayed to hold the boat, Mike and I went up. We had brought a hundred feet of rope purposely for such a situation. Anyone hunting this way should go so equipped.

We gutted the little buck, which turned out to have seven points, and then the two of us eased him down the cliff on the rope, and almost to the water. Stones and rocks clattered, and I was glad I wasn't below. This is something to be extremely careful of. We snubbed the rope around a tree, and I went back down. I set up a camera and fixed it so all Terry had to do was snap the shutter. Then I eased the boat in, got hold of the deer and yelled up to Mike to loosen the rope very gently. We had, of course, carefully checked to make sure no loose rocks would come down when he gave me slack.

As the weight of the deer burdened my arms, I was instantly overbalanced. The deer's head slid down the rock face. The boat was thrust away and scooted out from the bluff. I staggered. The boys laughed uproariously, and I knew darned well they were hoping the buck and I would both go overboard. The water wasn't deep, but it sure looked cool. Hugging the buck, I did a crazy little dance.

"Sit down, Dad," Terry yelled. "You're rockin' the boat." He was in stitches.

"Get his picture, Terry, when he hits the water!" Mike yelled from above.

About then, the deer and I were in a heap on the boat bottom. But we were still dry. This time going back downstream, Mike made it pretty obvious that I should row, carting in my own deer. By now his buck was cooled out enough for us to skin it and cut it up. Terry was determined to have venison right away. That was to be part of the fun of the hunt—hanging up the deer and eating it in camp.

While I was trimming away on the deer, the boys got a fire going. Next thing I knew, they had whittled sticks and were each roasting one of the small tenders from inside the buck's back over a heap of coals they'd scratched aside. Then they sprinkled on a little salt and hunkered there beside their fire, munching away. As I stowed the meat in an ice chest we'd brought along, and hung up my buck, I reflected that this was about the best stuff for kids—and their father—that I could think of. I rather wished that civilization would just go away and that we could go on hunting for our food and drinking from the waterfall where we'd quenched our thirst during the morning.

That evening we threw some foil-wrapped potatoes into the coals, and cooked more venison to go with them. Then we crawled into our sleeping bags, for Terry was especially primed to get started early next morning. I should comment that in many states, the law prohibits youngsters from hunting, at least for big game, until they're somewhat older. Several states, for example, set the age at 14, or 16. But Texas, at this time at least has no such laws.

I do *not* approve at all of 6-year-olds shooting deer. But up around age 10 or 12, much depends on the boy and on how much the parent has trained him. I let Mike shoot his first deer at 11, restricting him to a neck shot. At 13, he had hunted with me on several good hard hunts, had killed several deer, all but one with neck shots, and had become a good sensible hunter. However, I had been able to spend much time with him. The same thing may not be true in all cases, so I think that in general the age-limit laws are a sound idea.

Terry had previously killed only one deer, and, of course, he had been badgering me about it, since Mike was away out ahead of him. I had agreed that Terry could hunt on this trip and had boned him up on the .243, which incidentally is a perfect rifle with which to start youngsters. The recoil is light, and yet the rifle is such a flattener on game that a kid can make a small error and still not get into trouble by wounding something. Nonetheless, I had, as with Mike, restricted Terry to a head or neck shot.

212

"That way," I'd explained to him, "you'll either miss it or kill it—clean either way."

It seemed to me I had just fallen asleep when something was banging on my back. I rolled over and stared sleepily. Daylight was barely outlining the trailer windows. Terry was whacking me, but holding a finger to his lips to "shush" me.

"For heaven's sake go back to bed," I whispered. "It's not time to go yet." I suppose maybe it was for him, but I was sleepy.

"But, Dad," he hissed. "There's a deer right out there." Then he pointed.

I looked, pulling the curtain back gingerly. Sure enough, a small deer, antlerless, was about 50 yards away, looking toward camp. This ranch had a quota of antlerless deer, and we had permit tags for two if we wished to take them. I knew that to Terry this deer probably looked as good as any buck he'd ever seen. Since the area we were in—and many others throughout the United States—needed does harvested, I didn't want my boys to get the idea that there was any stigma attached to shooting a deer that has no antlers.

"Think you want that one?" I asked.

"You bet!"

Fortunately, the deer was on the side away from the trailer door.

"All right," I said. "Ease out with the gun, take a rest on that cedar limb where the saw hangs. And aim for the *neck,* mind you!"

As I watched Terry maneuver into position, I realized that I was the one breathing hard. I squinted at the neck of that little deer. It didn't look much bigger around than my arm. He'd never do it. But then the rifle cracked and the deer dropped.

Terry let out a yell. Mike reared up out of his sleeping bag bug-eyed. I grinned and pointed out the window. Terry was racing to his deer, not conscious of frost or rocks on his bare feet, and with the shirttail of his pajamas flying.

Mike hooted. "Go get the boat, Terry, and bring it in. This is a boat hunt—remember?"

It seemed to me that this trip, all told, had been a pretty good lot of fun, even though the last one was a dry-land deer.

Fine Points of Deer-Hunting Lore

The buck was standing with its rump toward me. My problem was that brush in the way made it necessary for me to get around to the left in order to get the shot I wanted. Then I'd be where I could put the bullet behind the left foreleg. The day was damp and overcast, perfect for a stalk. There was no wind, and as I appraised the situation, I sensed that my chances of putting this one in the locker were excellent.

Thickets of mountain cedar were interspersed with thinly grassed openings here. As I cautiously advanced, I saw a mourning dove walking in the grass and among the stones, pecking away. Mourning doves very often feed high and on the ground during late fall and midwinter in some areas. But because I was so intent on the deer, that dove made no impression on me—until it and all its buddies, about a dozen of them, flushed.

For some reason doves feeding on the ground late in the season invariably flush noisily. The startled whistle of their wings can be heard a long way. A dozen pairs of wings seems to simply shout, "Look out! Something's after us!" The buck never even looked back. It fled in a panic.

If I had been as sharp as I should have been, I'd have backed off gingerly when I saw the single dove. Then I'd have tried my approach from the other side. I'm sure the buck had not the slightest inkling I was there. He simply took off impulsively. I doubt that he ran far. But the cover he entered was impossible for me to make a stalk in, and so he might as well have known what frightened him and run a mile. He was irretrievably lost for that day.

This small incident wouldn't be particularly important except for the fact that it points up a whole vast area of deer-hunting lore that's practically unexplored by the average deer hunter. And this "advanced course" stuff is sometimes more important than the fundamentals. Far too many deer hunters put their trust each year in a few basic

214

principles—and luck. The fellow who digs deeper is the one who has buck heads hanging clear around the den wall, not just in one place!

An experience of a recent season was a forcible reminder. During the first three days of the season, I had killed two bucks—the legal limit where I was hunting. After that, I hunted turkeys in the same area. I had several weeks of turkey season ahead of me. The turkeys gave me a bad time, right to the last minute. I knew I couldn't run down a turkey, so most of the time I sat. Sitting day after day, I put in the hours studying deer while waiting for a turkey. I correlated and relearned a lot of things I had previously noted. And I learned a lot of new things. Every deer hunter should be required to sit this long, not hunting, just observing. He'd be a changed hunter, with new concepts and knowledge.

So now, to begin, think of a buck living in the woods—any kind of woods—the kind you hunt in, for example. He appraises his surroundings by the same senses with which you appraise yours. His senses are keen. Most of the time he is more alert than you. And so it's old-hat, repeated year after year, that a deer can hear, see, and smell everything. But, does this mean that everything he hears, sees, or smells alarms him? Of course not. And so the advanced deer hunter must know what will and won't alarm the deer from among the thousands of messages the animal's basic senses bring him. "Luck," remember, translates simply as an instance when the deer made an improper appraisal!

Let's consider first what a deer sees. I know a hunter who, last season, put on a camouflage coat and pants and sat down in a clump of brush. A deer rounded the clump fairly close to him, took one horrified look, and almost broke a leg in wild panic. Does this prove camouflage is ineffective? Not at all. It proves something every deer hunter should know: the human face is a horrible object for a wild animal to contemplate at close range.

I made some experiments on this very subject one year. I put on a camouflage suit that had a hood. The front of the hood had a flap that could be dropped in front of the face or flipped back over the top of my head. I sat in an enclosed blind—a small wooden shack on stilts, with a shooting window. I sat on a stool and leaned my arms on the window sill so I stuck well out of the blind. Deer in areas where such blinds are used often are moderately skittish around them, until they're positive everything is safe. They peer, prance, and fidget until they assure themselves that no human is inside.

I had the camouflage flap down before my face. There was a breeze. The flap kept waving back and forth. Six deer, two of them bucks, finally worked in close to the blind. By "close" I mean within 20 paces. I had presumed that even though this "lump" of mottled something (me) in the window might possibly go undetected, the flapping motion of the cloth would catch the deer's attention instantly and send them racing off. Nothing of the kind happened. Conditions were such that the deer did not scent me, and I made no sound. This minor, small area of flapping above them was, somehow, a natural motion to them, if indeed they saw it, possibly like a waving tree branch. When I moved my head, however, they were instantly startled.

They didn't run. They stared uneasily. They hadn't the slightest idea what I was. One buck even took several steps *toward* me, sniffing, trying to correctly identify this "thing." After a bit, all six deer went back to feeding. When no deer was looking, I very cautiously raised the flap. Next time one looked, it saw my face. Wow! It lit out as if it intended to run forever. The others, not knowing why, ran with it.

Don't conclude, now, that the difference in *color* between my face and the camouflage was responsible. Actually, I have no awesome respect for a deer's eyes generally, except where motion is concerned. Hunters who claim a deer can "see that red coat a mile" should pause to consider that red, even if the deer can see it, which may be questionable, doesn't necessarily frighten it. If that were true, deer in the maple woods in New England would be panic-stricken all fall! The eyes of deer have only a modest number of cone cells that send color images to the brain.

Indeed, you can be dressed in bright scarlet and stand or sit—if you're absolutely immobile—within 30 yards of deer that don't scent you. I've tried it. They'll stare at you and give no sign of fear whatever. You're just a strange object, that's all. But movement is something else. A very still, apparently inanimate object that suddenly moves would startle anything, even you or me. But the point is, the deer will not be disturbed by the color ordinarily (regardless of how close it is), except possibly by the *shine* of blaze orange. Nor will your face frighten deer if it's far enough away and blending with the immediate surroundings. The eyesight of a deer is just not very good for distant detail.

Because yellow clothing was the new fad for hunters some few years ago, I tried it mainly to see how the deer reacted. I wore a bright yellow coat. It very definitely drew the attention of deer more quickly in the area where I hunted. Why? Because it was the color yellow? Not necessarily. Intensity undoubtedly is what draws attention. Also, if deer, as many scientists believe, are nearly color blind, they may see both red and yellow in related shades of gray. The yellow

216

would be almost white, the red much darker. The yellow coat, in most environments, is more "disturbing" to deer simply because its intensity and contrast to surroundings draws their attention more quickly. This does not mean it more quickly *frightens* a deer. The animal has no more reason to fear a yellow coat than a white rock.

I found, in fact, that the deer whose attention I drew in yellow were not unduly afraid as long as they did not wind me, hear me, or see me move. Movement is the main consideration, period. I leaned far out the blind window, immobile, dressed in a yellow coat and camouflage headnet. The deer, after a brief staring, were not alarmed at all. The reason full camouflage, including headnet, is the best outfit for hunting deer (I'm not speaking of safety of the hunter, which is another consideration) is that the camouflage is not so likely to attract a deer's attention. Nor is inadvertent or conscious movement of the hunter in camouflage quite so likely to be noted.

To illustrate how astutely dress can be planned, let me tell you about a friend of mine who hunted one season in the Colorado high country and purposely wore yellow. The reason? He hunted the quaking-aspen patches while the leaves were canary colored and the ground partly strewn with them. Even the light reflected in the quakey patches is yellowish when sun is bright, as anyone who has hunted in them knows. Yellow in this case *was* camouflage.

The hunter's biggest problem with deer eyesight is that more often than not the hunter doesn't realize deer are observing *him.* Deer are "edge" animals, whitetails emphatically more than mule deer. They follow the woods edges, the borders of forest openings, feeding and traveling. They do not cross open places often without standing first just inside the edge and carefully scanning for danger. Obviously they can see out far better than the hunter can see in.

But there's a way you can compensate at least partially for this handicap. Get the binocular habit. Far too few deer hunters carry binoculars for any purpose other than to gauge good heads or to bring a far-off object in closer. A great many hunters carry poor and all but worthless binoculars. Hunters who carry a good glass and form the habit of frequently looking through it have a "third dimension" in which to hunt. You'll be amazed, if you've never really concentrated on it, how far *into* a piece of cover you can see by thoroughly glassing it with a top-grade glass. You can, in fact, see almost as well as the deer can see out. By proper use of the glass along the edges, you can see deer from a distance before they spot you. Then you may be able to outwait and outwit them.

What complicates the hunter's problem with deer eyesight is that deer have great ears. A deer's hearing is very acute, especially when it's facing you with a breeze favoring it. What the hunter with only surface observation does not realize is that a deer's large ears when cocked toward one direction automatically work to the animal's disadvantage in the opposite direction. Let me illustrate for you how such little gems of lore can be helpful.

An armadillo, a porcupine waddling along, a grouse scratching, or any small creature feeding or traveling in fall woods is noisy. Deer sometimes will run as if possessed when they hear such things. It all depends on how sudden the sound is. But much of the time, such woodland sounds merely make the deer curious. I know a hunter who was wondering how the dickens to get into shooting position on a buck that was screened by trees. Then the man had the good fortune to hear an armadillo scratching around on the far side of the deer. The deer cocked its ears toward the noise, and the hunter made his sneak. The direction of the deer's ears and its concentration that way covered the small sounds my friend made.

Now let's consider just what a deer can hear. And of that continual amalgam of sounds that sift into a deer's consciousness, which are the ones that frighten it? Everything depends on how the deer "reads" the sound.

I spent several days in a blind one season experimenting with the whitetails to see what sounds I could get by with. I found that I could clear my throat, like a rutty buck grunting, and deer within only a few yards would pay utterly no attention. I learned that I could put my hat over my face and cough or sneeze in muffled fashion and up to a point deer nearby would be only curious or skittish. Sometimes they wouldn't even look up toward the high blind. I know hunters who are using deer calls in an interesting way. Whenever these men happen to pop a stick as they walk, they utter a low blatt, to reassure any deer that may have heard the misstep.

This practice could be overdone, certainly. But it's not as silly as it may sound. Remember that a deer, especially a whitetail, may bolt at some sound and not necessarily know what made the sound. The sudden "fright" is an automatic reaction. Actually it is doubtful that the deer is really frightened. Deer callers of experience often get a fleeing deer to pause and look back by making a low bleat, or by hitting the ground with a stick to imitate a stamping deer.

Deer, of course, are to some extent individuals. What frightens one deer may fail to disturb another. Such differences may be the result of the conditioning and life experiences of individual deer. I remember one season that I hunted for several weeks at a certain deer stand around which, every afternoon, a doe and twin fawns fed. That doe almost drove me nuts she was so nervous. She had those two big lubbers of fawns made into ninnies, too. They jumped and walled their eyes every second.

Now maybe I'm looking for devils where none hide, but I predicted that those fawns would grow up to be just as high-tensioned as their mama. I also knew that most deer don't range far and that it was likely these would be right here the next season. I cannot prove, of course, that they were the same deer, but at that stand the next year was a spike buck that acted just like that doe. As a little spike, he should have been dumb and trusting. Instead, he'd have been as difficult to kill as a big buck. If I were hunting such a spot each year, and could convince myself that all the progeny from that beginning were likely to be such crazy animals, darned if I wouldn't pick a new place.

More important: if I were planning to hunt such a stand seriously and that doe and fawns showed up each day, I'd purposely get up and scare her so badly she'd run clear out of the country. Why? Because while I watched her during my experiment for several weeks, out of curiosity, she was a constant alarm bell to every other deer that came within range. Plainly she was a liability. Maybe that's cutting it fine, but big bucks almost always come only by the "luck" of fine cutting!

I found one year during my experimentation that I could get by with some astonishing sounds while deer were nearby *if* I contrived to make the noises seem like something they weren't. In this case I was in country that has foxes and the odd bobcat. There are also squirrels, both tree and rock, and turkeys. Just for fun when deer were near, I'd make a thump or a scratching noise, let's say, and as a deer jumped with tail starting up or whirled to look, very much disturbed, I'd—while with headnet on and well concealed and immobile—make a low growl, snarl, or catspitting sound. I was astonished that 90 percent of the time the deer paid very little attention, even when I got real loud about it.

I don't think this hearing business needs to be discussed further from this angle to have a sharp hunter understand how he may utilize a deer's excellent hearing to allay rather than arouse its suspicions. In all of this advice, I'm presupposing that the deer is not meanwhile alarmed by knowledge brought to it through another of its senses besides hearing.

In somewhat the same way a camouflage headnet helps thwart a deer's only moderately good eyesight, certain things can be done legally to thwart his much better sense of hearing. One common mistake of hunters is actually a simple-minded error. It might be called the "ostrich theory." The hunter is operating on a still, windless day. The woods are dry, leaves down, weeds dried and crackly. No human being can possibly make a quiet boot-footed stalk on such a day. We all have heard the old Indian tales about silent walkers, but they're tales, nothing more. Yet hunters keep right on cracking their way around, making believe the deer don't hear them.

Such situations require enough self-discipline to sit down, shut up, and stay put. Or they require real ingenuity. I know an archer who commonly makes his close stalk in his sock feet when walking conditions are precarious. I know another hunter, a rifleman, who never walks when the woods are still and dry. He finds a hill from which to survey surrounding country, and then he waits for the deer to make the noise.

There is also the possibility of hunting from a pickup or jeep. I am not attempting to judge how sporting or unsporting this may be. I am simply recording that it is commonly done, where the practice is legal. Driving a vehicle along a woods trail does not disturb deer like a man on foot. At the very least, whenever possible in "near-civilization" deer hunting, getting someone to drive you by pickup, or other vehicle, to your stand spooks deer less than walking.

There is another most important angle on the business of both sight and sound that really deserves a whole chapter in any advanced deer course. It is "The Art of Sitting Still." Have you ever sat still or stood still in the deer woods? By "still" I mean *still*. I have hunted with very few deer hunters who even know how. Most of them don't realize what an art it is. They've either been lucky or else have scared off deer constantly and never knew it. Keep in mind, always, that when you hunt in an area, whether sitting or moving, and see no deer, it's probably your fault, not an absence of game. Many of the animals you've driven off didn't run; they just faded or walked over the hill, away from the disturbing "messages" their senses brought.

One reason for sitting very still is that the longer you sit, the more of your scent there is around you. The more you hitch and twist, the more you spread it.

You cannot sit still if you're uncomfortable. Even the fit of your boots, your underwear, and your shirt is important. So is your position, the position of your gun, the feel of the ground or limb or log you sit on, and the tree against your back. If you select a spot from which you can see plainly a certain slice of territory, and only by craning and hitching can some marginal areas be watched, then you're asking for failure. To be still, you should just see so much, without moving an iota—and not try to see more.

The positions of your hands and your feet are most important. A hand braced against a limb may snap off a piece of rough bark at the wrong instant. A twig or branch in a certain position may bump the gun barrel as you raise it. A dry leaf beneath a boot may crackle and cause a miss. All of these things should be thought of ahead of time. They are awfully minor—and thus the more embarrassing when they ruin a chance.

If an insect is on your face, or your scalp itches, your hand must move with inexorable slowness up and again down. No one on a deer stand who jerks a hand up (or makes any movement other than in slow motion) knows how to sit still. The expert "sitter" knows that a sudden sound to the right or left must not bring his head swiftly swiveling. Slow motion again. And a deer behind you, but working around, shouldn't be looked at any more than an experienced water-fowler would pop his head out of a duck blind to see how close the flock is.

Probably the ultimate in poor "sitting" is the hunter who fails to place his back against something to keep from being silhouetted, or the one who, dressed darkly, sits against light grass, or vice versa.

Of course, no end of care about preventing a deer from being frightened by what it sees and hears will do the least bit of good if that one best sense the animal has is not somehow thwarted. A deer's eyes and ears are quite unimportant compared to its sense of smell.

I have an old friend whose home location I won't divulge for fear of hurting his feelings. He lives in a shack and works in the woods. He eats very simply, mainly off the country. He may bathe inadvertently when a hard rain catches him or he falls into the lake, but I doubt if he ever does so on purpose. His shack smells like a coon's den, and he smells like a mixture of earth, woods, and animal. He is a deer killer extraordinary. Yet he is not an especially careful hunter. I am firmly convinced deer don't wind him, or if they do are not especially disturbed, because he smells like he belongs. Laugh if you must, but let me go further.

Crude as it may sound and look on paper, hunters sweat. Some sweat worse than others. Most do not live in the woods like the old gent I just mentioned, so they exude man odors with a "city label." Some of these hunters are scrupulously clean in their habits, bathing regularly. Some aren't. A great many, in addition to bathing, use synthetic "deodorizers." So here we have the sweaty man, the well-soaped-and-scrubbed man, the deodorized man. All three, to a deer, smell to high heaven, and all three, conceivably, will never see Mr. Big because that sharp old critter will wind them from afar and never show so much as an antler tip.

One time I had a favorite seat on a low live-oak limb from which I hoped to kill a buck. A gentle breeze was on my right shoulder. Several deer came out 200 or more yards to my left and one was a pretty fair buck. Because does kept in the way, I never did get a shot.

Those deer, even with the breeze toward them, never suspected I was there. For one thing, the day was chill. I was not perspiring. Somehow the currents didn't waft "me" to them. The next afternoon just before going hunting I took a shower. The soap smelled real nice. I used a deodorant after my shower, and put on all clean clothes replete with that "nice clean smell." I got on my limb and found I was dressed too warmly. The day was almost hot. The same breeze was in the same place and the same deer presently emerged from their thicket, some 200 yards from me. By this time I was perspiring freely, and with bath soap, clean clothes, and deodorizer, brother, I was a wondrous mixture of smells. The deer worked around until they were precisely in line with the breeze. I was getting into shooting position when, *whammo!* That buck whirled and the does whirled, all facing toward me. They threw up their heads and drank in the message on the breeze, and then did they ever strip their gears getting gone.

Because scent is such an imponderable, and so little understood, it is a tremendous problem to a hunter. Most of us go deer hunting "too clean." Some people who have thoroughly studied this amazing phenomenon of scent claim we should be very careful what we eat for as much as several days before hunting, that we should not wash our hands previous to a day in the woods, should never wear just-cleaned, or brand new, clothing—and so on. I am not going to scoff, because nobody can prove how many big bucks have *not* been killed because, for one of these reasons, they winded the hunter.

For that matter, what does "winding a hunter" mean? It means that the deer smells something not only unnatural and to him possibly unsavory but also something that conjures up a picture of danger. It is quite possible that a deer, let us say, in the hardwoods of northern Wisconsin (where leeks abound in spring and deer eat them) or in Tennessee (when wild onions load the air with fragrance in April and are nibbled by deer) might not be disturbed by the onion smell wafting in infinitesimal amounts from a hunter's breath. But in areas where the onion smell was strange, conceivably it might panic the deer. I don't believe we should scoff at such theories. After all, there's still

222

an awesome amount to be learned about the science of smell—and for that matter, about deer hunting!

The best preventive of deer-frightening man-smell to date is the air currents themselves. The hunter who never forgets to keep the wind in his face whenever possible will go far toward licking the problem of a deer's super-acute nose. To illustrate how tremendously important this is, I cannot resist telling of my experience in a picture-taking blind. A friend of mine, an avid photographer, had built a comfortable blind, even with bunks. He kept grain in front of it daily, just so he and his friends could take photos of deer, turkeys, and other wildlife. This well-made little building was just about airtight, except for the door at the back and the two ports of very small dimensions from which the camera lenses were thrust. He even had a shed at the back into which the vehicle was driven, so occupants were never seen getting out of it.

He and I sat all day one Sunday in that blind, with a stiff little breeze hitting it quartering-on from behind. Deer would come out of heavy cedars about 100 yards directly in front. Because the area from us to cover was completely open, they would all go to our left, where they could approach the blind from thin brush—and also pick up the breeze. They had absolutely no reason to fear this area. They had been fed here for months. No one had ever been allowed to shoot here.

We hunched at the small portholes, which were big enough for camera lenses. The breeze, I suppose, stole in the cracks around the back door, swirled over us with the lightest brushing, and oozed out the all-but-plugged portholes. The deer walked along unconcerned until they reached the exact place where the breeze direction pointed. Then they suddenly went wild, all but falling over backward trying to get away. This happened time after time, all day long. I have never seen a more convincing exhibition of how finely a deer's nose operates. Explore this scent angle with utmost diligence and your deer-kill record unquestionably will improve.

It may sound contradictory, but I have never been fully convinced that the smell of smoke, for example, bothers deer much, if at all. I may be wrong, or partly so. Many expert deer hunters say you must not smoke in the woods. I think the deer certainly smell the smoke, which to them may be a danger signal. But I think what *frightens* them is the smell of *man* along with the smoke. After all, smoke smells have been common in the forest for untold centuries. And today millions of deer live within range of smoke smells from farm houses, cabins in the woods, and so on. A deer has no knowledge of tobacco. It is just another plant burning. Indians actually burned certain plants to *at-*

tract deer. Many hunters don't want to build camp fires because "the smoke will frighten the deer." I believe the camp smell and noise are what bother them, or any unknown smell that might be connected with danger. A mild whiff of smoke never has meant dire difficulty for deer. They don't even run from a forest fire until it gets rather close to them. The worst effect of smoke is that it may alert deer to possible danger.

And so don't be misled into thinking that just because a deer's nose is his best sense-organ defense against the hunter that everything he smells worries him. And don't think that everything he sees and hears worries him. Quite the contrary: certain sights, sounds, and smells make deer curious or interested. The problem of the advanced deer hunter is to sort the disturbing from the nondisturbing. Upon a correct appraisal of what will and won't alarm a deer, from among the thousands of messages the animal's basic senses bring it, hinges almost totally the hunter's success or failure.

How My Sons Improve
My Deer Hunting

The day after Christmas dawned very bright, still, and crisp in the Texas hill country where I live. I was sitting on a high ledge of rock, braced against a big Spanish oak. I could see across the sharp canyon below me and observe a substantial sweep of the opposite slope. It was fairly open, with only scattered small cedars, but where the canyon curved around away from and in front of me on my left, at the base of the slope, the cover was dense.

Not a deer was stirring. This seemed odd. It should have been, I thought, a perfect morning. I was reflecting that it takes a lifetime to learn in depth about deer hunting. As an outdoor writer, whose hunting has been both business and pleasure, I have put in 40 years or so at it. And always, just when I think I have everything figured, the deer don't do what they're supposed to. This morning I was especially disappointed, because my boys, Mike and Terry, were out with me for the first time that season. Now that both of them are grown, we don't get in as many hunts together as we used to.

I was just about at that point in my reflections when I heard a deer snort. The sound came from off across there where the boys were. In the stillness of the morning it was loud and clear. I was slightly irritated. Mike and Terry were supposed to be darned well expert at prowling carefully. This place belonged to us, they knew every foot of it, and I felt I'd taught them in great detail over their growing-up years of our deer hunting together. They weren't *supposed* to blunder into deer and spook them.

About then the deer snorted again—three times in quick succession. That meant it was running. A clatter of rocks rattled across the canyon, and at that instant I saw the deer. There were three. All were adult does. They pulled up spang in the open, broadside to me at maybe 200 yards, and kept looking back, as if wondering what had startled them. That told me where the boys were all right.

We don't live on our ranch, where we were hunting. No one does.

It's a wild, mint-condition piece of Texas hill country. The deer, of course, are whitetails, and most years we have too many. Most seasons, we're allotted one doe permit for each 50 acres. We need to harvest does. On our licenses we can each take two bucks and a doe, one buck and two does, or all three does if the permits last.

I eased up the .243 Winchester Model 70 and took a rest in the crotch of a dead cedar that I'd purposely sat behind for that reason. I'd let the boys do the buck hunting today. I turned the 3x-9x Redfield variable scope up to six and held very carefully so as not to ruin any meat—if I could make this good. I was going to try for the neck, a small target indeed at that range. Fortunately, when the rifle cracked, we had venison.

Even though this was a doe, there was nonetheless the old excitement and gratification over a well-made shot. I clambered down and climbed the slope. As I got to the deer, the boys were coming along the edge of the cover, both grinning ear to ear.

"Good shot!" Mike said.

Mike, an ardent outdoorsman, was then 23, a six-footer, through college, and with a family of his own. It had been difficult this year for him to get home for our annual deer hunt.

I said, "I'm glad enough to have the venison, but you guys keep bumbling around and you'll spook everything in sight. I could hear them snorting clear over here."

Mike grinned and winked at Terry, and Terry guffawed.

"What's so funny? I gave both of you credit for being better prowlers than that."

"That wasn't the deer," Terry chuckled. "That was *Mike!*"

Terry, then going on 20, was in his second year of college but still living at home. They both broke into laughter now, gleeful that they had fooled the Old Gent.

"We saw the deer in the cover but didn't want to shoot," Terry finally explained. "They never knew we were there. Mike's been practicing up so he can snort just like a deer."

"It'll put 'em out every time," Mike said. "It doesn't mess things up except in that immediate area. And almost always I've noticed that as long as they can't wind you, deer flushed out this way will stop to look back."

"From where we were, we knew they *had* to run right out where you could see them." Terry added. "Pretty smart, eh?"

"Brag a little!" I told him. "If you guys are that clever, you must know how to dress out a doe better than I do. I'll just watch."

As they worked on the deer, we went through our usual banter. But the fact was that they *had* worked a mighty slick trick. Most hunters trying to drive deer make a big racket and have them running every which way. This method, using a sound well known to deer, moved them but didn't terrify them. I had to admit that in all my years of deer hunting I'd never experienced this one. I had learned something —from my own kids.

The more I thought about it, the more I realized that I had learned a great deal from my sons over the years, and we had learned a lot together. Although neither of them was born in Texas, we moved there just about when they were starting school. There was no age limit in the state on when youngsters might begin deer hunting. I was really not eager for them to start too young. I felt—and still feel—that helping a kid of five or six hold up a rifle to kill a deer is just plain ridiculous. Yet a good many Texans start their youngsters that young.

I wouldn't go for it. I did take my boys along with me when they were fairly young. But by the time Mike was 10, the heat was on me. Fathers of all the other kids in school with him let their youngsters hunt. So that year I carefully coached Mike in gun handling, safety, accuracy, sportsmanship, and all the rest. I took him on his first deer hunt, leaving my own rifle at home.

Once Mike was launched, it was tough to put Terry off, even though he was nearly four years younger. I recall with amusement his first deer, when he was nine. It was a rather small deer. I got him into position, with a good rest. Both of us were standing. I had my glass on the deer. To give him the largest possible target I instructed him to shoot it in the ribs. But I had overlooked the fact that from his lower stance he couldn't see the ribs.

"All I can see is its neck" he whispered in a trembling voice.

I presume I sounded impatient. I didn't want him to foul up the first time around. "So," I hissed, "shoot it in the neck!"

Through the glass the neck looked awfully small. I groaned inwardly. But when the gun cracked the deer folded—and I had another deer hunter on my hands.

Much of what I learned from my boys simply accrued while I was teaching them. I'd suddenly realize something I hadn't known previously, or possibly had known but not with any emphasis or not in all its facets. Like the time I was explaining about cover. As the boys and I walked together, I mentioned that whenever there's cover, whether you're after mule deer or whitetails, you should make a habit of moving within it because even a man's moving shadow, if he ducks bush to bush in the open when sun is low, may alert and spook a deer. We were walking just inside a stand of trees and the sun was to our left and low. To our right was the open area we were avoiding.

One of the boys said, "Dad, look out there," pointing into the opening.

I was astonished. There was my own shadow, rifle and all, flickering between other shadows along the grass. We weren't inside the cover *far* enough. The boys, being shorter, didn't project shadows as far as I did. It was a lesson we all learned right there and have followed since. I remember later hunting mule deer in open mountain country and watching another hunter who thought he was stalking some deer. Meantime he was throwing a downhill shadow to his right 40 feet long that ran his targets over the hill.

Sometimes a question led to new knowledge. I'd stop and think and decide I really didn't know the answer. The boys and I would all discuss our opinions. Then we'd start looking for confirmation. First thing you know, we had all learned some valuable and unusual deer-hunting lore. One of the most important bits of lore to be unearthed this way has to do with buck rubs.

I had pointed out buck rubs, explained about them, and assured the boys at a tender age that if you find several fresh rubs in any general area, it is a positive sign a buck *lives* in this vicinity. I explained that deer when not unduly disturbed do not roam widely. Many careful experiments have traced deer—in recent years even by radio-signal collars—and found that a square mile is a lot of territory for an individual deer. Thus several fresh rubs meant the area would bear watching. Sooner or later, the buck would probably be seen. I had also shown Terry and Mike the difference between buck rubs and others.

For example, our country (and some other places) has a good many horses. Horses rub their necks on trees, usually with head held down. Thus the height is about that of a deer rub. The difference is that horses invariably select a solid tree four or more inches in diameter, with rough bark. They're scratching their necks. Most deer rubs are on saplings of seldom more than an inch in trunk diameter, one that will give and bend, one that has bark the antler beams can shred, and one that has branches to fight against.

This discussion immediately brought an unexpected question from the boys: "What *kind* of trees?"

"Any kind," I replied. But suddenly I knew my answer wasn't correct. I'd seen rubs commonly, I remembered, on small balsams up north, and said so. Those, in fact, are ideal. I'd also seen rubs often on small Ashe juniper in our hill country. But invariably only on a tree with a single trunk, one that was springy but still had enough substance.

"If we knew what kinds of trees get *most* of the rubs," Mike offered, "we'd always know where to look and could find buck home grounds easier."

It was a darned good point. We started observing more closely. The two shrubs that get the big play in our area, we discovered, are single-stem junipers (cedar) and shin oak with trunks one or two inches in diameter. Although we have much scrub persimmon, we've never seen a rub on this and seldom on live oak. Both, I believe, are too hard and unyielding. This line of thought got me started checking in other places.

In the brush country of southern Texas I discovered that a green-barked small tree well-equipped with thorns called retama is a prime rubbing tree for bucks. Where it grows, almost all rubs thereabouts are found on it. Obviously the varieties of favorite rubbing trees will differ from place to place, depending on what's available. Observe which are the hot ones, and you can zero in on this important sign far more easily than by the usual shotgun method of looking everywhere.

One deer-hunting trick that is often just about surefire in farm country (which takes in a vast area, especially of whitetail range) was discovered by both of the boys independently of each other during the same season. The trick is based on a deer habit that I knew well but just never had thought about as a way to bag one. It was Mike who first showed it to me.

I'd gone up to visit him and his family and have a brief hunt. They live within 60 miles of Fort Worth, in an area of modest-size diversified farming-ranching tracts. The place Mike leased at that time had 110 acres. It had open fields, brushy fence rows, and a good woodlot with ample cover and a pond at its edge. Deer are not really abundant there, but there are enough, and of good size and plenty sharp. We were walking in the woodlot the afternoon I arrived, just before season, when Mike showed me a tree in which he proposed to sit next morning.

I didn't agree at all. "You've got only a tiny opening to watch in thick woods. That's a handicap. Ought to watch a field."

He smiled. "Just got a hunch."

The next morning was so cold I decided to stay in. Sitting would be a bitter chore. I didn't stay in for long. Shortly after the sun was up, Mike came for me. He had a big buck down.

When I saw it, shot from only a few yards away from his tree seat,

I was astonished. Some luck! But he insisted it wasn't luck at all, and he urged me to take a short walk with him. Within 75 yards we came to the edge of the woods and a fence separating it from a field.

"I walked all the fences a couple weeks ago," he told me. "Deer can jump any of them, anywhere. But I reckoned that when they're undisturbed they'd habitually jump only at one or two *low* spots, like where a top wire is down or bent. Look."

He pointed to a sag in the fence. Obviously deer had been jumping here all year. Weeds were cut to pieces, and gouged-out spots on either side showed where they landed.

"I figured that either way they were headed, to or from the woods, they'd aim for the fence here and would skirt or cross that small opening before or after. That sag in the fence was as good as bait!"

That wasn't the end of it. When I returned home, Terry had a buck hanging in our backyard. At our home place, we have 27 acres, mostly woods, and a couple of small ponds. Usually we don't hunt the home place. But we'd seen two fair bucks, and I'd asked Terry to see if he could collect one, a tricky job because they're terribly skittish.

"How'd you manage it?" I asked, amazed that he'd brought it off.

He insisted I come with him in the jeep to where he'd made his stand. You guessed it. A top wire was sagging and there was a plain trail on either side. This was where deer jumped into, and out of, our place.

"It was real simple," Terry said. "I just sat 50 yards away and waited."

When we first bought our Bushwhack Creek Ranch some years ago, 20 miles from our home place, we often began a hunt by making a first cruise through the long dimension of it in a slow-moving vehicle, watching and glassing for deer. That ranch trail runs generally east-west. Getting in at the east end is difficult and very rough going. But for a morning run, I pointed out to the boys, it was mandatory. Otherwise we had the low-slanted sun in our eyes. Conversely, an evening hunt of this sort had to move from west to east. Furthermore, I showed them, using a scope directly against the sun is all but impossible.

I gave little thought to the matter after they had learned these simple facts, until one fall when I took Mike to west Texas on a mule-deer hunt. The country was almost wide open, with only a few clumps of sotol and scattered Spanish bayonet on the slopes. Very late one afternoon we got the glass on a nice buck a long way off. I told Mike to have a go at making a stalk on his own. He ducked up a draw,

230

out of sight of the deer, and I stayed by our vehicle, keeping watch of the deer.

The day was very still, so breeze direction was no problem. But imagine my chagrin and annoyance when I suddenly saw Mike right out on the open slope, crouched and moving toward the buck. True, it would have been a long haul clear around to come over the ridge into range. I assumed he'd simply become too eager and excited. I saw the buck stare at him, and Mike would stop. Then the deer looked away and Mike moved a few steps. This routine kept on until Mike was within easy range, and still he continued.

I was about to conclude that this must be a dumb buck indeed, as well as a dumb kid hunting it. Then, from a range of about 60 yards, I guessed, the deer stared, big ears wide, and Mike raised the rifle and killed it. All of a sudden it hit me what Mike had been doing—a variation on our low-light hunting, thinking not of light so *he* could see but so the deer *couldn't*.

"It was blinded!" he told me in high excitement when I got there. "I was remembering our ranch and hunting with low sun behind us. That buck had the bright, low sun right spang in its eyes all the way. It never knew what I was, and I couldn't resist trying to see how close I could get."

Purposely putting sun directly in a deer's eyes was, I suppose, something I knew in a vague way, but I had never paid close attention to the idea. To be sure, deer have excellent eyesight. But they can't see any better than you can when looking straight into a low sun. Ever since that incident, we've made numerous successful stalks just this way. You simply stop when the deer stares. If you keep your shadow straight in front of you, the deer doesn't see its movement. When you must make a sneak in the open or with little cover, this is one of the sharpest tricks in the book.

One of the most valuable opportunities we've all had has been to hunt on our own property incessantly. It has been a kind of laboratory. The habits of deer are pretty much the same everywhere. Only the differences in terrain make them seem to differ. When you know a piece of country in infinite detail, you're able to deduce what deer will do under any given circumstance. That's one reason why hunters who are sharp students of the outdoors and who hunt the same place year after year seem uncannily "lucky."

Something that Terry brought to my attention one time at our ranch was that we always saw deer in the same general places—and also that there were some places where we *never* saw deer. I hadn't even thought of the situation just that way.

"It's like fishing," Terry observed. "Like you say, a lot of lake bottom doesn't have any fish." We started being more meticulous in our observations, and we discovered that almost without fail the deer on any given sector of the place traveled precisely the same routes. I don't mean trails. They moved along certain ridges, crossed the creek at certain general stretches, went from point A to point B along general routes that didn't deviate in the least.

Obviously there might be exceptions. But the *basic patterns* of their lives and movements were quite routine. By learning those, we eliminated some territory where test after test taught us hunting was not likely to be productive. The gist of it is that knowing where *not* to spend hunting time, whether for whitetails or mule deer, is just as important as knowing where *to* hunt. And again, it was Terry who zeroed me in on something in this field I'd never previously considered.

He fiddled around on our home place and on the ranch a number of times, watching the routes where deer moved most and the areas they used most for feeding and bedding. He also got interested in watching where deer ran when he jumped them. Then one fall he and I were hunting one day and we saw a buck that had seen us first and gone bounding away. There was a gully beside us that curved around several meanders to tie into a canyon that curved toward us. Terry suddenly took off up that gully like a scared jackrabbit.

I couldn't imagine what he had in mind. The buck, I was pretty sure, had gone over the ridge from which it had seen us. But in a few seconds I heard a shot. When I got to Terry, he was really teed off. He had seen the buck and missed it. But he was at least gratified that he'd been correct about where it would go.

"Probably this is old stuff to you," he told me. "But I've noticed that anyplace where deer travel naturally, like from one canyon to the next or one patch of woods to the next, they'll go the same exact routes when they're scared."

True. Again, it was something I was aware of but hadn't paid enough attention to. Thinking back, I could remember numerous times when the same sort of thing had happened. You just *knew* where a spooked deer was going to go. But Terry's refinement, I think, was in checking the general travel routes and the high-use areas beforehand, so he could avail himself of short cuts to head off or intersect a fleeing deer. Whitetails will always take the long way—unless terribly pressed—in order to stay in cover, and that's why knowing short cuts can help a hunter. Mule deer are more likely to pursue more direct flight paths.

232

The great thing about hunting with youngsters, especially when they're starting, is that they have a fresh, unprejudiced approach. They aren't afraid of looking foolish when they present a quirky idea. I tried in the beginning to impress upon my kids that a deer wasn't anywhere near as big in real life as in their mind's eye. Mark well that it is very important for any deer hunter to *know* how big a deer is, that is, how tall. Scads of hunters look for deer where they don't have a chance of seeing one. The cover is too high. Yet many hunters seem to think a deer would tower over it. Or they look for animals a whole lot bigger than deer really are.

My admonitions led the boys to pressure me into actually digging out some figures. For example, small whitetails aren't over 30 inches high at the shoulder, large ones seldom over 40. Many mule deer are only a yard high or a bit less at the shoulder, and the outsize ones are seldom higher than 42 inches. What this investigation led to was that the boys asked for some literal comparison. Mike wanted to know where the top of the shoulder of a fair-size whitetail would come to on me. By measurement with a tape, we found the height was just barely above my hip joint. Terry said the best idea was to measure him and Mike. Then they could look at each other and compare themselves to deer.

Kid stuff? Ha! It was a brilliant idea. Measure off the length of your leg sometime, the distance from ground to belt line, and to your shoulder. Compare it to deer—few of either species will stand at shoulder very much above the belt line of an average man. Then compare *that* information to brushy cover in which you hunt. You'll understand much better how to look for deer and why they're not easy to see. A good buck with its head up can be concealed totally in cover only shoulder high on an average hunter!

Both the boys also got me interested in measuring the ears of deer, which may seem a little ridiculous. But I'd explained to them that when a deer is looking toward you with its ears cocked, if the antlers are well outside its ears, you're looking at a very presentable buck. To the kids, this general rule wasn't good enough. How long were deer ears? Some years ago, I didn't really know. I know now, thanks to prodding from inquisitive kids. Whitetail ears run from 7 to 8 1/2 inches, mule deer from 11 to 12. Whitetails cock their ears up somewhat; mule deer hold theirs, when listening, out straighter from the head. Skull width differs among races of whitetails and mule deer. In general, however, eartip-to-eartip distance on whitetails with ears cocked will be 12 to 14 inches. On mule deer the distance is usually 14 to 16 inches. These average measurements, we learned, allow you to judge pretty well, when hunting a fair to good buck, whether or not you want to shoot.

While we were all on the measuring kick, we did a few tapings on the thickness or width of deer bodies. Many hunters see deer running straight away. Husky whitetails average 14 to 16 inches from side to side through the body. Mule deer generally have a couple of inches more. So a quick glance comparing antler spread to body or rump width is a good way of judging trophy size. I presume I never would have got into any of this except for insistent questions from the boys. Kids enjoy finding questions the Old Gent can't answer. That aroused my Irish ire to find out!

Reminiscing, it seems to me that for the dedicated deer hunter it is the open-mindedness toward amassing endless small bits of lore that finally transforms an average hunter into an authentic expert. But by then he knows he should never stop trying to learn. In my experience at least, there is one influence above all others that can keep a hunter ever acquisitive. It is the endless "whys" of his offspring, the answers to which a proper father is forced to dig up. And it doesn't hurt if you have the patience and good sense to listen to *their* ideas. Youthful appraisals are fresh and provocative—if the Old Gent will only listen!

My All-Time Favorite Venison Recipes

The longer a fellow lives, the more I suppose he likes to regale listeners with stories of events from his past. Most of us, I'm sure, like to tell about what we did when we were kids and then follow up with stories about our own kids when they were growing up. I'm as bad as the next. I suppose probably I've repeated many times the incident I'm now about to relate, but it fits here so properly that I can't resist.

My wife, when I met her, was strictly a city girl, working in downtown New York and living in a nearby suburb. She hadn't done much cooking, and certainly nothing wilder than a prime-beef sirloin. But by the time we'd been married a year, she'd had everything from woodcock to snowshoe hare to venison carted into her kitchen. Because she didn't have any idea at that time about how to ruin game by bedeviling it with a hundred combinations of condiments soaked into it, poked into it, and layered on it, she simply hauled off and cooked it. The result was that we ate venison that tasted like venison, woodcock that was authentic, and so on.

By the time several years later when we had two small boys to feed, Ellen had become a truly excellent cook and a superb game cook. She had fiddled with some of the complicated recipes that claimed to "bring out the delicate flavor," and she'd discovered that a ruffed grouse, for example, or a tenderloin of deer already had a delicate flavor that didn't need much "bringing out." She also discovered that most of the overintricate recipes for handling game were not devised as "bring outs" at all but as "coverups."

We ate a tremendous amount of game those early years. I hunted just as often as I could during every season. It was fortunate that this was part of my business and that I was successful in hunting, for in those early years we were not exactly affluent. At any rate, by the time the boys were of school age, they had routinely eaten wild creatures week after week, even to roast raccoon and broiled bear chops. To them, meat meant mostly wild meat, except for an occasional smoked ham or fresh pork roast as a change.

Then one time in an expansive moment of shopping Ellen dropped a substantial percentage of the week's budget on a fine-quality leg of lamb. Her mother had often cooked lamb, and she was extremely fond of it. We came to the table with some fanfare to launch this very special meal, with the mint sauce and all the proper trimmings. I carved and laid the pink slices on the plates.

The boys were sniffing and frowning, full of uncertainty about this break in routine. Their looks were dubious, but each at last took a tentative bite. They glanced knowingly at each other, and Mike said to his young brother, Terry, "Hmmm. I guess it's fit to eat, but it sure is gamey-tasting old stuff."

We joked many times later that when they got through third grade we started breaking them to beef. I have often thought in the years since that what we eat as kids we continue to relish all our lives. It certainly is true that venison, which was a staple to the colonists and probably not at all distasteful to them, does have its very own flavor. To a person raised on the best cuts of beef, venison might come as a taste shock of sorts. It is also true that there is a vast difference between individual deer and the quality of the venison a hunter turns them into. But it is just as true that there is beef oh so tender and with a marvelous flavor, and beef so tough you couldn't shoot a hole in its gravy and with a flavor a coyote would question. It all depends on how well it has fed and on what, and who did what to it after.

But venison in general is excellent meat. It's the blasphemy the cooks lay on it that turns many a first-time venison eater against wild meat. I don't know how many deer our family has gone through. In my hunting-season travels as a writer, I have collected, on story assignments, as many as eight in a season. During the fall previous to the time I write this, I took four deer: two mule deer and two white-tails. Now, six months later, my wife and I have whittled down the stack in the freezer appreciably. We have venison as often as twice a week, sometimes oftener.

We do not worry it with intricate conglomerations. Ellen has tried a lot of those. They simply overwhelm. Mostly we treat venison the way we'd treat beef. Except in rare instances of a poorly fed or poorly handled animal, if the result was any better it would have to be listed among sins to be confessed.

Venison can be hung a few days to "age," but it should not be hung as long as beef. Many hunters hang a deer with the hide on. I won't say this will ruin it. But I will say the quicker the hide comes off, the better the venison. On our own ranch, we often skin and butcher a deer immediately. I have shot a deer, gutted it, pulled it up to hang from a tree limb with a rope I carry, and had the hide off and the animal rough-butchered in as little as 45 minutes. The meat cools out very swiftly this way. Getting body heat out in a hurry enhances venison quality.

I realize that most deer hunters nowadays cart their animals to processing plants. Some of these do a good job, some ruin the meat. We take care of our own. I have described in another chapter the simple ways of cutting up a deer. Years ago I used to cut either wing chops or single chops from the loin. But for at least the past 20 years, I have boned out the backstraps on every deer I've killed. On a small whitetail, this gives you two boneless loin centers about 16 to 18 inches long and 2 1/2 to 3 inches in diameter. On a big deer of either variety, the dimensions, of course, are larger. I start the cut after the shoulder has been removed, high up at base of the neck, and take out the straps clear to the top of the ham.

We have a fireplace in our home that we actually use to heat with. Often I have taken a whole backstrap, oiled it, and laid it on a grill over coals in the fireplace. This piece of meat, turned several times as it cooks, is beautiful. We like it pink in the middle, but, of course, you should experiment to get it done as you enjoy it. It is put on the table whole and then is cut crosswise in slices about 3/4 of an inch thick.

That whole backstrap bit is a "house specialty" just occasionally. Our usual treatment of backstraps is as inch-thick fillets. I'll tout this as the absolute superlative in venison. If we think the deer may be a little tough, each fillet—all of them laid on a cookie sheet for example —is stippled with a fork and then some tenderizer dusted on. They are then set in the refrigerator for a short time. Usually, however, this process is unnecessary.

The fillets can be broiled. However, even though we're not big on fried meat or fried fish, this cut of venison is an exception. Broiling is inclined to dry the meat a bit. Instead, use an iron skillet if you have one—they distribute heat so well—and a very small amount of butter or margarine. The skillet should be hot, but, of course, not so hot that the margarine burns. Drop in the fillets and sear them quickly, turning them so that the original top side (now the bottom side) gets seared before juice begins to come out. Three or four minutes on each side will leave the fillets pink in the center and juicy. I suppose you can use condiments if you must, when you eat them. Once I even saw a guest put catsup on some and never asked him back. We use only salt and pepper. This is venison that will make you ponder how to line-breed deer to develop animals that are all backstrap!

If you have a barbecue pit, or a big barbecue cooker, or have a business place near you, as we do, that does barbecue to order, you might want to try this delicious way to handle a venison ham. I favor a mule deer as best because the hams are larger than those of most whitetails. Even the ham of a desert mule deer, a mature buck, will weigh around 22 pounds. Ordinarily I cut hams in two, crosswise. Keep in mind whenever you work with venison in roast sizes that— except in special instances where you use a sauce—a big roast is far better than a small one. Roasts of three pounds dry out too much. A big one resists drying much better.

I take a butt section of around 12 pounds, or else a whole ham from a smaller deer maybe 15 pounds or so, to a place near us that has an enormous barbecue pit. The fire is of wood. Charcoal barbecuing is something I'd look shy at, except in an open cooker and on items like ground burgers. I get the ham to the place the night before and have the proprietor get it onto his fire as soon as it's started, about 7 A.M.

Now I'm not talking of "barbecue" as a process during which some hideous red mess of sauce is incessantly splattered over the meat. You could barbecue a cardboard box with such junk on it and it would taste the same as the deer. Authentic barbecue is done by simply brushing the meat with oil very occasionally—just enough so it doesn't get crusty outside. And an expert operator, of course, keeps the heat very low and the hood down. A large pit, one that handles 100 pounds or so of meat, does the best job.

I go back to pick up the venison ham about 6 P.M. The meat can be eaten hot. Or it can be cooled, refrigerated, and sliced cold. Either way, it is unbelievably delicious. This is a fine way to serve a haunch to a party of guests, sliced still warm. Then use the leftover cold.

On a good-sized whole deer ham, a cutting method that is not common but presents an unusual roast is to cut the shank off short and then slice lengthwise near the large bone so that on the "bulge" side a chunk of meat of four or five pounds is cut off. This piece is a boneless roast. The other piece (with the bone in it) can be used as a larger roast. The boneless piece is an excellent cut to use as I will describe in a moment.

Beforehand, however, I want to mention shoulders. The shoulder of a deer, especially of a small deer, can be a perplexing cut. I remember when I used to have shoulder steaks cut at a process plant. They never were much account. I've also boned out shoulder meat and used it ground. But my wife has a method of preparing a shoulder—the same recipe as for the boneless ham cut I just mentioned—that not only is delicious but also utilizes this piece (particularly on small deer)

238

to its best advantage. Otherwise, the way in which the shoulder meat is attached to the bones offers a rather stringy and difficult problem.

You need a Dutch oven for this. And this is one instance in which Ellen does use what I suppose might be called a cooking sauce. Mix together a can of undiluted mushroom soup, at least a half-cup of mushrooms (sliced, or small whole ones), and as much chopped onion as you wish. We like quite a lot. Exact measurements are kind of ridiculous anyway in cases like this. For example, if you like lots of mushrooms, have at it. Now comes the red wine. We're a little bit picky about wine. The term "cooking wine" is meaningless. It could mean sweet, dry, heavy, light, pleasant, or terrible. My recommendation here is for a good Cabernet Sauvignon or a Beaujolais. Use a cup of it.

Salt and pepper the roast, put it into the Dutch oven, pour the mixture over it, and put the lid on snugly. Place the Dutch oven in your kitchen oven and set the heat at 350 degrees F. Ordinarily, three hours should turn out a tender piece of meat. If you decide it needs longer, no harm done. Just be sure the liquid doesn't get too deleted. We rather like venison done this way to be extra-tender—a shoulder roast, for example, so it loosens from the bone. The gravy can't be resisted, even if you're dieting.

For haunch roasts, and for saddle roasts cut out of a whole loin roast, the simple approach beats involved methods. Because there's no fat, or seldom any, and because the fat of deer when present often does have an unpleasant flavor, pinning strips of bacon to a roast after it has been salted and peppered helps keep it moist. Ellen just wraps the roasts in foil and puts them in the oven. If you like onion, sprinkle dry onion flakes or chopped fresh onion over it.

Foil wrapping is an excellent and simple way to handle various cuts of venison. Some hunters have large deer cut somewhat like beef. If you do this—it really never works as well as it does on beef—you may have what would be called a chuck roast. A venison chuck is rather often on the tough side. Try using tenderizer on it for a half hour. Then sprinkle a half envelope of onion-soup mix onto a sheet of foil, place the roast on it, and sprinkle the rest of the dry mix over the top.

Lay slices of carrot—maybe using a half dozen carrots—over the meat, and add several celery stalks. The closed bundle, with some space left at the top for steam, now goes into a pan and into a 300-degree F. oven. The time you give it depends, of course, on the roast size. If it is thin, a couple of hours should do. Otherwise, leave it in for three. Obviously the foil should have no punctures in it.

239

Along the Mexican border and in Mexico the jalapeno pepper is a staple seasoning. The flavor of this pickled hot pepper is indeed unique, and it is used delicately on various meats. My wife learned to flavor mushroom soup with jalapeno juice well stirred into it and then use this mixture over a shoulder or other roast in a Dutch oven or comparable covered baking dish. The venison flavor is excellent this way, with a hint of "hot" that you can barely identify.

When I asked Ellen as I was writing this how much jalapeno juice to use, she replied, "Some." It recalled to my mind how my mother and my Irish maternal grandmother described recipes years ago using a "dab" of this and a "pinch" of that and "some" of the other. When I pressed Ellen to tell me precisely how much jalapeno juice, she added, "Well, not too much, of course. But not too little either." Is that plain?

One error many hunters make with venison is insisting that not a single scrap go to waste. This is ridiculous. When beef is butchered it is true that there is not much waste evident. The "waste" goes into a lot of things you eat processed and hope you never know what they're made of. There is utterly no sense in the view—especially the faddish modern environmentalist view—that nothing should be wasted, especially when applied to a deer carcass. For example, many people I know scrape up everything but loose hair to use in ground meat, bits of stew meat, or chili meat. This is just a good way to pick up bad flavors. On a small deer, for example, the flank meat is literally worthless. The same goes for rib trimmings on a small deer. Some, of course, can be saved. But don't try to utilize worthless scraps. And never go short on trimming away shot-up and bloodied meat. All of these odds and ends ruin the good parts.

That gets us to the subject of ground venison. The way I butcher a deer, there's very little to grind. The neck, which we've never thought much of as a roast, can be ground. On a large deer, rib trimmings also can be used. The same goes for the tougher parts of the shoulder and haunch lower ends. Sometimes I grind this meat with strips of bacon. I squint at the pile of trimmings and guess at one bacon slice for an amount of venison that will make a large burger patty. Then when I make up the patties at cooking time, I mix in some Worcestershire sauce. This makes a delicious deer burger. Again, if you are an onion fan, shake in and mix in some dry onion flakes. These burgers are best ground and mixed as you are ready to use them, if you have a food grinder in your kitchen.

No hunting season is complete without at least one big venison stew. The reason I said a moment ago that you shouldn't save scraps is that too many persons think of stew meat as whatever worthless old barely edible chunks are left over. Well, in our household a venison stew gets top-quality meat. A stew shouldn't be considered some kind of trumped-up leftover but a regal dish in its own right. The only place I draw the line is at cutting up backstrap for stew. Otherwise, no part of the deer is too good for the superb brown stew we usually have each season. I should add that a proper venison stew is not a one-day affair. It is to be nurtured, added to, and cherished for the better part of a week, if you can keep people from putting it to death at the first sitting.

I don't pretend to have set rules for putting together a stew. Or at least any rules should be loose. I'll give you a basic guide for the way ours goes together, but you should feel free to switch ingredients and amounts as you wish.

For every pound of meat, gather a couple of tablespoons of chopped onion, a sprinkle of paprika, half a tablespoon of lemon juice, a half tablespoon of Worcestershire, a small garlic clove, a bit of sugar (not more than a teaspoon), a small amount of tomato juice (maybe two or three ounces), and a shade more than a teaspoon of salt. Coarse pepper goes in as you like it. To all of this per pound of meat you'll need about 2 1/2 cups of boiling water when it goes together.

Cut the meat into cubes, or however, maybe inch size. Flour the meat and brown it in a Dutch oven or other large stew pot, using as little cooking oil as possible. Then turn the heat down, pour the boiling water over the meat along with the seasonings noted. Put the lid on and let the meat simmer for a couple of hours, adding more water if it seems to be needed.

Now, in go the vegetables. Really there shouldn't be specified amounts, but again for each pound of meat the following will be about right: a cup of onion chunks or small onions and a half cup of chopped celery. Carrots depend. Some people like them diced. We use big chunks, what would amount to at least half a cup. Potatoes we also use in fair-size bites, not tiny cubes. At least a cup. Again, however, carrots and potatoes should be as many or as few as you want.

Let the simmering continue, the pot covered, until the vegetables are done. There are now two ways to go. Some proper cooks like to pour off the juice and thicken it with flour and water mixture or with corn starch, and then put it back. However, it can as easily be thickened in the pot. The stew is now ready to serve.

You should feel free as you go along to try additions or subtractions. Further, bear in mind that even though this stew will be delicious first time around, it will be even better the next day and the next. That's why it may be best not to use more vegetables than you'll eat at a sitting, so they aren't all mushy. Add some fresh ones, and a little water and seasoning, each day.

In our part of Texas, which is quite literally the whitetail capital of the United States, with an annual kill in the few hill-country counties of well over 100,000 deer, practically everyone makes at least some venison sausage, and many a hunter puts an entire deer into sausage. The idea got started many years ago because hill-country Texas was settled chiefly by German immigrants. Their love of sausage, plus live-off-the-land frugality and the abundance of deer, launched the "Sausage Age" in this neck of the woods.

All you need to make pan sausage is a grinder. Electric kitchen-style food grinders are not especially expensive and serve many needs. Most have a coarse and a fine grinding plate. The best sausage makers in my neighborhood use all lean pork, not fat. The ratio is one pound of pork to two pounds of venison. Trim all tendons and stringy places out of the venison, and use good cuts, not scrapings. Weigh the meats for proper ratio, cut them into grindable small strips or cubes, mix them around together, and sprinkle on the seasoning.

You have to experiment with seasoning. Some sausage fans like sage only, some a bit of garlic or onion, some a sprinkling of ginger. For 10 pounds of mixed meat, the usual common seasoning is 3 to 4 ounces of salt, 1 ounce of pepper (plus a teaspoon of red pepper to boot if you like your sausage a little bit hot), and a half ounce of sage. If you try ginger, keep it to a half ounce. Be sure the seasoning is well mixed, and then evenly sprinkle it over the meat. Grind the meat twice, coarse, then fine. If you like garlic, try it, but go easy. When the sausage is ground, it is ready for cooking, can be packaged and frozen, and kept for several months.

In general, smoked sausage is of two kinds, moist or dry. Most grinders have a stuffer attachment, and you can buy casings in a market. Tie a stout string to one end of a casing, stuff the casing, tie the string to the other end so you form a sausage ring and a loop for hanging the sausage. Season as you would for pan sausage. But take my word for it: dry sausage is sensational with just salt and pepper, plus a dab of cure mixture you can buy at a locker plant or a meat market.

After the rings are ready, they must be hung in a cool place. We hang them on a broom stick in our pump house. Then they drip as the salt takes water and meat liquids out through the porous casing.

For moist sausage, which must be cooked, the rings should hang at least 12 hours. For dry sausage, twice that, and if you have a temperature around 40 degrees F. or slightly lower, twice again does best.

Then start the smoking. You don't want a real hot fire. Just damp chips over charcoal or a commercial sawdust mixture. For dry sausage that has hung long, give it a couple of hours of smoking each morning for three days. Moist sausage that has not hung so long can be smoked the same or longer.

Both sausages keep well frozen, and the dry kind will keep in a refrigerator, or hung in a cool place, for several weeks. The dry kind needs no cooking and is a marvelous snack to carry in a hunting-coat pocket and take into the woods with you. Sometimes it is a toss-up at our house whether to grind shoulders *and* hams or just shoulders. Venison sausage properly made of good cuts is instantly addictive.

Over the past few seasons a surprising interest has arisen nationwide in the old Indian and cowpoke method of preserving meat by making jerky. Nowadays beef jerky, often selling for $10 or more a pound, is advertised widely. "Jerky," the word, is thought to have come from what Peruvian natives long ago called any dried meat—*ccharqui.* North American Indians dried venison and buffalo. And during the early days of the cattle industry in the West, and especially over the warm-climate areas of the Southwest, jerky made from beef was a staple. Every cowboy carried beans, coffee, and jerky in a saddle bag, and many were sustained by it for weeks on end.

Certainly any jerky enthusiast needs good teeth to handle it, but there's no doubt that it is tasty, an excellent dry food to carry on a hunting trip, and an authentic conversation piece to serve to guests as you regale them with tales of your successful deer hunt. Any deer hunter can easily make his own venison jerky.

There are several methods. A simple one is to cut strips of venison one or two inches wide, a quarter-inch thick, and up to ten inches long. Be sure you remove all fat. Mix up black pepper, salt, and sugar (two parts pepper, three each of the others), and sprinkle it heavily over the strips, as you place them layer on layer in a glass baking dish. Refrigerate for overnight. If you want a smoky flavor, liquid smoke can be added when you do the sprinkling. After the refrigeration period, lay the strips on crushed foil spread over an oven rack. Set the oven so it doesn't get hotter than 150 degrees F., preferably less, perhaps with the door open if necessary.

Obviously eight oven hours will take a substantial amount of energy, so it's really better to make jerky the way the old hands did it. Cut larger strips, as much as three inches wide and half an inch to as much as an inch thick. Be sure there's no fat attached. Knot a loop of twine into a hole pushed through one end of each strip. Dip a few strips at a time into boiling water. Be sure to keep

243

it boiling. The outside of the meat will quickly turn whitish. Remove as each does, and drain.

Now spread thickly on all sides a half-and-half mixture of salt and coarse pepper. Hang the strips on a stick, or a smoker rod, using the loops. Keep the strips from touching. If you own a smoker, check the length of time needed to smoke sausage, and give the jerky the same. If you live in the country and have or can rig up a smokehouse (a small shed of any sort will do fine) set up a charcoal bucket with damp wood chips for smoke. Of course, you must keep replenishing the chips, and the smoking and drying process takes time. You can tell by testing a strip. The thick ones may require up to three days.

Jerky strips thoroughly dried all the way through will keep a long time if you keep them well aired and away from dampness. Thicker strips that are softer inside actually taste better, and they can be frozen.

Shaved jerky—sliced cross-grain into very thin chips—is a marvelous snack, and shavings stirred in as you scramble eggs will keep camp mates or guests talking about the occasion for days.

I have tried to be selective and sparing in recommending these recipes for venison. The rather simple approaches are intended to emphasize that you should be kind to deer meat in your kitchen. These favorite recipes of mine are meant merely to serve as a guide. There are hundreds of venison recipes scattered hither and yon, all too many of them apparently having been concocted as punishment, not succor.

I cannot think of a more fitting way to end this book than by quoting a deer-hunter friend who considers the aftermath of the hunt, the eating, as equal in value and enjoyment to the sport. He is fond of saying, when explaining to guests why it is they relish his venison dishes so much, "Too many hunters, and their wives, think a deer needs killing twice—once in the woods and once in the kitchen!"

Index

Acorns as deer food, 99, 100, 108, 126
Age, hunting and, 212–13
Antler-rattling, 74, 131, 134–44
  scent in, 81–82
Antlerless deer, 55–56
Antlers, influences on size of, 183
Apples as deer food, 81, 100, 112
Arid country, 102–3
  See also Desert country
Aspen
  as deer food, 111
  as habitat, 120–21

Backstraps, cooking of, 237
Ballistics, 39–40
Barbecues of venison, 237–38
Barbee, Jim, 75, 163
Barometric pressure, effect on deer, 17
Binoculars, 47–48, 129, 190, 199, 203, 217
Bolt-action rifles, 41
Boats, in hunting, 89, 205–13
Boone and Crockett Club, 23, 184, 188
Boots, *see* Footwear
Bottomland hardwoods, as whitetail
    country, 117
Breeding, 24–25, 189
Breeding season, *see* Rutting season
Broadside shots, 57–58
Brush rifles, 36–37
Buck scrapes, 32, 149
  in antler-rattling, 138–39
  in mixed woodlot country, 115
  stand hunting by, 131
  tree species and, 228–29
Bucks
  distinguishing from does, 152–54
  mule deer, 91–92
  sounds by, 148–49
  tail movements of, 150–51
  tracks of, 31
  vocal sounds of, 72
  whitetail, 92, 173–74
  See also Antler-rattling; Buck scrapes
Bullet speed, 38–40
Bullets, deflection of, 36–37
Burnham Brothers, 73
Burro deer *(eremicus)*, 201
Bushwhack Creek Ranch, 230

Cactus country, 78, 97, 105, 110, 119–20,
    196–97
Calling, *see* Deer calling
Camouflage clothing, 44–45, 215–16
Camp sites, 42–43, 83–84, 87
Carmen Mountains whitetail, 161, 196
Cattle, observation of, 25
Cedar as deer food, 110
Chamness, Wally, 81
Clothing
  appearance to deer, 28–29, 215–17
  camouflage, 44–45, 215–16
  color of, 43–44, 216-17

headgear, 45
  jackets, 43, 44, 51
  "Mackinaw" jackets, 43
noise and, 43–44
  nylon 43–44
  safety colors, 43–44
  scent in, 30
  underwear, 45
Cold weather, footwear for, 46
Columbian blacktail deer, 37, 185, 187
Compasses, 50
Cooking game, 235–44
Coues deer, 88, 119, 185, 187, 188, 196
Crooki, see Desert mule deer
Crowded conditions, 22, 171–75
  stalking vs. sitting, 132
  See also Spooked deer

Daily routine of deer, 17, 27–28, 97, 105,
    124–25, 161–62
Dakota whitetail, 189
Day packs, 50–51
Deer
  appearance and health of, 25
  body language of, 145–46, 150–52
  difficulties in looking up, 6
  as individuals, 218–19
  measurements of, 233–34
  vocal sounds of, 71–72, 149
  See also Daily routine of deer; Mule
    deer; Senses of deer; Whitetail deer
Deer calling, 71–80, 131, 218, 225–26
Deer food, 81, 88, 107–11, 168, 197
  season and, 99–101
Deer management, 55–56, 190
Deer population, growth of, 21–22, 190–91
Desert, 50, 194–204
  as mule deer habitat, 122–23, 194–95
  water in, 51–52, 106
  as whitetail country, 102–3, 119–20, 194,
    196
Desert mule deer, 122–23, 186, 200–1
Does
  distinguished from bucks, 152–53
  physical movements of, 145–46
  snorting by, 147–48
  tail movements of, 150–51
  vocal sounds of, 147, 149
  whitetail, 173–74
Dogs, in hunting, 117, 130
Dolan Creek Ranch, 164
Domestic animals, observation of, 25
Doves, 214
Driving, 116, 117, 119, 128–29
Droppings, 31, 89, 90, 95
Dry camps, 87–88
Duck calls, 73
Dunham Brothers (Co.), 46

Ears of deer, 145
Edwards Plateau deer, 207
Elk bugles, 73

Prowling, *see* Stalking

Rain, deer activity in, 13–14
Ramsey, Bob, 134
"Ream" method, in field-dressing, 62
Record-book deer, listings of, 191–93
Recreational vehicles, 84
Retama as buck scrape, 229
Rib shots, 56–59
Rickenbacker, Eddie, 5
Rifles
    actions, 41
    brush rifles, 36–37
    caliber for deer, 34–40
    open sights, 35
    See also Shotguns
Roasts, venison, 239
Rock hurling, 163–64
Rocky Mountain mule deer, 123, 185–86,
    201
Ross, George, 5
Routes of deer, 232
Rubs, 31–32
Running shots, 35–36, 57–58
Rutting season
    antler-rattling in, 135–39, 142, 144
    does in, 145–46
    hunt timing and, 17–20
    statistics in determining, 23–24
    weather and, 26–27, 93–95, 126–28,
        136–37

Safety
    in antler-rattling, 140–41
    for deer, 105
    in field-dressing, 60
    in high stands, 7–8
Safety colors, 43–45
Sagebrush, 110
Sausage, venison, 242–43
Saws, 50–51
Scents
    as deer calls, 80–82
    human, 30, 221–23
    musk, 6, 80–81, 138
    in tree-stand hunting, 6–7, 133
    See also Senses of deer—smell
Scopes, 35–36, 47, 176
Scrapes, *see* Buck scrapes
Senses of deer
    hearing, 29, 217–20
    sight, 6, 28–29, 176, 216–17
    smell, 29–30, 221–24
Shadows, in stalking, 227–28
Shin oak as mule deer habitat, 122, 168
Shotguns, 35, 117
Shot placement, 56–60
Shoulders, cooking, 238–39
Signs
    buck scrapes as, 32, 115, 131, 138–39,
        149, 228–29
    droppings as, 31, 89, 95
    shed antlers as, 89
    tracks as, 31, 89, 93, 95
Sitka deer, 185
Sitting still, 220–21

6mm rifles, 40
Skinning, 65–67
Slings, 164
Slings, rifle, 48–49
Smoking, *see* Tobacco smoke
Snakes, protection against, 47
Snorting, 72
    as deer call, 225–26
    meaning of, 147–48
Snow
    deer reaction to, 90–91
    tracking and, 93, 95
"Socks and rubbers," 46
Soil, effect on deer, 23, 183
Southern mule deer, 201
"Solunar Tables," 16–17
Sounds of deer walking, 149–50
Spine shots, 58–60
Spooked deer
    mule deer, 177–80
    whitetails, 173–77
Sport, hunting as, 53–56
Stalking, 98
    fundamentals, 129
    rutting and, 126–28
    time of day and, 132
    See also Driving; Stalking vs. standing
Stalking vs. standing, 124–25
    analysis of deer needs and, 133
    in crowded conditions, 132
    in farm and woodlot country, 130
    moon phases and, 27
    observation of cattle and, 25
    in open country, 130
Stamping
    by deer, 152
    as deer call, 75, 218
Stances of deer, 152–53
Stand hunting, 115, 124–28
    antler-rattling and, 142
    near buck scrapes, 32
    desert, 119, 197–99, 203
    time of day and, 132
    See also High stands; Tree stands
Statistics, use of, 22–23
Stew, venison, 240–42
Stilson, Keith, 167–68
Stockman knowledge, utilizing, 24–26
Storms, deer activity in, 13–14, 90–91
Swamp hunting, 7, 27, 101

Tailbone shots, 56
Tails of deer, movements of, 150–51
Tarsal gland, 138
Temperature
    in mule deer hunting, 168
    and rut timing, 94–95
Territory of deer, 107–8, 135, 138–39, 228
Texas whitetail, 189
.35 caliber Remington, 37
.30/30 caliber, 35–37, 39
.30/06 caliber, 38–39
Tidal effect, 16–17
Time of day, hunt timing and, 14–15, 82,
    176
Thermal currents, 102–3

247